Security Issues and
Privacy Concerns in
Industry 4.0 Applications

Scrivener Publishing
100 Cummings Center, Suite 541J
Beverly, MA 01915-6106

Advances in Data Engineering and Machine Learning

Series Editor: M. Niranjanamurthy, PhD, Juanying XIE, PhD, and Ramiz Aliguliyev, PhD

Scope: Data engineering is the aspect of data science that focuses on practical applications of data collection and analysis. For all the work that data scientists do to answer questions using large sets of information, there have to be mechanisms for collecting and validating that information. Data engineers are responsible for finding trends in data sets and developing algorithms to help make raw data more useful to the enterprise.

It is important to have business goals in line when working with data, especially for companies that handle large and complex datasets and databases. Data Engineering Contains DevOps, Data Science, and Machine Learning Engineering. DevOps (development and operations) is an enterprise software development phrase used to mean a type of agile relationship between development and IT operations. The goal of DevOps is to change and improve the relationship by advocating better communication and collaboration between these two business units. Data science is the study of data. It involves developing methods of recording, storing, and analyzing data to effectively extract useful information. The goal of data science is to gain insights and knowledge from any type of data — both structured and unstructured.

Machine learning engineers are sophisticated programmers who develop machines and systems that can learn and apply knowledge without specific direction. Machine learning engineering is the process of using software engineering principles, and analytical and data science knowledge, and combining both of those in order to take an ML model that's created and making it available for use by the product or the consumers. "Advances in Data Engineering and Machine Learning Engineering" will reach a wide audience including data scientists, engineers, industry, researchers and students working in the field of Data Engineering and Machine Learning Engineering.

Publishers at Scrivener
Martin Scrivener (martin@scrivenerpublishing.com)
Phillip Carmical (pcarmical@scrivenerpublishing.com)

Security Issues and Privacy Concerns in Industry 4.0 Applications

Edited by

Shibin David, R. S. Anand, V. Jeyakrishnan, and M. Niranjanamurthy

Scrivener
Publishing

WILEY

This edition first published 2021 by John Wiley & Sons, Inc., 111 River Street, Hoboken, NJ 07030, USA and Scrivener Publishing LLC, 100 Cummings Center, Suite 541J, Beverly, MA 01915, USA
© 2021 Scrivener Publishing LLC
For more information about Scrivener publications please visit www.scrivenerpublishing.com.

Wiley Global Headquarters
111 River Street, Hoboken, NJ 07030, USA

For details of our global editorial offices, customer services, and more information about Wiley products visit us at www.wiley.com.

Limit of Liability/Disclaimer of Warranty
While the publisher and authors have used their best efforts in preparing this work, they make no representations or warranties with respect to the accuracy or completeness of the contents of this work and specifically disclaim all warranties, including without limitation any implied warranties of merchantability or fitness for a particular purpose. No warranty may be created or extended by sales representatives, written sales materials, or promotional statements for this work. The fact that an organization, website, or product is referred to in this work as a citation and/or potential source of further information does not mean that the publisher and authors endorse the information or services the organization, website, or product may provide or recommendations it may make. This work is sold with the understanding that the publisher is not engaged in rendering professional services. The advice and strategies contained herein may not be suitable for your situation. You should consult with a specialist where appropriate. Neither the publisher nor authors shall be liable for any loss of profit or any other commercial damages, including but not limited to special, incidental, consequential, or other damages. Further, readers should be aware that websites listed in this work may have changed or disappeared between when this work was written and when it is read.

Library of Congress Cataloging-in-Publication Data

ISBN 978-1-119-77562-1

Cover image: Cyber Security - Funtap P | Dreamstime.com
Cover design by Kris Hackerott

Set in size of 11pt and Minion Pro by Manila Typesetting Company, Makati, Philippines

10 9 8 7 6 5 4 3 2 1

Contents

Preface

The scope of this book is to envision the need for security in Industry 4.0 applications and the research opportunities for the future. This book discusses the security issues in the Industry 4.0 applications for research development. It will also enable readers to develop solutions for the security threats and attacks that are common in Industry 4.0. The chapters will be framed on par with the level of advancements in industry in the area of Industry 4.0 with its applications on additive manufacturing, cloud computing, IoT, etc. This book will help researchers and industrial specialists to reflect on the latest trends and the need for technological change in Industry 4.0.

Smart water management using IoT, cloud security issues with network forensics, regional language recognition for Industry 4.0, IoT-based healthcare management system, artificial intelligence for fake profile detection, and packet drop detection in agriculture-based IoT are covered in the book. Leading innovations such as smart drone for railway track cleaning, everyday life–supporting blockchain and big data, effective prediction using machine learning, classification of dog breed based on CNN, load balancing using the SPE approach and the impact of cyber culture on media consumers are also addressed.

Industry 4.0: Smart Water Management System Using IoT

S. Saravanan[1], N. Renugadevi[2*], C.M. Naga Sudha[3] and Parul Tripathi[4]

[1]Department of Mechanical Engineering, K. Ramakrishnan College of Technology, Tiruchirappalli, Tamil Nadu, India
[2]Department of Computer Science and Engineering, Indian Institute of Information Technology, Tiruchirappalli, Tamil Nadu, India
[3]Department of Computer Technology, Anna University MIT Campus, Chennai, Tamil Nadu, India
[4]Artificial Intelligence Group, Centre for Development of Advanced Computing (C-DAC), Delhi, India

Abstract

Industry 4.0 will provide increased automation, self-monitoring and improved communication in most industrial sectors in the near future. This can be achieved through a variety of sensors and different cloud platforms controlled through Internet of Things (IoT). The Industry 4.0 era has given innovative solutions to water service providers for distribution, monitoring, leakage detection and water metering. The existing method of managing water in municipalities requires manual attention. Further, water wastage, infrequent water cleaning, and at times contaminated water are considered the main drawbacks in the conventional municipality water management system. The quality of drinking water is one of the vital key elements for a healthy life. Therefore, the concept of Industry 4.0 can be employed to convert a manual into an automated system for managing municipality water. Hence, this paper surveys several research works on automated water management systems. From the extensive survey, it has been decided to propose a Smart Municipality Water Management System (SMWMS) to ensure good public health without water-borne diseases. This SMWMS assists the municipality in water conservation and in safeguarding public health; it can be widely employed in different applications such as the residential, agricultural and industrial sectors, to name a few.

Corresponding author: renugadevin@iiitt.ac.in

Shibin David, R. S. Anand, V. Jeyakrishnan, and M. Niranjanamurthy (eds.) Security Issues and Privacy Concerns in Industry 4.0 Applications, (1–14) © 2021 Scrivener Publishing LLC

Keywords: Industry 4.0, Internet of Things, water industry, municipality water, water quality

1.1   Introduction

The right moral compass is trying hard to think about what customers want.

– Sundar Pichai

1.1.1   Industry 4.0

With the blossoming of technologies in the Internet era, the term Industry 4.0 has been coined as a new stage in the evolution of Internet technologies. It has made automation a buzz word in almost all sectors. Industry 4.0 mainly deals with the integration of three components, namely Internet of Things (IoT) with Cyber-Physical Systems (CPS), Big Data Analytics and Communication Infrastructure [1]. The main scope of Industry 4.0 is to increase efficiency along with the effectiveness of the production field. In order to satisfy customer requirements, Industry 4.0 has to manage a huge amount of data which can be met with Cloud Computing techniques. In [2], Industry 4.0 is defined as "the combination of physical machines and devices integrated with smart sensors are utilized to control and predict for betterment of future decisions". It is defined as the CPS communication enabled over IoT which helps the real-time application to provide Internet of Services (IoS). These IoS are offered to the entire participants (both internal and external organizational service providers) who are involved in production and utilization of the supply chain. Industry 4.0 mainly highlights the possible ways to establish communication between human and machine through which the automation can be enhanced in an efficient way. Human-to-Machine (H-M) communication will initiate the emergence of smart factories with more business interaction models. Complex integration of CPS and IoT devices are equipped with network capabilities which can be used to sense, identify, process and communicate between them [3].

1.1.2   IoT

A combinational flavor of IoT and Industry 4.0 will ultimately lead to a smooth relationship between customers and suppliers. With this new flavor, domination of manufacturers and retailers will be avoided. Customers can make their own decisions on customization of their quality products which maintains the supply and demand cycle. However, a cyber-security threat is a great challenge in establishing Machine-to-Human (M-H) communication. The supply-demand cycle and efficient usage of resources which are considered as main characteristics of Industry 4.0 make the environment (production, cities, factories) become smart [4].

1.1.3 Smart City

Stock and Seliger [5] have described Industry 4.0 applications on smart cities, smart factories and smart products. A city which is connected by various factors, namely smart governance, smart people, smart health, smart communication and smart mobility, is defined as a smart city [6]. According to Jokob Julian, who is an architect and urban thinker, smart cities are a gift, a chance to transform old and slow systems and structures into a smart future. "Smart cities are developed in a vision of transforming the lives of digital citizens to meet their requirements," Julian writes. Every country has started smart city projects with their own framework in order to improve their citizens' quality of living.

1.1.4 Smart Water Management

When the well is dry, we'll know the worth of water.

– Benjamin Franklin

Global Risk Perception Survey Reports from the World Economic Forum highlight that there will be a greater societal impact of the water crisis over the next 10 years [4]. It will lead to a higher rate of water stress areas where water available for consumption will be on demand. In recent years, the water level consumed has been twice that of population growth. Therefore, there is a tradeoff between demand and supply of water. As everyone is aware about water scarcity in recent decades, it has its adverse consequences on food production also. Even though the future is uncertain, it is certain to have the hope that the situation can be changed. Water demands are increasing due to a huge increase in water consumption per capita among industrial sectors. Water is the first and foremost necessity of human life. Therefore, water policy has become a priority issue at the international level. If the proper water management is not maintained, a country's economic development will be at risk. With these facts in consideration, a spotlight on water conservation has spread all over the world.

With the help of smart water management, one of the five basic elements of nature can be conserved for the future. Further, many IoT-related researches are to be focused on effective monitoring of water quality. While researchers promote the ideas towards water management, there arises a need to maintain the sustainability of water for future usage with the successful deployment of IoT, Cloud Technologies and Big Data.

1.2 Preliminaries

This section briefly explains the preliminaries related to Industry 4.0, namely IoT and Smart Cities. Out of various appliances involved in SC, Smart Water Management System (SWMS) is highlighted.

1.2.1 Internet World to Intelligent World

A tremendous shift of technology from the Internet world to the intelligent world is conveyed by the trending phrase "Internet of Things". As modern societies have turned to round-the-clock connectivity, IoT fits their needs. Recently, many researchers have redefined the term IoT according to the applications developed. It includes transportation, healthcare, mining and many more. A mathematical language of IoT is expressed by the conceptual framework of 2020 as [7], *IoT= Sensor + Network + Data + Services.*

IoT services will be gained from all living and nonliving things which either request or offer a service. The inter-connectivity between all the things is made possible with microcontrollers, sensors and actuators. IoT provides promising smart solutions which have arisen due to dramatic urbanization as shown in Figure 1.1 [8]. Several scientific and engineering applications have emerged rapidly with the help of IoT. Solutions on IoT can be addressed with the recent technologies such as Robotics, Radio-frequency identification (RFID), Wireless Communication, Cloud Computing and Micro-Electromechanical Systems (MEMS).

1.2.2 Architecture of IoT System

Various architectures on IoT are designed with respect to the smart functionalities provided by the system. In this typical system, middleware is the main component as it combines infrastructure and services together. In this Figure 1.2 [8], the combining factor of the Real World Data with the

| World Population | | 7.25 | 7.33 | 7.41 | 7.48 | 7.56 | 7.63 | 7.71 | 7.78 | 7.85 | 7.92 | 7.99 |
| Smart Devices | | 15.41 | 17.68 | 20.35 | 23.14 | 26.66 | 30.73 | 35.82 | 42.62 | 51.11 | 62.12 | 75.44 |

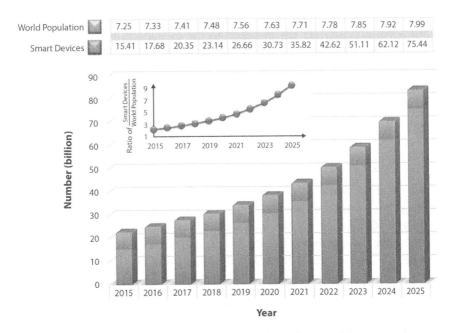

Figure 1.1 Comparison between the estimated world population and the projected number of smart devices connected to the Internet: 2015–2025.

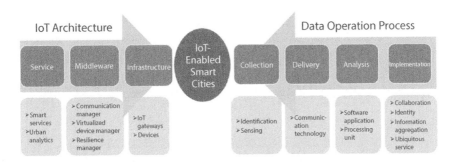

Figure 1.2 Characterization of the technologies in IoT-enabled smart cities.

semantic web for providing services is through Linked Sensor Middleware (LSM). Also, nowadays various IoT architectures have been designed with Cloud-based Middleware infrastructure.

Generally, primary components involved in IoT architecture are application, sensors, processors and gateways. The major zone of IoT framework for users to utilize the gathered data is application. Sensors help in sensing the environment and to learn the functionalities of assembled things in order to make the actuators respond. The brain of the IoT framework is considered as processors which help to extract the information from raw data collected from sensors. Assigning the property to the gathered information is performed through gateway. Its working is similar to that of a router which will allow the processed data into LAN, PAN, WAN. In simple words, a gateway is used for a steering process which is performed on data collected [9].

1.2.3   Architecture of Smart City

IoT services in smart cities are of great interest and are implemented not only for the welfare of human lives, but also to reduce the operational costs in administration. Some of the major administration policies are in the hands of local bodies such as corporations and municipalities. Services offered through smart cities include smart water management, smart lighting, and smart waste management. These advantageous developments through IoT can be used within smart homes, grid stations and also in workplaces for efficient management of energy usage as shown in Figure 1.3 [9].

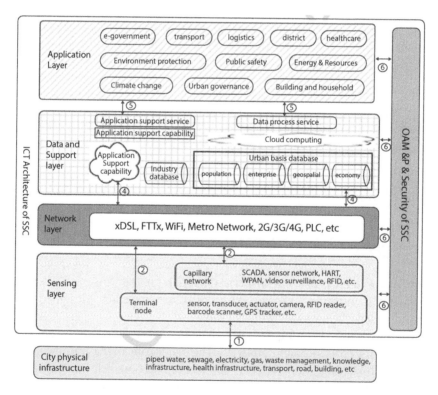

Figure 1.3 Smart city architecture.

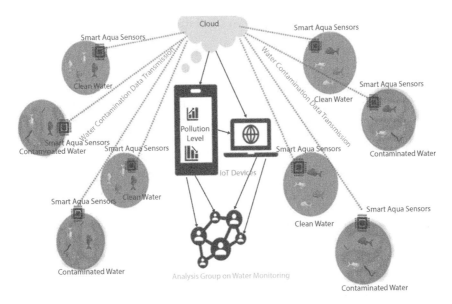

Figure 1.4 IoT with Smart-Aqua sensors via cloud.

A smart city mission is initiated in all nations for renewal of citizens' lives through digital technologies. Also, the Government of India has aimed to develop at least 100 smart cities. Smart cities are equipped with innovative technologies such as 5G, Wireless Sensor Networks (WSN) and well-established Information Technology (IT) infrastructure. These technologies provide necessary services like water supply, transportation, recycling, and electricity in a smart manner, i.e., via connection of sensors, actuators and gateways to WSN. This connectivity helps to monitor, record and control the environment, which will help to satisfy the needs of the citizens. For instance, if a smart water monitoring system is considered, pollution level in water can be easily monitored through mobile phones (end devices) and IoT sensors (Smart Aqua Sensors) which are connected via the cloud as shown in Figure 1.4 [10]. Analysis of data on water monitoring can also be processed in order to display the results.

1.3 Literature Review on SWMS

This section presents a literature review on SWMS. It is mainly divided into four subsections, namely Water Quality Parameters related to SWMS, SWMS in Agriculture, SWMS using Smart Grids, and Machine Learning (ML) Models in SWMS.

1.3.1   Water Quality Parameters Related to SWMS

When all other high-level services offered by smart cities are considered, SWMS gains the highest value. Research studies are particularly emerging in the drinking water management system for the welfare of the public and also in the field of agriculture. In [11], requirements for the smart water distributed system and water quality parameters such as technological, quality, quantity and topological parameters are discussed. A smart application is designed for the residents to get updates on water level and water quality using Raspberry Pi and MQTT protocol. Residents can use smart applications and can toggle the motors on and off accordingly. A turbidity sensor is used to determine the water purity.

In other countries like Pakistan [12], an IoT-based water management is focused on rural areas and urban areas according to the requirements. In rural areas, due to lower population, automation of IoT is deployed in the irrigation sector, whereas in urban areas, monitoring of water quality in real time is deployed as such areas have high population levels. Water-quality is monitored using the controller module, where the data collected in the cloud is analyzed and the action is performed if the quality falls below threshold value. Ubidots and Thingspeak are the cloud platforms which are used for data storage in the cloud. In rural areas, as cellular connectivity is limited to 2G, implementation of cellular-based connection is impossible. Therefore, an IoT system which can provide sustainable operation is deployed. With this technique, water theft and water distribution policy violation can be eliminated. An actuator-based water distribution system is remotely controlled without any user intervention, which will avoid conflicts over water distribution.

Multi-Intelligent Control System (MICS) can be designed in the IoT framework with the help of the entire monitoring process. It is made possible with the help of smart layers such as smart alerts, smart communication and smart water level. These layers assist in automation of the entire process involved in water management [13].

1.3.2   SWMS in Agriculture

A district which constitutes farms, processing and supply companies is termed as an Agro industrial district. In agriculture sectors, quality irrigation is possible using SWAMP (Smart Water Agricultural Management Platform) architecture. Among SWAMP, FIWARE is the most preferred open-source platform. The main component of FIWARE is Orion Context Broker (OCB) which manages and responds to the system with

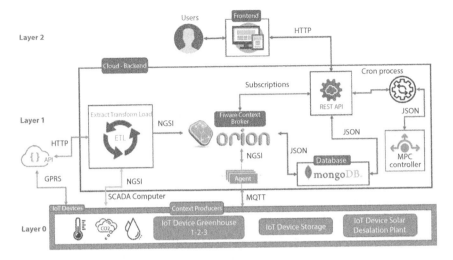

Figure 1.5 Working of OCB in agriculture.

the information collected from the surrounding IoT system as shown in Figure 1.5 [14].

Energy constraint is considered as one of the main drawbacks of IoT. To overcome this disadvantage, solar energy is utilized in Smart Agriculture. The main functionalities involved are sensing of temperature, checking the crops' condition, detecting the movement of things in fields which are monitored through DHT 11 sensors, moisture sensors, and PIR sensors [15]. In agricultural sectors, sustainable productivity can be obtained through moisture analysis, water contamination level, and soil health analysis and water quantity level.

1.3.3   SWMS Using Smart Grids

In Singapore, the aim of the Public Utilities Board (PUB) is to supply fresh drinking water to the society throughout the day through the smart water grid system [16]. It is made possible to design smart grid water systems by using the sensors and advanced analytical tools. Smart water grid facilitates the decision support system along with real-time monitoring, which helps to manage the water supply network efficiently. A smart water grid system highlights the five important features of WSN, namely, asset management, water conservation, water quality management, automated water reading and leak management. The system is correlated with the network system and the customer's end. Minimization of the leakage problem and efficient water quality can only be done with the help of enhanced asset management and leak preventive management. Real-time water consumption information can be extracted from the automated meter reading for helping the customer and to provide information regarding water conservation between them and company principles. The only theme is to embrace data analytics tools for developing a new technology to fulfill the requirements of water efficiency and customers of smart water grid systems.

Although IoT gives growth to our society in the advancement of technologies, the system faces an issue when there is a lack of energy. Therefore IoT gets connected to the smart grids to give better results. For any smart city, IoT and smart grids are undoubtedly the important features. These include practice of smart devices like advance meters, sensors and actuators through which the automation devices are used for controlling, monitoring. Emergencies in the power grid are rapidly increasing in the coming era of the energy sector. However, it can be proven that the combined IoT and smart grid system raises various types of network-based systems at power generation side and transmission level [17].

With such advanced technologies and their development, research based on cyber-attacks attracts more attention, since it involves interoperability and connectivity issues. In the coming era, almost all the private and government services will stretch out their focus on the smart grid as their energy sector consists of residential, commercial and industrial infrastructure developed based on IoT architecture and regulatory standards. However, our next-generation IoT technologies and their complications in the energy management system should be explored by the energy stakeholders. Hence, cost of energy required is minimized; utility peak gets minimized in all the sectors, as the new power plant is constructed, aimed as a support for a strong business platform with large opportunities [18].

1.3.4   Machine Learning Models in SWMS

Various literature surveys on SWMS have been summarized in Table 1.1 [19-25]. Monitoring the water quality and classifying them according to the contamination level is performed through ML methods along with IoT. When the water is classified under impure category, the level of contamination has to be tested. In water parameters such as chloride, sulphate and alkalinity contents were analyzed. With the presence of these chemicals, water quality is predicted through neural networks [19]. Big data and Artificial Intelligence (AI)–based Support Vector Machine (SVM) play an important role in categorization of water. When drinking water is analyzed, an ML-based prediction method is implemented and also IoT sensors are

Table 1.1 Research on IoT-based SWMS.

Research	Purpose	Device/method used	Models
Water Contamination [19, 24]	Water Contamination Assessments	ML with Fast Fourier Transform	SVM and Color Layout Descriptor
Water Quality Parameters [19, 25]	Water Contamination and Quality Analysis	Neural Network, ML-based classification, IoT devices	SVM, IoT sensor models
Drinking Water [10, 22]	Drinking Water Analysis	ML-based prediction and classification	Decision Tree, K-Nearest Neighbour, SVM
Water Level [21, 23]	Water Level Detection	IoT device	Raspberry Pi
Water Meter [20]	Water usage measurements	IoT device, WSN	Arduino and NodeMCU

deployed in video-surveillance for the classification of polluted water and clean water [20]. In 2020, an intelligent water management system has been designed and implemented through Thingspeak cloud platform, where the water leakage has been detected via Blynk application [21]. Also, water metering is attached through which the amount of water consumed can be measured in real time.

1.3.5   IoT-Based SWMS

Many contributions have been made on SWMS using ML methods. A few researches on IoT-based SWMS are summarized in Table 1.1.

1.4   Conclusion

This chapter has contributed a deep dive into the review of existing research works on SWMS. A systematic framework on review of Industry 4.0 with a smart water management system is explained in the introductory part in Section I and then followed by IoT and SC. Among the applications of SC, importance of conservation of water resources is discussed in detail. Section 1.2 discusses preliminaries on three parts namely, Internet to Intelligent World, Architecture of IoT and Architecture of SC. Under subsection 3, a literature survey on SWMS is focused on water quality parameters related to SWMS, SWMS in agriculture, and SWMS in smart grids and ML models on SWMS. Finally, a summarized table of review on IoT-based SWMS research is presented. Overall, the paper focuses on what SWMS means and what are the possible research directions on which future researchers can focus. As there is a lack of well efficient real-time tests in water resources, more research has to be performed in the water management system in collaboration with cross-disciplinary sectors. The future scope of SWMS relies on integration of Big Data, IoT and Cloud technologies to maintain the sustainability of water resources. It will also assist in adding the value chain which will help stakeholders to become well-versed in understanding Industry 4.0 and come up with the solutions.

> *We don't want to push our ideas on to customers; we simply want to make what they want*
>
> *– Laura Ashley*

References

1. K Lova Raju and V Vijayaraghavan. IoT technologies in agricultural environment: A survey. WIRELESS PERSONALCOMMUNICATIONS, 2020.
2. Industrial internet consortium ii, fact sheet. http://www.iiconsortium.org/docs/, 2013 (accessed 15 July 2020).
3. Li Da Xu, Wu He, and Shancang Li. Internet of things in industries: A survey. IEEE Transactions on industrialinformatics, 10(4):2233-2243, 2014.
4. A. Varghese and D. Tandur. Wireless requirements and challenges in industry 4.0. In 2014 International Conferenceon Contemporary Computing and Informatics (IC3I), pages 634-638, 2014.
5. Tim Stock and G Seliger. Opportunities of sustainable manufacturing in industry 4.0. *Procedia* Cirp, 40:536-541, 2016.
6. Vasja Roblek, Maja Mesko, and Alojz Krape_z. A complex view of industry 4.0. Sage Open, 6(2):2158244016653987, 2016.
7. BM Alhafidh and William Allen. Design and simulation of a smart home managed by an intelligent self-adaptive system.

8. Amir H Alavi, Pengcheng Jiao, William G Buttlar, and Nizar Lajnef. Internet of things-enabled smart cities: State-of-the-art and future trends. *Measurement*, 129:589-606, 2018.

9. Oladayo Bello and Sherali Zeadally. Toward efficient smartification of the internet of things (IoT) services. *Future Generation Computer Systems*, 92, 10 2017.

10. Silvia Liberata Ullo and GR Sinha. Advances in smart environment monitoring systems using IoT and sensors. *Sensors*, 20(11):3113, 2020.

11. V. Radhakrishnan and W. Wu. IoT technology for smart water system. In 2018 *IEEE 20th International Conference on High Performance Computing and Communications; IEEE 16th International Conference on Smart City; IEEE4th International Conference on Data Science and Systems* (HPCC/ Smart City/DSS), pp. 1491-1496, 2018.

12. S. Safdar, M. Mohsin, L. A. Khan, and W. Iqbal. Leveraging the internet of things for smart waters: Motivation, enabling technologies and deployment strategies for Pakistan. In 2018 IEEE SmartWorld, Ubiquitous Intelligence Computing, Advanced Trusted Computing, Scalable Computing Communications, Cloud Big Data Computing, Internet of People and Smart City Innovation (Smart World/SCALCOM/UIC/ATC/CBDCom/IOP/SCI), pp. 2117-2124, 2018.

13. An experimental setup of multi-intelligent control system (mics) of water management using the internet of things (IoT). *ISA Transactions*, 96:309-326, 2020.

14. J. D. Gil, M. Munoz, L. Roca, F. Rodriguez, and M. Berenguel. An IoT based control system for a solar membrane distillation plant used for greenhouse irrigation. In 2019 Global IoT Summit (GIoTS), pp, 1-6, 2019.

15. G Sushanth and S Sujatha. IoT based smart agriculture system. In 2018 *International Conference on Wireless Communications, Signal Processing and Networking* (Wisp NET), pp. 1-4. IEEE, 2018.

16. Public Singapore. Managing the water distribution network with a smart water grid. *Smart Water*, 1:1{13, 07 2016.

17. Future effectual role of energy delivery: A comprehensive review of internet of things and smart grid. *Renewable and Sustainable Energy Reviews*, 91: 90-108, 2018.

18. Edward Curry, Souleiman Hasan, Christos Kouroupetroglou, Willem Fabritius, Umair ul Hassan, and Wassim Derguech. Internet of things enhanced user experience for smart water and energy management. *IEEE Internet Computing*, 22(1):18-28, 2018.

19. Mohammad Saeid Mahdavinejad, Mohammadreza Rezvan, Mohammadamin Barekatain, Peyman Adibi, Payam Barnaghi, and Amit P Sheth. Machine learning for internet of things data analysis: A survey. *Digital Communications and Networks*, 4(3):161-75, 2018.

20. Vilen Jumutc, Rocco Langone, and Johan AK Suykens. Regularized and sparse stochastic k-means for distributed large-scale clustering. In 2015 *IEEE International Conference on Big Data (Big Data)*, pp. 2535-2540. IEEE, 2015.

21. K. Gupta, M. Kulkarni, M. Magdum, Y. Baldawa, and S. Patil. Smart water management in housing societies using IoT. In *2018 Second International Conference on Inventive Communication and Computational Technologies (ICICCT)*, pp. 1609-1613, 2018.
22. Mohamed Amine Ferrag, Lei Shu, Xing Yang, Abdelouahid Derhab, and Leandros Maglaras. Security and privacy for green IoT-based agriculture: Review, blockchain solutions, and challenges. IEEE Access, 8:32031-32053, 2020.
23. Swapnali B Pawar, Priti Rajput, and Asif Shaikh. Smart irrigation system using iot and raspberry pi. 2018.
24. O. Elijah, T. A. Rahman, I. Orikumhi, C. Y. Leow, and M. N. Hindia. An overview of internet of things (IoT) anddata analytics in agriculture: Benefits and challenges. *IEEE Internet of Things Journal*, 5(5):3758-3773, 2018.
25. Parvaneh Asghari, Amir Masoud Rahmani, and Hamid Haj Seyyed Javadi. Internet of things applications: A systematic review. *Computer Networks*, 148:241-61, 2019.

2

Fourth Industrial Revolution Application: Network Forensics Cloud Security Issues

Abdullah Ayub Khan[1], Asif Ali Laghari[1]*, Shafique Awan[2]
and Awais Khan Jumani[3]

[1]Department of Computer Science, Sindh Madressatul Islam University, Karachi, Sindh, Pakistan
[2]Department of Computing Science & Information Technology, Benazir Bhutto Shaheed University Lyari, Karachi, Sindh, Pakistan
[3]Department of Computer Science, ILMA University Karachi, Sindh, Pakistan

Abstract

This chapter studies the cloud security issues in network forensics and a large-scale machine-to-machine (M2M) communication impact on the fourth industrial revolution. The parameters help to gather, analyze, and document information about incidentals security and network-based crime activities. It also supports the solving of a complication related to the network traffic in the cloud, virtual machine dynamic migration, virtual resources of cloud clients, provides an environment like multi-tenancy, does not infringe on the security and protection of other cloud users, and most important, avoids transferring costs of large sets of data and processed directly. Cloud security and M2M communication permit the discovery of the best conceivable security configuration, improve communication, self-monitoring, and diagnose cloud security issues without the need for human intervention. Restrictions and crucial points are emphasized to arrange for initial forensics investigations and also further studies in this area. This chapter presents a model that is generic in nature for network forensics in the cloud environment as well as defines prototype artifact that articulates the M2M communication security issue that impacts on fourth industrial revolution application. We validate the architecture prototype with an implementation based on the OpenNebula Hypervisor web-based interface and the NetworkMiner analysis framework.

Corresponding author: asif.laghari@smiu.edu.pk

Shibin David, R. S. Anand, V. Jeyakrishnan, and M. Niranjanamurthy (eds.) Security Issues and Privacy Concerns in Industry 4.0 Applications, (15–34) © 2021 Scrivener Publishing LLC

Keywords: Network forensic, digital forensics, cloud forensics, cloud computing services, M2M communication application, fourth industrial revolution, impact and issues in Industry 4.0 cloud application

2.1   Introduction

Nowadays, several organizations use cloud resources offered by a cloud service provider as an external IT-infrastructure for their organization. Cloud computing has emerged as a highly powerful and most popular field over the past few years, the significant aspect of which is getting more focus on virtual crime and cyber-threat activities that are IT-based services [1]. As a result, digital forensics has gained increasing importance as a cloud investigation technology. Cloud computing security imposes several new challenges in between M2M communication technology [2, 3]. In this chapter, we address critical cloud security issues, network forensics investigation challenges, machine communication interruption, and the impact on industry 4.0 application.

2.1.1   Network Forensics

Network forensics (NF) is a crucial sub-branch of digital forensics (DF), itself a branch of forensics science, in which experts and law enforcement capture, record and analyze network events, and discover the source of attacks and cyber incidents [4] that enhance security in the cyber environment. Simson Garfinkel writes, "network forensics systems can be one of two kinds either catch-it-as-you-can or stop, look and listen to system" [5]. Catch-it-as-you-can is a network approach in which packages pass through a certain traffic point, catch packages, and subsequently store analysis in batch mode. The approach requires a huge amount of memory storage that usually involves a Redundant Array of Inexpensive Disks or Redundant Array of Independent Disks (RAID) system. On the other side, Stop, Look, and Listen is a network approach in which individual package analysis is carried out in an initial way; only certain information stores in the memory for future analysis. Undoubtedly, this type of method used less memory storage but needs more processing power to tackle the incoming traffic on the network environment.

In computer forensics, data is more often seized in disk storage, which makes it easier to obtain; unlike DF, NF is more difficult to carry out data while it is transmitted across the network and then lost in a short time [6]. Anyone planning to apply NF tools for analysis data needs to know about the privacy laws; privacy and data protection laws restrict active tracking as well as analysis of network traffic without explicit permission. In the network and IT infrastructure, NF is used in a proactive fashion to dig out flaws; however, the scope includes shoring up defenses by the officers of information security and IT administrators against future cyber-attacks.

2.1.2 The Fourth Industrial Revolution

The digital transformation of production, manufacturing, and several other related industries that value process creation have led to the fourth industrial revolution [9], is a new phase in the organization and control of chain value interchangeably [7]. Industry 4.0 is concerned with those areas that are not usually classified such as smart cities where industry applications cannot perform their own rights [8]. In the first industrial revolution, the advent of mechanization, water, and steam power made a huge and positive impact on the traditional industry. In short, the first revolution boosted industrial production; the second industrial revolution revolved around using electricity, mass production, and assembly lines. Industry 3.0 was the revolution of electronics, IT systems, and automation at the industrial level that led to Industry 4.0, which is [10] associated with the cyber-physical system.

The Industry 4.0 briefly elaborates the automation growth trend and data exchange in industrial technology as well as processes within the manufacturing industry, such as Artificial Intelligence (AI), Cloud Computing (CC), the Internet of Things (IoT), the Industrial Internet of Things (IIoT), Cyber-Physical Systems (CPS), Cognitive Computing, Smart Manufacture (SM), and Smart Factories (SF). The mentioned automation creates individual manufacturing systems; the machines in industries are augmented with multiple sensors and network connectivity to monitor an entire process of the production and make decisions autonomously [12]. However, augmentation of machines and wireless connectivity can highly advance industrial and manufacturing systems, create robust response times, and allow for a near real-time machine-to-machine communication. Nevertheless, the revolution relates to the digital twin technologies; these technologies make real-world virtual versions of installations, processes, and real-time applications that can enhance testing to make cost-effective decentralized decisions.

The virtual copies allowing the cyber-physical machine to communicate with each other also create a real-time data exchange for human staff and automation interconnectivity between transparent information, processes, and technical assistance for industry 4.0 manufacturing [11]. Industry 4.0 demonstrates the business models, for example, offline programming for arc welding, take adoptive controls, and the overall processes of product design architecture and automotive industry 4.0 businesses implementation as well as a variety of smart factories all around the world.

2.1.2.1   *Machine-to-Machine (M2M) Communication*

A new concept evolved in Industry 4.0: machine-to-machine (M2M) communication, which is becoming an increasingly important technology in the entire domain. M2M refers to the concept where two devices exchange information with each other, such as sending and receiving data. The communication that occurs between devices is autonomous; no human intervention is required for the overall process of exchanging information. The wireless connectivity [13] between interrelated devices automatically exchanges and analyzes data in the cloud. The Internet of Things (IoT) enabled integrating several M2M systems and cloud computing that process all data by using the cloud web platform.

This chapter highlights the distinct types of connectivity used between machines for communication. The most used connectivity [16] is: (i) Radiofrequency identification (RFID), which has a maximum range up to 10 meters that indicate the limitation of this type of connectivity; (ii) Bluetooth and Wireless-Fidelity (Wi-Fi), the most useable and reliable wireless connectivity for communication, with the range limitation from 10-20 meters in the case of Bluetooth and approximately 50 meters in the case of Wi-Fi; and (iii) low-frequency connectivity [15], which has a range of up to 1000 kilometers, such as GSM network and satellite.

In general, the applications and the area of M2M connectivity that can be applied and used widely most probably apply to all domains. Likewise, it is successfully utilized in the artificial intelligence industry [14], allowing devices to communicate with each other and make autonomous decisions. Some established and used crucial industrial M2M applications that enhance the productions in the manufacturing industry are: (i) intelligent stock control, (ii) data collection for processing, (iii) just-in-time implementation, (iv) automated maintenance, and many more.

2.1.3   Cloud Computing

The National Institute of Standard and Technology (NIST) defines cloud computing as "a model for enabling ubiquitous, convenient, on-demand

network access to a shared pool of configurable computing resources"
[17]. Cloud computing is considered as a new business model throughout the world, computing as a utility [18]; there are five essential characteristics of the cloud: (i) on-demand self-service, (ii) resource pooling,
(iii) rapid expansion, (iv) broad network access, and (v) measured service.
Furthermore, cloud computing has three service models [19] for cloud
users, such as software, platform, and infrastructure. In the same manner, Forensics-as-a-Service is the emerging technology in the area of cloud
computing that facilitates investigators to perform digital crime investigation tasks utilizing the services of the cloud. Cloud categorizes four distinct deployment models, public, private, commercial, and hybrid models,
a proper way to deliver cloud services to cloud users. In cloud computing,
this is intended to serve as a way of making broad comparisons of cloud
deployment strategies, services models, and describing the actual baseline
[20], for using cloud computing in the best manner.

2.1.3.1   Infrastructure-as-a-Service (IaaS)

Infrastructure-as-a-Service (IaaS) is one of the types of cloud service models, the computing infrastructure that manages the overall cloud services
over the internet. On-demand quickly scales up and down infrastructure
services [21], working on the mechanism like a pay-as-you-go platform
where cloud users pay only for what they use. This avoids the expense
of buying additional physical IT-infrastructure and managed complex
server and other data center resources. In a cloud environment, IaaS offers
resources as an individual service component, cloud service provider [22]
manages the IT-resources in a virtualized environment, and the users can
focus only on installation, configuration, and software maintenance. The
cloud service providers enable users to elastically utilize virtual server and
storage resources by a pay-per-use method, forming networks that tie them
all together [23]. By renting IaaS from a cloud service provider, essentially,
cloud users not only have on-demand hardware services but also provi-
sioning software services that automate it.

2.1.3.2   Challenges of Cloud Security in Fourth
Industrial Revolution

The IT revolution has brought an important transformation in the industrial manufacturing processes with high impact [27]; this envelopment

promotes the latest technology trends such as cloud-based systems, Internet of Things (IoT), Big Data Analysis, and others in the fourth industrial revolution. However, new innovative solutions carry challenges and limitations, such as unexpected risk, security vulnerabilities, infringing privacy, and many more [24]. Increased reliance on innovations may gain a competitive advantage [25], but on a certain note, security issues have been one of the most insignificant challengeable aspects for conducting successful business communication and transaction between machines on the cloud platform [26]. This chapter, highlighting the reflections and emphasizing the security issues and limitations of industry 4.0, raises awareness towards good security practice within the fourth industrial revolution:

- Inadequate Access Management
- Multi-tenancy
- Data Loss
- Data Breaches
- Infringing Privacy
- Cost of Transferring

The chapter is structured as follows. The next section presents the generic model architecture for network forensics and cloud security issue in the industry 4.0 application. Section 2.3 discusses the model implementation, implementation platform used, such as Open Nebula and Network Miner for analysis of security threats. Section 2.4 focuses on the machine-to-machine communication impact on industrial 4.0 applications, and also describes an application scenario of cloud computing security in the domain of industry 4.0. Finally, we conclude our chapter in Section 2.5.

2.2   Generic Model Architecture

This chapter considers cloud-based IT infrastructure in which a cloud service provider (CSP) executes virtual machine (VM) [28], cloud users get full control over the services like software, running on the VM, and these VMs are managed by the virtual machine monitor (VMM) [28]. CSP manages the physical machine with the help of hypervisor and provides resources on-demand to the cloud users [29]; the users have no right to access them directly. Multiple cloud users can share the same infrastructure or IT resources. In the event of malicious attacks, users' virtual machines can easily be compromised.

The proposed architecture performs as the autonomous authorized third party of network forensics investigation, which forensically investigates cloud-based virtual resources (such as security threats as well as data acquisition, multi-tenant, and infringing privacy) with the support provided by CSP. The factor which we assume here is that we can only trust the cloud provider and the IT infrastructure, whereas cloud users' VMs are untrusted. However, the behavior of a virtual machine needs to be modified for secure M2M communication; a malicious attacker manipulates data (gains access to the user's virtual machine). Therefore, we do not collect forensics data while the process is running on the user virtual machine rather than apply forensics investigation directly. The virtualized cloud infrastructure guarantees virtual machine isolation [28]; it is completely clear that the attacker does not access other VMs itself or VMM running on the same physical host.

Several types of research have been published that relate the situation of the trust in the cloud infrastructure, justified through a technical mechanism. Susan F. Crowell says [30] regarding the VMs trust, for virtual machine trust isolation in an IaaS cloud environment, embodiments of the invention monitor level of suspicious activities on the particular virtual machine using embedded node agents. Crowell addresses the critical problems of VMs over the cloud, for example, to create a trustworthy cloud infrastructure by designing a security audit system: verify clients' data confidentiality and integrity [32], measure virtual machines root-of-trust [31], enforce by a technical mechanism not only by Service Level Agreements (SLAs) contracts.

In this chapter, we present a model for network forensics to investigate security threats (malicious attacks) when machines communicate with each other in a cloud environment. The forensics process model (shown in Figure 2.1) depends on five process-layers that interact with the control manager, and the adaptation of the process-layers from the flow of the process of the NIST network forensics model [33]. The process-layers perform independent tasks regarding the incident investigation of cloud computing security issues. The investigational tasks execute a parallel and distributed manner in a multitenant environment. We already discussed the multitenancy in the above section 2.1.3.2.

In this section, we describe the purpose of an individual process-layer; the first process-layer is the collection of data or data collection layer, in which overall data is captured. The control manager interacts with the data collection and decides when to start or stop the data capturing process. The data collection coordinates with the migration of VM in the cloud

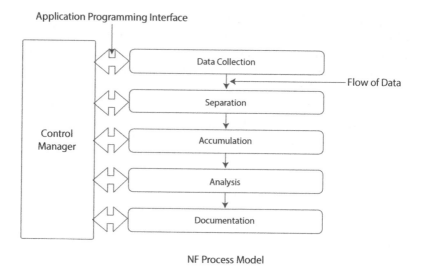

Figure 2.1 Network forensics process model for cloud investigation.

environment and the control manager simultaneously collects data traffic of VM migration. On the next process-layer is the separation or filtration; the actual task of the process-layer is to filter captured data by cloud user. The main advantage is that each set of data maintains data accordingly to the single cloud users. Additionally, separation can compress user-specific collected data; reduce the size, and filtering forensically network data traffic.

In the third process-layer, the accumulator or aggregate layer deals with the adds data from multiple sources of a single cloud user. The cloud user utilizes resources from distinct physical locations such as load balancing then the accumulator collects all data from multiple source location. Furthermore, this layer helps to collaborate with all the network data into a single set. The fourth layer is data analysis, analysis of the preprocessed data set for the detailed investigation. The control manager configures the complete transmission from data capture to the accumulation layer, analysis process-layer is run as a cloud service in the cloud environment. The last process-layer is documentation, which presents the analysis results and consequence to tackle the entire security threats.

The proposed forensics network architecture for secure machine communication translates the conceptual blocks of separate services as described in Table 2.1.

Table 2.1 Network forensics architecture conceptual block of the model.

Name of network forensics process-layer	Task description
The Control Manager	• Manage cloud infrastructure; • An interface configures and controls the forensics process; • Authorize forensics request; • Target cloud users VMs; • Delegate to a third party.
Data Collection/Collection of Data	• Execute on the local VM; • Monitor physical host; • Collect network traffic at the VMM level; • For an update, dynamically reconfigure; • Start/stop data collection.
Separation/Filtration	• Filtering data individual cloud user; • Investigate distinct nodes on the particular physical host; • All forensics investigations independently investigated; • Separate datasets to a single cloud user; • Filtering and reduce the network traffic size; • Monitor specifically cloud users; • The proposed architecture uses VMs lookup table; • Filtering ID, Mac addresses for further investigation.
Accumulator/Aggregation	• Filtration process-layer provides data; • Collect data; • Capture from the several locations; • Combine data.
Analyzation	• Potentially support multiple possibilities; • Transfer the accumulator layer output to the investigator; • A user of the cloud deploy analysis as a cloud service; • Run analysis on the cloud.
Documentation	• Produce a report on the basis of analysis results; • Presentation of analysis outcomes.

2.3   Model Implementation

In this section, we have implemented the model of the prototype archi-tecture described in section 2.2. In the implementation phase, we extend some crucial components that are usable for network forensics investiga-tion on the cloud environment; the prototype implementation of the pro-posed architecture assumption are as follows:

- An account of individual cloud user VMs managed by CSP;
- Cloud users able to run/stop the process of data collection for forensics investigation;
- Monitor the VMs for cloud security perspective and also ensure the M2M secure communication;
- Inside the cloud, a web-based system created and used to analyze the collected data.

In this chapter, we clarify that the users are able to work with the VMs, to change their status individual and also monitor the overall activity param-eters of VMs. Our proposed architecture slightly extends the software management for control of network forensics by adding some application programming interface. Using OpenNebula [34, 35], an open-source active community-based cloud management system, it supports more distinct and independent VMMs products. The main objective is to create an inter-face of analysis tool to capture malicious threats that run as a service in the users' cloud VMs. In this scenario, NetworkMiner [36] an open-source network forensics analysis framework, helps to analyze collected foren-sics data within the cloud [38]. The next couple of sections briefly elabo-rate on the complete mechanism of the OpenNebula and NetworkMiner analysis tool.

2.3.1   OpenNebula (Hypervisor) Implementation Platform

In the model architecture, the control manager is the add-on extension of the OpenNebula application programming interface (shown in Figure 2.2) that we already discussed in section 2.3. The cloud user request to the control manager for accessing on-demand VMs for the different physical host, the control manager instance OpenNebula can manage users request regarding cloud storage, networks, and software services.

The authentication gives the user access to VMs within the cloud [37]. All the physical hosts share multiple virtual machines, and these

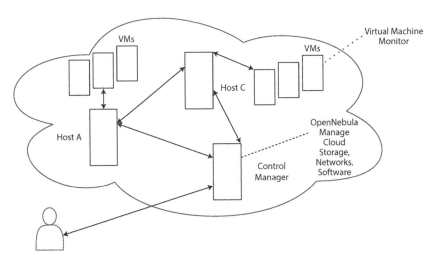

Figure 2.2 OpenNebula: a community-based cloud management system that manages resources of the cloud physical host, VMs, VMM, control access, and authentication between cloud users.

machines monitor by virtual machine monitors (VMM). OpenNebula perform overall management of a cloud system; it helps the network investigator to analyse forensically captured data of vulnerabilities, risk, cyber-threats, and malicious attacks on cloud network environment for further investigations.

2.3.2   NetworkMiner Analysis Tool

NetworkMiner analysis is an open-source network forensics analysis tool that aims to collect malicious attacks or threats over the cloud; these things help in the forensics investigation. In the implementation phase, cloud user direct data collection and separation or filtration layer, where it can start/stop/reset cloud VMs that running as a forensics service.

The collaboration of the layers performs both the tasks, for example, VMM and network forensics task. NetworkMiner received collected data from OpenNebula and then run accumulator and analysis forensics process-layer as a cloud-based service for aggregate as well as analyze provided captured data. The documentation layer performs visualization of the analysis output. Our modified has additional forensics components (shown in Figure 2.3) that ensure safe machine communication and also help for further investigation.

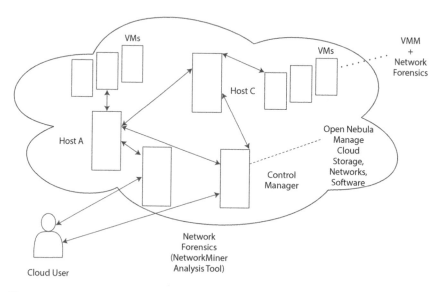

Figure 2.3 NetworkMiner analysis tool cloud-based forensics services.

The actual cloud environment provided by OpenNebula and Network Miner is as under:

- The first is to start data collection, trigger to start the forensics process on the cloud network;
- Next is stop data collection, trigger to stop the network forensics process;
- Virtual machine identity (VM-ID) used by OpenNebula for setting the action parameter of an individual virtual machine;
- OpenNebula translating VM-ID into MAC network address;
- Filtering the MAC address;
- Help to capture the PCAP file (Package capture file) used for tackle network traffic;
- An additional component of network forensics Network Miner analysis tool manages the entire VMs analysis (VMM); the main task is to collect, separate, accumulate, and analyze data for proper communication;
- The control manager triggers the overall system action.

In the next section, we calculate the performance matrix of OpenNebula and NetworkMiner, and also compare both the accuracy and efficiency of the tools to the other well-known network forensics tools.

2.3.3   Performance Matrix Evaluation & Result Discussion

Performance evaluation of the proposed architecture is to verify our network forensics cloud-based system performs well enough as compared to the previously published model. The setup of measuring the performance impact on the running VMM manages all VMs in the cloud environment with network forensics. The process consumes computational and power resources to evaluate the model performance, communicate resources that would capture, aggregate and analyse, and transfer network traffic.

In the experiment, the proposed model architecture intended to quantify the performance matrix by comparing both the scenarios: (i) without network forensics and (ii) with network forensics (shown in Figure 2.4).

The performance measurement was done by setting the tune of the host system, as well as mention the crucial software specification of the hosts, described below:

- System Software: Linux Ubuntu 18.04;
- Application Software: OpenNebula and NetworkMiner;
- System Specification: x64 2.4GHz Octa-Core 7th Generation CPU with 32GB RAM connected via highly powerful ethernet connectivity up to Gigabit.

Evaluate almost 8 VMs parallel with network forensics on a single virtual machine monitor, VMs hosts a web-based service interface that runs tasks as a computationally intensive. This web-based service interface calculates both the great common divers, for example, with or without

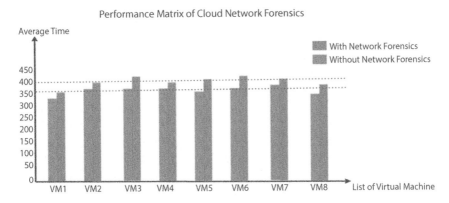

Figure 2.4 Measurement of the performance of network forensics while running cloud infrastructure systems.

network forensics, output results show in Figure 2.4. Iteratively calculate the request of cloud users to call a function over several times. Moreover, users' web services and NetworkMiner analysis run a separate interface.

- Call Function: More than 2,800 times with minimum 20 concurrent requests;
- The time it takes to calculate the call function of cloud users is less than 2 minutes;
- The average performance of VMs is almost 89%;
- Average performance reduction between 3% to 18%.

Recently, cloud service provides offered Forensics-as-a-Service. Similar to the other cloud services, FaaS is a business service model for digital investigators. One is the addition of cloud resources for the analysis of forensics data by cloud users, and the second is the most prominent aspect that, not account for VMM plus network forensics cloud-based system. Estimate the sets of forensics transferred data to the accumulator that aggregate and then the analyzation process-layer.

In the next section, we have taken a real-world scenario of cloud security impact on M2M communication and how we can utilize the cloud application in the fourth industrial revolution.

2.4   Cloud Security Impact on M2M Communication

For an authorized and secure communication channel an autonomous system is required [38], many parts of a system where a machine can communicate with others, such as (i) daemon to backend, (ii) service to service, (iii) IoT tools, and (iv) CLI (client to internet service). Establishing an authorized trust system between client [39], means authorization process attempts to build trust in the cloud environment by authorizing a client. In this case, a cloud client can simply utilize cloud applications, services, and securely processes cloud infrastructure. There is no need to typically authenticate like username/password, two-way authentication, social login, and others. However, provide protected, and secure machines communication, cloud client grant credentials, this credential has two pieces of information, one is the client ID, and the second is secret. This piece of information can request access for secured resources. The cloud-based services access mechanism of secure M2M communication are as under:

- The cloud client request to the authorizing server by sending the client ID and secret along with the audience, get access to cloud infrastructure (access distinct virtual machine);
- The authorized server validate request (if successful);
- Send response by giving the access token;
- By providing the access token, cloud users request secured resources from the server.

In this chapter, we have proposed our architecture on the basis of daemon to backend secure communication channel for machines.

2.4.1   Cloud Computing Security Application in the Fourth Industrial Revolution (4.0)

The fourth industrial revolution is the transformation of industrial and manufacturing products, introducing the new stages in the organization, valuing creation processes, and controlling the organizational value chain. Cloud computing (CC) is one of the biggest aspects to boost manufacturing products. CC brought about a remarkable overhaul of the enterprise's phenomena, a significant investment to establish IT infrastructure. In almost every business, CC benefits in many ways. The most prominent features are the flexibility to pay for resources, 24/7 availability, on-demand means resource elasticity, based on need only. Moreover, when it comes to Infrastructure-as-a-Service (IaaS), an existing infrastructure on the pay-as-you-go platform, an obvious choice for enterprises saving on the cost of investment to acquire, control, available, manage, and maintain server all the time. Infrastructure becomes a commodity; the majority of businesses use the services of the cloud to enhance the manufacturing productions, whether or not they know about the cloud.

To show the advantage of cloud computing in industry 4.0, we have adopted the real-world scenario to make the concept clear. Consider your business has multiple locations, you might have trouble connecting the team, and trying to collaborate on the same project, because of the distance between them. The same issue arises when your employees work remotely. The thing is how we can tackle the situation; cloud collaboration tools allow your people to access the same project and connect several people remotely in a single go. Accessing the real-time project reduces time and money and has many advantages: the ability to upload documents and send via email remotely; decreasing the time for updating; easy to monitor and get updates on the project completion; enhancing communication, reducing cost, and increasing productivity.

Consider another aspect: your company rapidly grows, but you do not have a way to scale your infrastructure. With the rapid enhancement of organizational production growth, you want to hire employees, but you do not have an idea of when and how large it will become. When you purchase convectional internal infrastructure, and potentially you want employees to maintain, that will increase the cost of purchases and hiring employees. In this situation, the cloud is the better solution; no matter how quickly you grow, cloud service provider simply provides scale on-demand IT infrastructure as per need and pay for what you used. The prominent feature in this scenario is protected machine communication; it is a trustable remote service; it provides a secure channel to access IT resources; you can rely on it.

2.5   Conclusion

The rapid growth of cloud computing, especially the use of cloud-based IT infrastructure in recent years, creates new challenges for network investigators. Essential means for remote prevention in the cloud-based industry 4.0 environment, tackle the security threats between machine communications that enhance the need of forensics in the cloud. In a cloud environment, it is hard to determine the location of virtual resources, which may change even a certain time frame. Network forensics needs to be limited in a multitenant environment, the reason behind the specific system under observation. We have analyzed the critical problems with a specific concentration on forensics for the cloud service models, and proposed a generic model for secure communication between M2M in a cloud-based environment. For the sake of prevention, we developed a system architecture and integrated implementation of network forensics modules that identify security challenges and its impact on the fourth industrial revolution application, with the support of the OpenNebula cloud management infrastructure. The security issues that our method solved are: First, facilitate cloud users by providing a mechanism of remote network forensics for data acquisition, processes, and monitor means overall control the physical location of virtual resources independently. Second, another limitation in cloud computing that is infringing privacy and security; the proposed approach ensures the separation of cloud users in a multitenant environment. The last is to remove the cost of transferring network collected data, impalement external investigation tools that analyze and control internal cloud services by network investigators. This contribution eliminates the disadvantages of traditional cloud-based services that run locally on the internal infrastructure of the industry.

References

1. Sun, Panjun. "Research on cloud computing service based on trust access control." *International Journal of Engineering Business Management* 12 (2020): 1847979019897444.
2. Siddiqui, Shadab, Manuj Darbari, and Diwakar Yagyasen. "A comprehensive study of challenges and issues in cloud computing." In *Soft Computing and Signal Processing*, pp. 325-344. Springer, Singapore, 2019.
3. Chong, Ngo Yang. "Cloud Computing Challenges in a General Perspective." *Journal of Computing and Management Studies* 3 (2019).
4. Meghanathan, Natarajan, Sumanth Reddy Allam, and Loretta A. Moore. "Tools and techniques for network forensics." arXiv preprint arXiv:1004.0570 (2010).
5. Garfinkel, Simson. "Network forensics: Tapping the internet." *IEEE Internet Computing* 6 (2002): 60-66.
6. Sikos, Leslie F. "Packet analysis for network forensics: a comprehensive survey." *Forensic Science International: Digital Investigation* 32 (2020): 200892.
7. Frank, Alejandro Germán, Lucas Santos Dalenogare, and Néstor Fabián Ayala. "Industry 4.0 technologies: Implementation patterns in manufacturing companies." *International Journal of Production Economics* 210 (2019): 15-26.
8. Bassi, Lorenzo. "Industry 4.0: Hope, hype or revolution?." In 2017 IEEE 3rd *International Forum on Research and Technologies for Society and Industry (RTSI)*, pp. 1-6. IEEE, 2017.
9. Lasi, Heiner, Peter Fettke, Hans-Georg Kemper, Thomas Feld, and Michael Hoffmann. "Industry 4.0." *Business & Information Systems Engineering* 6, no. 4 (2014): 239-242.
10. Vaidya, Saurabh, Prashant Ambad, and Santosh Bhosle. "Industry 4.0–a glimpse." *Procedia Manufacturing* 20 (2018): 233-238.
11. Agolla, Joseph Evans. "Human capital in the smart manufacturing and industry 4.0 revolution." *Digital Transformation in Smart Manufacturing* (2018): 41-58.
12. Bahrin, Mohd Aiman Kamarul, Mohd Fauzi Othman, Nor Hayati Nor Azli, and Muhamad Farihin Talib. "Industry 4.0: A review on industrial automation and robotic." *Jurnal Teknologi* 78, no. 6-13 (2016).
13. Varghese, Anitha, and Deepaknath Tandur. "Wireless requirements and challenges in Industry 4.0." In 2014 *International Conference on Contemporary Computing and Informatics (IC3I)*, pp. 634-638. IEEE, 2014.

14. Lee, Jay, Hossein Davari, Jaskaran Singh, and Vibhor Pandhare. "Industrial Artificial Intelligence for industry 4.0-based manufacturing systems." *Manufacturing Letters* 18 (2018): 20-23.

15. Lo, Anthony, Yee Wei Law, and Martin Jacobsson. "A cellular-centric service architecture for machine-to-machine (M2M) communications." *IEEE wireless communications* 20, no. 5 (2013): 143-151.

16. Wu, Geng, Shilpa Talwar, Kerstin Johnsson, Nageen Himayat, and Kevin D. Johnson. "M2M: From mobile to embedded internet." *IEEE Communications Magazine* 49, no. 4 (2011): 36-43.

17. Laghari, Asif Ali, Hui He, Asiya Khan, Neetesh Kumar, and RupakKharel. "Quality of experience framework for cloud computing (QoC)." *IEEE Access* 6 (2018): 64876-64890.

18. Armbrust, Michael, Armando Fox, Rean Griffith, Anthony D. Joseph, Randy Katz, Andy Konwinski, Gunho Lee et al. "A view of cloud computing." *Communications of the ACM* 53, no. 4 (2010): 50-58.

19. Laghari, Asif Ali, Hui He, Muhammad Shafiq, and Asiya Khan. "Assessing effect of Cloud distance on end user's Quality of Experience (QoE)." In *2016 2nd IEEE international conference on computer and communications (ICCC)*, pp. 500-505.IEEE, 2016.

20. Laghari, Asif Ali, Hui He, Imtiaz A. Halepoto, M. SullemanMemon, and Sajida Parveen. "Analysis of quality of experience frameworks for cloud computing." *IJCSNS* 17, no. 12 (2017): 228.

21. Kumar, Vishal, Asif Ali Laghari, ShahidKarim, Muhammad Shakir, and Ali Anwar Brohi. "Comparison of fog computing & cloud computing." *International Journal of Mathematical Sciences and Computing (IJMSC)* 5, no. 1 (2019): 31-41.

22. Manvi, Sunilkumar S., and Gopal Krishna Shyam. "Resource management for Infrastructure as a Service (IaaS) in cloud computing: A survey." *Journal of Network and Computer Applications* 41 (2014): 424-440.

23. Adhikari, Mainak, Sudarshan Nandy, and Tarachand Amgoth. "Meta heuristic-based task deployment mechanism for load balancing in IaaS cloud." *Journal of Network and Computer Applications* 128 (2019): 64-77.

24. Pereira, T., L. Barreto, and A. Amaral. "Network and information security challenges within Industry 4.0 paradigm." *Procedia manufacturing* 13 (2017): 1253-1260.

25. Zhong, Ray Y., Xun Xu, Eberhard Klotz, and Stephen T. Newman. "Intelligent manufacturing in the context of industry 4.0: a review." *Engineering* 3, no. 5 (2017): 616-630.

26. Preuveneers, Davy, and Elisabeth Ilie-Zudor. "The intelligent industry of the future: A survey on emerging trends, research challenges and opportunities in Industry 4.0." *Journal of Ambient Intelligence and Smart Environments* 9, no. 3 (2017): 287-298.

27. Stock, Tim, and Günther Seliger. "Opportunities of sustainable manufacturing in industry 4.0." *Procedia Cirp* 40 (2016): 536-541.

28. Gebhardt, Tobias, and Hans P. Reiser. "Network forensics for cloud computing." In *IFIP International Conference on Distributed Applications and Interoperable Systems*, pp. 29-42. Springer, Berlin, Heidelberg, 2013.

29. Wei, Jinpeng, Xiaolan Zhang, Glenn Ammons, Vasanth Bala, and Peng Ning. "Managing security of virtual machine images in a cloud environment." In *Proceedings of the 2009 ACM workshop on Cloud computing security*, pp. 91-96. 2009.

30. Crowell, Susan F., Jason A. Nikolai, and Andrew T. Thorstensen. "Virtual machine trust isolation in a cloud environment." U.S. Patent Application 13/969,705, filed February 19, 2015.

31. Scott-Nash, Mark E. "Roots-of-trust for measurement of virtual machines." U.S. Patent 9,053,059, issued June 9, 2015.

32. Ramarathinam, Aravind, and Srivatsan Parthasarathy. "Allocating identified intermediary tasks for requesting virtual machines within a trust sphere on a processing goal." U.S. Patent 9,342,326, issued May 17, 2016.

33. Kent, Karen, Suzanne Chevalier, Tim Grance, and Hung Dang. "Guide to integrating forensic techniques into incident response." *NIST Special Publication* 10, no. 14 (2006): 800-86.

34. Milojičić, Dejan, Ignacio M. Llorente, and Ruben S. Montero. "Opennebula: A cloud management tool." *IEEE Internet Computing* 15, no. 2 (2011): 11-14.

35. Ismaeel, Salam, Ali Miri, Dharmendra Chourishi, and SM Reza Dibaj. "Open source cloud management platforms: A review." In 2015 *IEEE 2nd International Conference on Cyber Security and Cloud Computing*, pp. 470-475. IEEE, 2015.

36. Dargahi, Tooska, Ali Dehghantanha, and Mauro Conti. "Investigating Storage as a Service Cloud Platform: pCloud as a Case Study." In *Contemporary Digital Forensic Investigations of Cloud and Mobile Applications*, pp. 185-204. Syngress, 2017.

37. Barrowclough, John Patrick, and Rameez Asif. "Securing cloud hypervisors: A survey of the threats, vulnerabilities, and countermeasures." *Security and Communication Networks* 2018 (2018).

38. Stergiou, Christos L., Andreas P. Plageras, Konstantinos E. Psannis, and Brij B. Gupta. "Secure machine learning scenario from big data in cloud computing via internet of things network." In *Handbook of Computer Networks and Cyber Security*, pp. 525-554. Springer, Cham, 2020.

39. Chang, David Yu, Messaoud Benantar, John Yow-Chun Chang, and Vishwanath Venkataramappa. "Authentication and authorization methods for cloud computing security." U.S. Patent 8,769,622 issued July 1, 2014.

40. Xue, Colin Ting Si, and Felicia Tiong Wee Xin. "Benefits and challenges of the adoption of cloud computing in business." *International Journal on Cloud Computing: Services and Architecture* 6, no. 6 (2016): 1-15.

3

Regional Language Recognition System for Industry 4.0

Bharathi V[1*], N. Renugadevi[2†], J. Padmapriya[3] and M. Vijayprakash[4]

[1]*Department of ECE, Indian Institute of Information Technology Tiruchirappalli, Tiruchirappalli, TamilNadu, India*
[2]*Department of CSE, Indian Institute of Information Technology Tiruchirappalli, Tiruchirappalli, TamilNadu, India*
[3]*Department of Marine Engineering, AMET Deemed to be University, Chennai, India*
[4]*Department of Civil Engineering, Mount Zion College of Engineering and Technology, Pudukottai, TamilNadu, India*

Abstract

In Industry 4.0, a Speech Recognition System (SRS) is used to develop an automated manufacturing unit and establish better communication between humans and machines. A SRS that translates the errors occurring in the automated system to the worker's language will help them to resolve major issues at the initial stage itself. Mainly, the industries in Tamil Nadu and Puducherry states require a Tamil SRS (TSRS) as the majority of operators and workers in these states speak only Tamil. TSRS can be used to recognize the Tamil keywords used frequently in the manufacturing sector. It has been inferred from the extensive literature survey that most of the SRS has been developed using HMM/GMM classification which recognizes only up to 30 Tamil phonemes and more words need to be explored. The SRS built using LSTM recurrent neural networks in various languages such as English and Chinese have given more accuracy and can recognize more words. Even SRS built for the Chinese Sichuan dialect with more phonemes than the Tamil language has achieved more accuracy using LSTM. Therefore, this paper reviews related research works using LSTM to design an efficient TSRS that can resolve the issues in the manufacturing sector of industry 4.0.

*Corresponding author: bharathiv@iiitt.ac.in
†Corresponding author: renugadevin@iiitt.ac.in

Shibin David, R. S. Anand, V. Jeyakrishnan, and M. Niranjanamurthy (eds.) *Security Issues and Privacy Concerns in Industry 4.0 Applications*, (35–54) © 2021 Scrivener Publishing LLC

Keywords: Industry 4.0, manufacturing sector, speech recognition system, Tamil language, LSTM

3.1   Introduction

Industry 4.0 has presented new methodologies to tackle the recent advancements in manufacturing systems. It enables new ways to create business models in manufacturing industries, thereby transforming the way of living in the new digital era. The main aim of Industry 4.0 is to increase productivity and efficiency by implementing a higher level of automation. This Industry 4.0 environment enables the smart manufacturing sector and collaborative systems to make better decisions to execute tasks and solve collision avoidance problems. From the outlook of production and service management, Industry 4.0 initiates intelligent communicative systems [1]. Some of these comprise complex interactions between two machines in addition to the Human-Machine Interaction. Internet of Things (IoT), cloud computing, big data and augmented reality, autonomous robots, and cyber security form the essential technologies required by Industry 4.0. IoT is the connection of two things, namely, internet and things. IoT network comprises interaction of Thing-to-Thing, Thing-to-Human and Human-to-Human that are connected to the internet. IoT architecture consists of various layers [1]. Among these layers, the Interface Layer allows the interconnection and management of the "things" easier. Thus, a clearly accessible interaction of the user with the system is provided while displaying the information.

Integrating human with the manufacturing systems is the prerequisite in achieving efficiency in manufacturing sector of industry 4.0. An interactive interface must be established between humans and machine/robots to analyze the interaction between the physical and the production world. Establishing interaction between Human–Physical systems is the major problem in the manufacturing sector. Human–physical systems implemented in the manufacturing sector include the modules mentioned in Figure 3.1 [2]. In a manufacturing sector, the physical module includes temperature sensors, humidity sensors and scanner module. Human can control the machines and robots by speech commands. The main aim of this interaction is to achieve accuracy and efficiency by controlling adaptive robots, planning the dynamic task and avoidance of active collision [2].

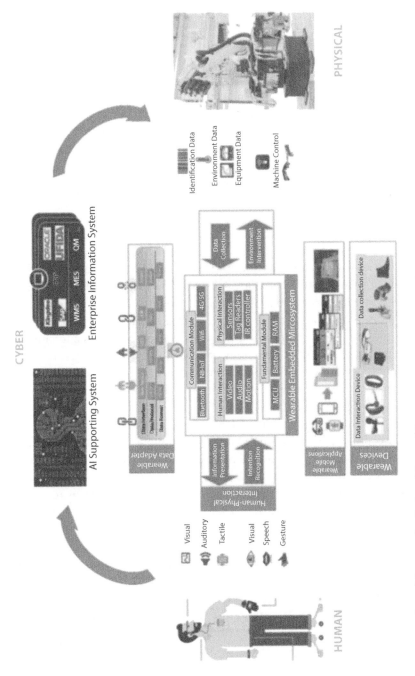

Figure 3.1 Technical framework of industrial wearable system.

An Automatic Speech Recognition system [4] can be defined as a technology that transcribes speech. Speech being the most instinctive form of human communication, the main objective of this technology is to correctly recognize the words spoken by a person with maximum accuracy. Also, this recognition should function with the speech of any human being irrespective of the gender, noise, vocabulary size, speaker accent and other characteristics. Once recognized, the same speech is to be converted into a written format. In general, the speech signals are quasi-stationary signals lasting for a duration of 5–100 ms, provided their characteristics are fairly stationary. The initial task of speech recognition is preprocessing, followed by feature extraction to retrieve the appropriate information from the speech sample. Feature extraction methods like Mel Frequency Cepstral Coefficient methods are used for extracting the cepstral coefficients.

Tamil is one of the traditional languages spoken in the world. It is the native language spoken by the people in TamilNadu, Puducherry Union Territory and in most of the southern parts of India. It is also an official language in Singapore, Malaysia, Sri Lanka, Mauritius, and Canada. Many precious literary works are available in Tamil which need to be taken to all parts of the world. Vasuki *et al.*, discussed and evaluated the identification of various emotions from the Tamil words uttered by adults and children from their speech with the accuracy of 82% in [3].

Many speech recognition-based applications are available now to make the process easier for people. We can make calls, and perform many other tasks, just by giving voice commands. SRS is a system which receives input in the form of spoken words, decodes it and either displays the recognized words or gives a command to the technological devices to perform a task automatically. With efficient recognition systems, even a difficult job can be done efficiently through recognized input speech. By doing so, we may reduce the time of consumption since it enables us to to perform multitasking. Also, currently all the manufacturing sector involves a high risk of electrocution or fire accidents that are a threat to workers. These accidents occurring in high voltage systems can be reduced if we operate things using speech recognition systems. In the southern part of Tamilnadu, most of the workers and operators who work in the lowest level of the top-bottom hierarchy are fluent only in Tamil. The main purpose of this proposal is to explore the research methodologies in designing an efficient Tamil speech recognition system which will help them to understand the automated systems well. The proposed block diagram is given in Figure 3.2.

Figure 3.2 Proposed human–physical interaction systems.

- Human–Physical interaction is the major problem in the automated industries.
- Data collection from physical system: Data collection is done by using sensor modules.
- From human to system: Artificial Intelligence is used to establish industrial human – machine interaction. The main aim is to design an automated system which understands naturally the human intention.
- From system to physical: the machine and process is facilitated by connecting the physical system to the industrial system through the sensors. Then, information is retrieved from the industrial system by ASR. Now, direct human–physical interaction can be performed easily. The human can give commands to the robot or the automated process "by giving instructions through the speech recognition system."

This chapter summarizes the role of speech recognition systems in the manufacturing sector and various speech recognition systems present for the Tamil language along with the methodologies that can be used in future to improvise the Tamil ASR systems. The following sections in this chapter include method of collecting databases, general ASR model, features extraction, existing recognition methods, methods which can be adopted to improvise the system, conclusion, and scope of future work.

3.2 Automatic Speech Recognition System

An important criterion in designing an efficient ASR system is to collect a speech corpus. The database taken into consideration in the existing research papers discussed here consists of Tamil characters, simple words, and some sample sentences. The speech corpus is collected under noiseless conditions and sampled at a rate of 16 KHz. Some of the datasets readily available for the Tamil language are listed in Table 3.1. An ASR system consists of the

Table 3.1 List of open source datasets for Tamil language.

Sl. No	Dataset	No. of speakers	Developer	Link
1.	Tamil Speech Data - ASR with 62000 audio files	1000	ILTPDC	https://tdil-dc.in/index.php?option=com_download&task=showresourceDetails&toolid=2003&lang=en
2.	Form and Function words, Command and Control words, Phonetically balanced vocabulary, Proper names, most frequent 1,000 words	450	Linguistic Data Consortium for Indian Languages	http://www.ldcil.org/resourcesSpeechCorpTamil.aspx
3.	MILE Tamil Speech Recognition - Speech samples and their transcriptions in Unicode text format	600	MILE Lab	http://mile.ee.iisc.ac.in/downloads.html
4.	4250 Tamil sentences	-	Open SLR	http://openslr.org/65

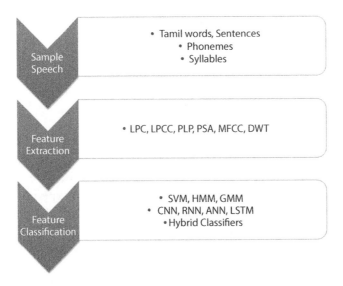

Figure 3.3 Automatic speech recognition framework.

modules namely, preprocessing, feature extraction and feature classification and evaluation. The main blocks used in an ASR are shown in Figure 3.3 [4].

3.2.1   Preprocessing

Preprocessing of a speech includes:

1. **De-noising**: removes unwanted interference or noise by designing appropriate filters for enhancing the signal's quality [4].
2. **Voice Activity Detection**: It is a technique to identify voiced, unvoiced and the silent regions in a speech signal. This is achieved by using a few parameters like zero crossing rate, energy of the signal and autocorrelation function [4].
3. **Framing & Windowing**: At first the signal is broken down into several frames of shorter duration for analysis, instead of analyzing the whole speech signal. There is a 50% overlap between adjacent frames. After framing, each of them is multiplied with a window function. The speech signal is mostly stationary for a time range of 10-30 ms. Windowing is the process of removing unnatural discontinuities in the speech segment [4].

There are a few types of window functions like Rectangular window, Hamming window, Hanning window, etc., the choice of which depends upon several factors. Hamming window is highly preferred in speech recognition systems as it has smooth transition along the edges and gives more accurate frequency spectrum of the original signal.

3.2.2   Feature Extraction

Selecting the best method to extract features from the sample decides the efficiency of the whole speech system. Since speech is a short and non-stationary signal, extracting features from it is quite an experimental task. Aishwarya analyzed the different features extraction techniques to recognize Tamil words from speech and the results were tabulated in [5]. In [6], the word- and tri-phone-based approaches to recognize the Tamil words from the speech were discussed. This chapter discusses various features that can be extracted from the speech signal. Some of the techniques available for speech feature extraction are Linear Predictive Coding (LPC), Linear Predictive Cepstral Coefficient (LPCC), Mel-Frequency Cepstral Coefficients (MFCC), Relative Spectral Filtering (RASTA), and Perceptual Linear Predictive (PLP) analysis; they are discussed below.

3.2.2.1   Linear Predictive Coding (LPC)

The steps used to find the LPC coefficients are mentioned in Figure 3.4 [4].

- **Pre-emphasis:** The numeric in the digitized speech signal, $s_i(n)$, is obtained through a lower order framework of digital systems, to level the signal and to make it less vulnerable to loss of formants while framing the signal. Implying difference equation (3.1) [4] in the entire digitized speech signal will eliminate the adverse effects present in the signal.

$$\hat{S}_i = s_i(n) - g\, s_i(n-1) \tag{3.1}$$

- **Framing:** Disintegrating the digitized speech signal at the difference equation of the pre-emphasis phase into a few frames; through separating the adjacent frames of the entire digitized speech signal with N samples each.
- **Windowing:** Windowing is done to expel unnatural discontinuities in the discourse section and the contortion in the basic range. The selection of window plays a vital role; here

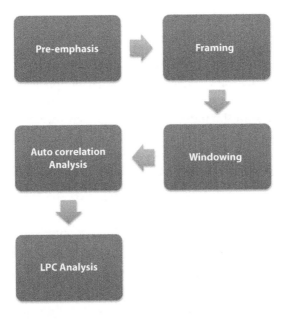

Figure 3.4 LPC framework.

the equation corresponding to Hamming window (3.2) [4] is given.

$$w(n) = 0.54 - 0.46 \cos\left[\frac{2\Pi n}{N-1}\right] \quad 0 \le n \le N-1 \tag{3.2}$$

- **Autocorrelation analysis:** To extract the similarity between the windowed speech samples, analysis of the dataset is executed. Each windowed frame of the signal is analyzed for similarity through this phase.
- **LPC analysis:** The LPC analysis would be carried out by evaluating the power and recurrence of the signal which was purposely analyzed to extract the speech samples in the entire range of the signal with the aid of assessed formants. Thiang discussed that the predictive coding method would be a linear method to recognize the speech signals by extracting the features accurately using ANN [7]. Inverse filtering is the process of extracting formants and deduction of the shifted display of the remaining signal is called residue.

3.2.2.2 Linear Predictive Cepstral Coefficient (LPCC)

The same process is carried out from pre-emphasis till the autocorrelation analysis and then cepstral coefficient must be addressed. Features are extracted by taking the Nth windowed speech sample as a reference and correlating with the linear combination of its previous samples. The features extracted from the numeric of the digitized speech signal are cepstral coefficients. The equation used to extract the cepstral coefficients are given below (3.3). The LPCC features are extracted from the Tamil and Telugu languages to recognize the emotion in the speech signals through the Neural Networks [8].

$$c_m = \begin{cases} a_1 & ; m = 1 \\ a_m + \sum_{k=1}^{m-1} \left(\dfrac{k}{m} \right) \cdot c_k \cdot a_{m-k} & ; 1 \le m \le p \\ a_m + \sum_{k=1}^{m-1} \left(\dfrac{k}{m} \right) \cdot c_k \cdot a_{m-k} & ; m > p \end{cases} \tag{3.3}$$

3.2.2.3 Perceptual Linear Predictive (PLP)

Three techniques are carried out to estimate the numeric in speech: 1) by obtaining the resolution for the spectrum with critical band, 2) equal pitch curve, and 3) pitch intensity. Spectral analysis for the numeric in the speech signal is outperformed by the obtained frames of M taken samples. Estimation of the numeric in the speech samples from the pitch intensity is done after traversing the samples through the N band filters with the implication of power law. This estimation is given for the next observation, i.e., to analyze the PLP. Then, Fast Fourier Transform (FFT) analysis is carried out and estimated vectors are obtained by emphasizing only the real values after taking inverse FFT.

3.2.2.4 Power Spectral Analysis

The frequency information of the numeric speech samples after windowing can be observed with the aid of the power spectrum obtained for the windowed speech samples. The occurrence of the frequency information in the numeric speech samples are obtained after applying Discrete Fourier

Transform. It provides the recurrence information of the numeric speech samples which were in the time domain. FFT has been utilized to expand the productivity in obtaining the numeric pitch in the discourse signal, since it contains just real point estimates. The subsequent information received after the filtering process contains both the relative magnitude and phase of the state-of-the-art signal in time domain. The fourier transformation would lead to better retrieval of the state-of-the-art signal which is in the time domain. In [9], power spectral features from the recorded speech samples were extracted and applied classification that resulted in the accuracy of about 75% for the word recognition.

3.2.2.5   Mel Frequency Cepstral Coefficients

This technique emphasizes only the amplitude spectrum instead of concentrating on both amplitude and spatial domain, since the pitch intensity of the numeric in the speech can be obtained from the amplitude spectrum. The steps implemented to extract MFCC features are mentioned in Figure 3.5 [4].

Framing and windowing of the numeric in the speech samples are carried out, then the FFT is implied on the windowed numeric speech samples for filtering purposes. Subsequently, the amplitude information from the filtering of the numeric speech samples are retained by not emphasizing the phase information of the filtered numeric speech samples. Scaling and smoothing are performed to retrieve the information only at the pitch with intensity of the numeric in the speech signal by eliminating other information. Then, the amplitude information of the speech samples is obtained by using Discrete Cosine Transform.

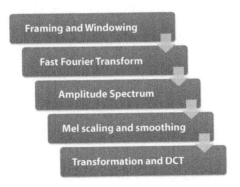

Figure 3.5 MFCC framework.

Karpagavali, in [9] explored the recognition of Tamil syllables using vowel onset points and features like MFCC, LPCC and PLP. The classification is done by using Multiple Layer Perceptron and Support Vector Machine algorithms and achieved the accuracy of about 90%. Abhishek Verma, discussed in [10] that the features were extracted with MFCC and Convolutional Neural Network (CNN) were applied which resulted in better accuracy of 97%.

3.2.2.6   Wavelet Transform

Time-frequency translation of a signal is processed with the help of wavelet transform. The basis function of the mother wavelet, i.e., the fundamental wavelet, is localized in time and frequency as well. The size of the window to group the samples depends upon the information present in the respective samples emphasizing the lower frequencies, since it contains more information than the higher frequencies.

Decomposition of the signals would lead to emphasizing the most concentrated information. In [11], features can be extracted through wavelets and wavelet packets for the Tamil words recognition from the speech. The numeric speech samples are decomposed and transmitted into low pass and high pass filtering, in which the approximated coefficients are obtained at the end of the decimation from the low pass filtering. Since the fundamental information will be in the low frequency signals, there is not much emphasizing on the high frequency signals. Analysis of the approximated coefficients is done for the windowed numeric speech samples.

3.2.3   Implementation of Deep Learning Technique

Deep learning technique has made remarkable progress in signal and information processing. Researchers are getting very high accuracy and efficiency in recognition and classification by implementing deep learning algorithms. In speech recognition systems, the most commonly used algorithms are Deep Neural Network (DNN), Recurrent Neural Network (RNN), Long Short Term Memory Network (LSTM) etc. M. S. A. Chowdhury, in [12] extracted the features by the Neural Networks and power spectral analysis and concluded that the better accuracy of almost 95% can be obtained.

DNN are the feed forward networks which propagate data only in forward direction. These networks are often optimized using gradient descent algorithms. Back Propagation is used as a learning algorithm to update the parameters in these networks. Deep learning networks are defined based on the purpose for which it is used, i.e., either for recognition or classification. There are many different deep learning algorithms; two of these popular algorithms are discussed below.

3.2.3.1   Recurrent Neural Network

RNN is a feed forward DNN with hidden layers that are connected recurrently in addition to the input and output layers. This shares parameter across different layers across the networks. The main aim of the RNN is to predict the future data sequence through the previous set of data samples. Recently, researchers have found that RNN can capture the long-term dependencies and have demonstrated that it can generate sequential text characters. It shows a remarkable efficiency in modelling sequential data samples such as speech and text. Major problems with these conventional RNN are vanishing gradients and exploding gradient problems. These problems are addressed with another RNN architecture called Long Short-Term Memory.

3.2.3.2   Long Short-Term Memory Network

LSTM is a smart network which is capable of remembering values having an arbitrary length of time. A forget gate adaptively forgets or resets the cell's memory and scales the cell's state before adding input into the cell. LSTM architectures give better performance than DNNs on a large vocabulary speech recognition task with many output states. Ying developed HMM-deep unidirectional LSTM model to recognize Sichuan Dialect with more classification accuracy in [13] and a special speech corpus for Sichuan Dialect by exploring unique and special phonemes, polyphones and different pronunciations that have been developed.

3.2.3.3   Hidden Markov Models (HMM)

HMM are used predominantly in ASR models. It is a stochastic finite state machine having a finite set of possible states with transition probabilities between these states. Each of these states is initialized with initial probability and the output probabilities will be different for each word or phoneme. For a sentence, HMM is found by concatenating the individually trained HMM of each word. The word sequence, dictionary defined and HMM training process will help to determine the word automatically. HMM has given a remarkable result by reducing the complexity and time for training large vocabulary. Some of the papers related to this are discussed in the next section. HMM was designed to recognize by estimating the continuous density probabilities and an accuracy of 90% was achieved [14].

3.2.3.4   Hidden Markov Models - Long Short-Term Memory Network (HMM-LSTM)

Compared to other dataset, the Tamil language has many phonemes, special words, and polyphones. For this kind of dataset, HMM- Gaussian Mixture Model (GMM) was proposed to construct the acoustic model in earlier days. But, GMM requires a large amount of data to find the probability values. Later, the GMM was replaced with DNN, which shows higher accuracy than GMM but this method can capture only a fixed number of preceding data. Nowadays, in place of DNN, CNN and RNN are used, which show high efficiency when compared with the existing methods. Especially when LSTM is implemented in place of DNN, more contexts can be identified. Here, the output is delayed to obtain future probabilistic values. Also, by increasing the number of hidden layers, higher representation of speech data could be achieved [13].

The speech feature sequence $S = (s_1, s_2 \ldots s_t)$ of length 't', a label sequence $L = (l_1, l_2, \ldots l_l)$ of length 't' and the corresponding HMM chain $X = (x_1, x_2, \ldots x_l)$ of length' l' are given for each utterance. All the historical information can be compressed by LSTM. Hence, here we combine HMM into LSTM to construct acoustic model. The phonemes are modelled using HMM and the posterior probabilities are estimated with the help of LSTM as $p(x_i/s_1, s_2, \ldots s_t)$. In HMM, the context of phonemes is considered, hence this method of modelling phonemes is called Context Dependent Phoneme Element Modeling (CDPEM). If we consider a context composed of three phonemes, then the model is called CDTPEM. Similarly, context of varying phonemes is considered and acoustic model is defined. The transition probability $p(x_i/x_j)$ is the output of HMM.

The speech feature vector S is given as input to the LSTM network. The posterior probability $p(l_t|s_1, s_2, \ldots, s_t)$ when the speech feature at time instant 't'(s_t) is input to the network. Here, the delay in the output for k steps is introduced to retrieve information from the future context. The delayed unidirectional LSTM estimates posterior probability $p(l_t|s_1, s_2, \ldots, s_{t+k})$. Also, here multiple hidden layers are stacked to extract higher level representation of speech data. SoftMax activation function is used to estimate the class posteriors. While decoding, the posterior probabilities are converted into emission probabilities using Bayesian equations.

3.2.3.5   Evaluation Metrics

In general, three metrics are used to analyze the performance of speech recognition system. They are Character Error Rate (CER), Word Error Rate (WER) and Sentence Error Rate (SER).

$$CRE = \frac{Insertions + Deletions + Substituions}{Total\ no\ of\ characters\ in\ the\ reference\ sentences} \qquad (3.4)$$

$$WER = \frac{Insertions + Deletions + Substituions}{Total\ words\ in\ correct\ transcript} \qquad (3.5)$$

$$SER = \frac{No\ of\ sentences\ with\ atleast\ one\ word\ error}{Total\ no\ of\ sentences} \qquad (3.6)$$

3.3   Literature Survey on Existing TSRS

This analysis emphasizes the databases with various forms of utterances in the Tamil language, for the applied classification technique and the obtained accuracy with the technique used to extract the feature. The numbers of the sample which have been taken for this are tabulated in escalating order.

From Table 3.2, it is evident that on comparison with all feature extraction techniques, 24-dimensional Mel frequency cepstral co-efficient feature vector shows greater accuracy. Also, the analysis of using different deep learning classifiers shows that CNN results in greater recognition rate, followed by Probabilistic Neural Network. A hybrid of DNN and HMM also shows promising results in recognition with a minimum word error rate.

Table 3.2 Performance of ASR systems using various extraction and classification techniques.

Ref. no	Aim of the paper	Database	Feature extraction technique	Classification technique	Recognition in terms of accuracy
3	Construction and evaluation of children & adult Tamil emotion corpora	Audio recordings of movies and plays	MFCC	GMM, SVM	82%
5	Comparison of Feature Extraction Techniques available in TSR	10 isolated Tamil words - 8000Hz -	LPCC, MFCC	PNN	8-LPCC = 82% 24-MFCC = 97%
8	Development of a feature-based emotion recognition system	229 Telugu emotional utterances. 218 Tamil emotional utterances.	LPCC and Hurst	KNN, ANN	LPCC with ANN/ KNN: >62%, Hurst with ANN/ KNN: >60%, LPCC + Hurst with ANN/ KNN: >64%,
10	Evaluation of different no. of feature maps in each architecture of different convolution layers	TIDIGITS database with 4558 samples	MFCC	CNN	97.46%
11	Recognition of Tamil Speech Query	FIRE dataset	DW-MFCC	ESVM_SOM	SNR,MSE = 92%

(Continued)

Table 3.2 Performance of ASR systems using various extraction and classification techniques. (*Continued*)

Ref. no	Aim of the paper	Database	Feature extraction technique	Classification technique	Recognition in terms of accuracy
15	Performance comparison of Tamil words recognition using different classifiers	10 isolated Tamil words with 5 repetitions (500 samples)	MFCC	PNN, HMM, SVM	PNN = 92% HMM = 97% SVM = 95%
16	Development of acoustic models for TSR	50 words (newspaper sub headings)- 30 phonemes- 10 speakers (1500 samples)	MFCC	HMM	Word Recognition rate >80% for Tamil word model and >90% for Tamil phoneme model
17	Tamil speech Utterances are segmented into Phonemes automatically	100 Tamil speech utterances – 25 words spoken by 4 persons	MFCC	STM, LBDP	STM = 77.8% LBDP = 79.4%
18	Recognition of vocabulary that includes selected Tamil words	100 names of railway stations in TamilNadu	MFCC	HMM, AAMM	HMM with 5 states and 4 mixtures in each state yields a recognition rate of 95%
19	Identification of spoken data in four local Indian languages	Voice recordings (news recording from Doordharshan network) The four languages include English, Hindi, Tamil, and Telugu.	MFCC	SVM, DTC	SVM = 76%, DTC = 73%

3.4 Conclusion

This chapter provides an analysis of the various techniques used for feature extraction and classification of Tamil speech signals. The database considered here are the phoneme, syllable, isolated word, and sentences of the Tamil language. Methods to extract features like MFCC, LPC, PLP, LPCC and WAVELET are discussed in detail and the deep learning recognition algorithms like RNN, LSTM are also explained in brief. It is inferred that most of the researchers have extracted MFCC for speech signals in deep learning models. Also, it is observed that the majority of the ASR models are designed using HMM. From the tables listed above, it is prominent that these models individually give more accuracy. So, it is worth trying by combining these models into hybrid structures like HMM-RNN, HMM-LSTM, etc. In future, the work can be extended by exploring other features like LPC, WAVELET with hybrid models like HMM-LSTM, since both HMM and LSTM are very powerful in speech recognition. Human – robots and Human and Physical systems' interaction will be effective if an ASR is established between them. This will improve efficiency and help to resolve the problems easily in manufacturing sectors of industry 4.0.

References

1. V. Alcacer, V. Cruz-Machado, Scanning the Industry 4.0: A Literature Review on Technologies for Manufacturing Systems (2019), *Engineering Science and Technology, an International Journal*, vol. 22, issue 3, pp. 899-919, https://doi.org/10.1016/j.jestch.2019.01.006
2. Kong, X.T.R., Luo, Huang, G.Q. *et al.* (2019) Industrial wearable system: the human-centric empowering technology in Industry 4.0. *J IntellManuf.* 30, 2853–2869. https://doi.org/10.1007/s10845-018-1416-9
3. Vasuki, P., Sambavi, B. & Joe, V. Construction and Evaluation of Tamil Speech Emotion *Corpus. Natl. Acad. Sci. Lett.* (2020)., https://doi.org/10.1007/s40009-020-00907-1
4. Lawrence Rabiner and Ronald Schafer. (2010). *Theory and Applications of Digital Speech Processing* (1st. ed.). Prentice Hall Press, USA.
5. P. Iswarya, Dr. V. Radha, "Comparative Analysis of Feature Extraction Techniques for Tamil Speech Recognition," *2013 International Conference on Emerging Research in Computating, Information, Communication and Apllications (ERCIC-13).*
6. R. Thangarajan, A. M. Natarajan, and M. Selvam. 2008. Word and triphone based approaches in continuous speech recognition for Tamil language. *WSEAS Trans. Sig. Proc.* 4, 3 (March 2008), 76–85.

7. Thiang. SuryoWijoyo. "Speech Recognition Using Linear Predictive Coding and Artificial Neural Network for Controlling Movement of Mobile Robot," in *2011 International Conference on Information and Electronics Engineering IPCSIT* vol. 6 (2011) © (2011) IACSIT Press, Singapore.

8. S. Renjith and K. G. Manju, "Speech based emotion recognition in Tamil and Telugu using LPCC and hurst parameters — A comparative study using KNN and ANN classifiers," *2017 International Conference on Circuit, Power and Computing Technologies (ICCPCT)*, Kollam, 2017, pp. 1-6, doi: 10.1109/ICCPCT.2017.8074220.

9. S., Karpagavalli & Chandra, Evania. (2016). Recognition Of Tamil Syllables Using Vowel Onset Points With Production, Perception Based Features. *ICTACT Journal on Soft Computing*. 06. 1163-1170. 10.21917/ijsc.2016.0162.

10. Haque M.A., Verma A., Alex J.S.R., Venkatesan N. (2020) Experimental Evaluation of CNN Architecture for Speech Recognition. In: Luhach A., Kosa J., Poonia R., Gao XZ., Singh D. (eds.) *First International Conference on Sustainable Technologies for Computational Intelligence. Advances in Intelligent Systems and Computing*, vol 1045. Springer, Singapore.

11. P. Iswarya and V. Radha, "Speech Query Recognition for Tamil Language Using Wavelet and Wavelet Packets," *Journal of Information Processing Systems*, vol. 13, no. 5, pp. 1135-1148, 2017. DOI: 10.3745/JIPS.02.0033.

12. M. S. A. Chowdhury and M. F. Khan, "Power spectral analysis and Neural network for feature extraction and recognition of speech," *2019 International Conference on Data Science and Communication (IconDSC)*, Bangalore, India, 2019, pp. 1-7, doi: 10.1109/IconDSC.2019.8816913.

13. Ying, W., Zhang, L. & Deng, H. Sichuan dialect speech recognition with deep LSTM network. *Front. Comput. Sci.* 14, 378–387 (2020). https://doi.org/10.1007/s11704-018-8030-z.

14. Geetha K and Chandra E, "Monosyllable Isolated Word Recognition for Tamil language using Continuous Density Hidden Markov Model," *2015 IEEE International Conference on Electrical, Computer and Communication Technologies (ICECCT)*, Coimbatore, 2015, pp. 1-6, doi: 10.1109/ICECCT.2015.7226056.

15. Iswarya, P. "Speaker Independent Isolated Tamil Words Recognition System Using Different Classifiers." (2015).

16. S. Karpagavalli and E. Chandra, "Phoneme and word-based model for tamil speech recognition using GMM-HMM," *2015 International Conference on Advanced Computing and Communication Systems*, Coimbatore, 2015, pp. 1-5, doi: 10.1109/ICACCS.2015.7324119.

17. Geetha, K & Chandra, Evania. (2015). Automatic phoneme segmentation of Tamil utterances. 1-4. 10.1109/ICACCS.2015.7324062.

18. Palanivel, S.. "Spoken Word Recognition Strategy for Tamil Language." (2012).

19. H. Venkatesan, T. V. Venkatasubramanian and J. Sangeetha, "Automatic Language Identification using Machine learning Techniques," *2018 3rd International Conference on Communication and Electronics Systems (ICCES)*, India, 2018, pp. 583-588, doi: 10.1109/CESYS.2018.8724070

4

Approximation Algorithm and Linear Congruence: An Approach for Optimizing the Security of IoT-Based Healthcare Management System

Anirban Bhowmik[1]* and Sunil Karforma[2]

[1]*Department of Computer Application, Cyber Research and Training Institute, Burdwan, WB, India*
[2]*Department of Computer Science, The University of Burdwan, Burdwan, WB, India*

Abstract

In the healthcare industry, privacy and security of patient information is the most crucial issue at present. Considering current legal regulations, every healthcare organization should impose a prominent security technique to maintain a secure electronic health records system. On the other hand, the realization of Internet of Things is the most notable advancement in the field of computer science and electronics. The healthcare services have increased with the help of IoT. Nowadays security flaws on patient information are a significant issue in the healthcare system. Electronic health records, i.e., collections of health-related information, are sensitive in nature, so it is very significant to impose advanced security techniques in the system. Here we have focused on security issues like technical safeguards. Our technique proposes an approximation algorithm-based security model for securing the diagnostics text data of patients and an authentication technique. For encryption, intermediate key, approximation algorithm-based session key are used. This new approach of session key generation provides beauty as well as extra robustness in our technique. The different types of experiments on this technique and their results confirms that our technique is very secure and efficient for data transmission in the medical sector.

*Corresponding author: animca2008@gmail.com

Shibin David, R. S. Anand, V. Jeyakrishnan, and M. Niranjanamurthy (eds.) Security Issues and Privacy Concerns in Industry 4.0 Applications, (55–88) © 2021 Scrivener Publishing LLC

Keywords: Internet of Things, intermediate key, session key, authentication, approximation algorithm

4.1 Introduction

Healthcare is defined as the act of taking preventative or necessary procedures to improve a person's well-being. This may be done with surgery, medicine, or other alterations in a person's lifestyle. These services are typically provided by hospitals and physicians through a healthcare system. At present it is seen that a healthcare service is necessary for life. The current trends in the healthcare industry are the digitization of healthcare workflow and moving to electronic patient records. An e-record of a patient means an electronic version of a patient's medical history like demographics, progress notes, problems, medications, vital signs, past medical history, immunizations, laboratory data and radiology reports, etc. These medical data are maintained by the provider over time. The quantity of e-clinical data has increased at a huge rate in terms of complexity, diversity and timeliness. The different types of medical information system have improved by using developed mobile Internet and Internet of Things (IoT). The key feature of different types of medical information system is that the patients can get their treatment from the healthcare providers directly. On the other hand, patients can also communicate with others that have the same symptoms. They also may form a group for exchanging their illness-related information, treatment experience, diets, medicines and specialist doctor recommendation. Patients may communicate to encourage each other to overcome the disease, regardless of the patients' locations and conditions. Sometimes, self-confidence and a friendly environment are more effective than drugs in patients' conditions.

Internet of Things (IoT) can be defined as a set of networking technologies that consists of different appliances, devices and electronic gadgets that interact and communicate among themselves. The world of IoT includes a huge variety of devices like smartphones, personal computers, PDAs, laptops, tablets, and other handheld embedded devices. The main aim of communication among IoT devices is to provide the facility for processing information in a centralized way and delivering it to the intended destination in a cost-effective way. In future the facility of IoT will provide a superior world for human beings.

4.1.1 IoT in Medical Devices

At present different healthcare systems widely use the IoT devices for smooth functioning, monitoring and assessment of patients' conditions and records [7]. PMD (Personal Medical Devices) are small electronic devices used for monitoring the medical condition of a patient. These PMDs are of two types according to their location, either internal (i.e., inside the patient's body) or external (i.e., attached to the patient's body externally). PMDs use a wireless interface to perform communication with a base station that is further used to read the status of the device, medical reports, and change parameters of the device, or update status on the device.

Unfortunately, most of these devices and applications are not secure for data or information communication. IoT may be prone to different types of attacks. The IoT devices are targeted by attackers and intruders and this may pose a risk for patients. Every healthcare system should ensure the security of network in order to protect the privacy of the patient from malicious attacks. To strengthen the sensitive information and other types of security, a proactive, preventive approach and measures must be taken by every healthcare organization with attention to future security and privacy needs.

4.1.2 Importance of Security and Privacy Protection in IoT-Based Healthcare System

Security is a most important issue in any healthcare system. The attackers aim is to steal the information, attack devices to utilize patients' resources, or shut down some applications that are monitoring a patient's condition. There are many types of attacks on medical devices that include eavesdropping, in which the privacy of the patient is leaked, and integrity error in which a message is altered. The IoT-based healthcare system provides huge benefits in society but it is also vulnerable to different types of attacks. These attacks mainly cause information leakage and loss of services in communication channel. The IoT consists of different types of devices and platforms with different credentials, and each device and platform needs security according to their characteristics. In an IoT platform, a lot of personal medical information is shared among various types of devices so the privacy of the user is a vital part [13, 14] of the healthcare system. Hence a secure cryptosystem is needed for data or information protection.

The different types of IoT attacks are physical attack, network attack, software attack, and encryption attack. In our paper we have emphasized only encryption attacks such as side channel attacks, cryptanalysis attacks, and man-in-the-middle attacks. The different algorithms in our cryptosystem which are described above provide a strong protection mechanism against different encryption attacks. The results section of our study proves the robustness of the proposed cryptosystem by using different data, graphs, comparisons, etc.

4.1.3   Cryptography and Secret Keys

Cryptography deals with the art of codifying messages, so that they become unreadable and can be shared secretly over public communication channels. It is the study of developing and using different types of encryption and decryption techniques. Here the plain text is converted into cipher text using an encryption algorithm so that hackers cannot read it, but authorized persons can access it. The decryption algorithm works in the reverse order and converts the cipher text into plain text. Cryptography is divided into two types: symmetric key and asymmetric key cryptography with respect to key.

4.1.4   RSA

The RSA algorithm is a suite of cryptographic techniques, and especially it is a public key encryption technique. It is widely used for security purposes when sensitive data or information are transmitted through the Internet. RSA was first publicly described in 1977 by Ron Rivest, Adi Shamir and Leonard Adleman of the Massachusetts Institute of Technology. In RSA cryptography, both the public and the private key are used in encryption for decryption purposes. RSA has become the most widely used asymmetric algorithm because it assures the confidentiality, integrity, authenticity, and non-repudiation of electronic communications and data storage.

4.1.5   Approximation Algorithm and Subset Sum Problem

An approximation algorithm is an algorithm that returns near optimal solutions. Depending on problem definition, it may be either a maximization or minimization problem. An algorithm for a problem has an approximation ratio of $p(n)$ if, for any input of size n, the cost C of the solution produced by the algorithm is within a factor of $p(n)$ of the cost C^* of an optimal solution: $max(C/C*, C*/C) \leq p(n)$. An algorithm that achieves an approximation ratio $p(n)$ is a $p(n)-$ approximation algorithm.

Definition: An instance of the subset-sum decision problem is (S, t) where:

$S = \{x_1, x_2, ..., x_n\}$ Set of positive integers and t a positive integer.

The problem is whether some subset of S adds up exactly to t. This problem is NP-complete.

The subset-sum optimization problem is defined as to find a subset of S whose sum is as large as possible but no greater than t.

We will define a class of algorithms, A_ϵ such that, $\forall \epsilon > 0$,

- A_ϵ is an ϵapproximation algorithm for subset-sum.
- A_ϵ runs in time polynomial in n, $\log t$ and $1/\epsilon$

Such a class of algorithms is known as a fully polynomial-time approximation scheme.

An Exponential time algorithm

If $S = \{x_1, x_2,...,x_n\}$ is a set or list and x a real number then define

$$S + x = \{x_1, x_2,...,x_n\} = \{x_1 + x, x_2 + x,...,x_n + x\}.$$

If $L = \{x_1, x_2,...,x_n\}$ and $L' = \{u_1, u_2,...,u_m\}$ are both sorted lists then define Merge–Lists(L, L') to be the procedure that returns the sorted union of the two lists. This procedure runs in time $O(|L'| + |L|)$.

Algorithm: (Exact-Subset Sums)

Step 1. $n \leftarrow |S|$

Step 2. $L0 \leftarrow < 0 >$

Step 3. for $i = 1$ to n

Step 4. L_i = Merge-Lists (L_i, L_i $+x_i$)

Step 5. Remove from L_i all elements bigger than t.

Step 6. Return largest element in L_n.

Step 7. Stop

4.1.6 Significance of Use of Subset Sum Problem in Our Scheme

The fundamental definition of subset sum.

The problem is to find subsets which are restricted on certain sum. Here we enumerate power set of a set which are categorized based on their sum. We consider the set of natural numbers within a range chosen by user as our problem domain.

A set of first n natural numbers. $X_n = \{1,2,3,...n\}$ where n is a positive integer. The set X_n is also known as the Universal set. This is our problem domain. The cardinality of the set X_n is n.

$$|X_n| = n$$

A set of all subsets of X_n is $P(X_n) = \{\emptyset,\{1\},\{2\},...,\{1,2,...n\}\}$. it is also known as power set. The empty set is denoted as $\emptyset$ or $\{\}$ or the null set.

Sum Distribution: In sum distribution (SD), we find the number of subsets which sum up to a certain integer S, where $X_n = \{1,2,3 ... n\}$ and $S\epsilon\left[0,\dfrac{n(n+1)}{2}\right]$. It is represented as $SD[n][S]$.

Before counting the subsets of a particular sum, we initialize the count as zero, ∀n, S $SD[n][S] = 0$.

Following are the base cases for sum distribution ($SD[n][S]$):

1. For $n = 0$ and $S = 0$, the corresponding subset is $\emptyset$. Since, zero-sum (Sum = 0) can be achieved only with subset $\emptyset$ and Sum ($\emptyset$) is assumed to be, as defined in Section 1.3, the count of occurrence of subset in $P(X_0)$ is taken as 1. Therefore, $SD[0][0] = 1$.

2. ∀i $\epsilon[1, n]$ and $S = 0$, $SD[i][0] = 1$. Since, zero-sum (*Sum = 0*) can be achieved only with subset, the count of occurrence of $\emptyset$ − subset in $P(X_n)$ is taken as 1. Therefore, $SD[n][0] = 1$.

3. $SD[i][j] = 0$, if $i < 0$ or $j < 0$.
   $SD[n][S] = 1$ $when$ $S = 0$ or $n = 1$.
   $SD[n][S] = SD[n − 1][S]$ $when$ $0 < S < 1$.
   $SD[n][S] = SD[n − 1][S] + SD[n − 1][S − n]$ $when$
   $$n < S < FLOOR\left(\dfrac{n(n+1)}{4}\right)$$
   $$SD[n][S] = SD[n] \cdot \left[\dfrac{n(n+1)}{2} - S\right]$$

4.1.7   Linear Congruence

Let $f(x) = a_0x^n + a_1x^{n-1} + \cdots + a_n (n \geq 1)$ be a polynomial with integer coefficient $a_0, a_1,...,a_n$ with $a_0 \not\equiv 0(mod\ m)$. Then $f(x) \equiv 0(mod\ m)$ is said to be a polynomial congruence (*mod m*) of degree n. If there exists an integer x_0 such that $f(x_0) \equiv 0\ (mod\ m)$, then the solution of the congruence is x_0.

Theorem1: If gcd $(a, m) = 1$, then the linear congruence $ax \equiv b \ (mod \ m)$ has a unique solution.

Proof. Since gcd $(a, m) = 1$, there exist integers u, v such that $au + mv = 1$. Therefore $a \ (bu) + m \ (bv) = b$. This gives a$(bu) \equiv b \ (mod \ m)$.

This shows that $x = bu$ is a solution of the congruence $ax \equiv b \ (mod \ m)$. Let x_1 and x_2 be solutions of the congruence $ax \equiv b \ (mod \ m)$. Then $ax_1 \equiv b \ (mod \ m)$ and $ax_2 \equiv b \ (mod \ m)$. This implies $ax_1 \equiv ax_2 \ (mod \ m) \rightarrow x_1 \equiv x_2 \ (mod \ m)$, since gcd $(a, m) = 1$. This proves that the congruence has a unique solution.

The concept of the above theorem is used in generation of intermediate key in our proposed technique.

4.1.8   Linear and Non-Linear Functions

A linear function has the form $y = f(x) = ax + b$. A linear function has one independent variable which is x and one dependent variable which is y. b is constant term or y intercept. a is the coefficient of the independent variable. It is also known as slope and it gives the rate of change of the dependent variable. A linear equation is used in our technique in intermediate key generation.

A simple non-linear equation is of the form $x^2 + by^2 = c$. A non-linear equation looks like a curve when graphed. Its slope value is variable. The degree of a non-linear equation is at least 2 or other integer values. The input and output of a non-linear system is not directly related. In this article a non-linear function is used in encryption process. The aim of the use of non-linear function is to create a non-linearity in cipher text.

4.1.9   Pell's Equation

Pell's equation is a Diophantine equation of the form $x^2 - dy^2 = \pm 1, x, y \in Z$, where d is a given natural number which is not a square [29].

Lemma: For each non-square positive integer d, there are infinitely many positive integers x and y such that $\left| x - \sqrt{d}y \right| < \dfrac{1}{y}$.

Theorem (Lagrange): *For every positive integer d that is not a square, the equation $x^2 - dy^2 = 1$ has a nontrivial solution* [29].

Here we focus on the integer solutions of Pell's equation. The two integers for a particular d provide a set of numbers for two or more number of d's which is used for key generation in this article.

4.2   Literature Survey

D. Boneh *et al.* [2], provided a comprehensive study on security issues in IoT networks in his work. Various security requirements such as authentication, integrity, confidentiality were discussed in this paper. This paper provides a comparison among different types of attacks, their behavior, and their threat level. These attacks are categorized into four levels: low-level, medium-level, high-level, and extremely high-level attacks; possible solutions to these attacks are suggested. P. Mania *et al.* [12], surveyed various types of healthcare applications based on wireless medical sensor network (WMSN). An IoT environment is suitable to implement these applications. Also, the different types of hybrid security techniques are discussed for handling the security issues of healthcare systems. E.T. Oladipupo *et al.* [5], has shown the analysis of the security vulnerabilities and the risk factors detected in mobile medical apps. These apps can be categorized into remote monitoring, diagnostic support, treatment support, medical information, education and awareness, and communication and training for healthcare workers. Categories are done according to its risk factor standards. Eight security vulnerabilities and ten risk factors of mobile security project have been detected and analyzed by the World Health Organization. X. Liu *et al.* [27] first proposed Medical Information System (TMIS) where novel authentication and key agreement protocol for accessing remote multi-medical server are introduced. However, V. Power Mohan [15] was vulnerable to internal attack, replay attack and the man-in-the-middle attack, impersonation attack and stolen smart card attack [16, 17].

Moshaddique Al Ameen *et al.* [28] proposed security and privacy issues in sensor networks application within the healthcare perspective. This focuses on the major social implications like secrecy and security and also analyzes these two issues. However, in this paper the authors do not provide any protocol or algorithm for security and privacy in a healthcare perspective either in same domain or cross-domain healthcare platforms. This paper does not examine physical level security and technical level security. It only looks at administrative-level security and provides some privacy measures without any protocol or algorithm. Clemens Scott Kruse *et al.* [29] analyzed and discussed prominent security techniques for a healthcare organization which is seeking to adopt a secure electronic health record system. But this work failed to provide any suitable robust algorithm or technique to prevent information or data breaches. Today's technical safeguard may not be sufficient for the next version of attacks. So, it is very important to establish a robust technical safeguard for medical data security. Xiaoxue Liu *et al.* [27] proposed a heterogeneous cross-domain AKA protocol with symptoms-matching in TMIS. In CDAKA protocol a patient who is in PKI-domain can communicate remotely with another patient who is in IBC-domain. This protocol is composed of four phases. The phases are registration phase, login phase, authentication and key agreement phase. Here two patients realize mutual authentication as well as session key establishment, but the generation of session key and authentication process is very complex in the sense that the communicating parties have to face four phases, but our technique provides a minimum number of phases for communication between patients.

Hai Tao *et al.* [32] proposed a secure data collection scheme for an IoT-based healthcare system named Secure Data with the aim of tackling security issues in an IoT-based healthcare system. Secure Data scheme is composed of four layers: 1) IoT network sensors/devices; 2) fog layers; 3) cloud computing layer; and 4) healthcare provider layer. For the first two layers, Secure Data includes two techniques: 1) light-weight field programmable gate array (FPGA) hardware-based cipher algorithm, and 2) secret cipher share algorithm. Mohamed Elhoseny *et al.* [33] proposed a hybrid security model for securing the diagnostic text data in medical images in an IoT-based healthcare system. The proposed model is developed through integrating either 2-D discrete wavelet transform 1 level (2D-DWT-1L) or 2-D discrete wavelet transform 2 level (2D-DWT-2L) steganography technique with a proposed hybrid encryption scheme. The proposed hybrid encryption schema is built using a combination of Advanced Encryption Standard, and Rivest, Shamir, and Adleman algorithms. The proposed model starts by encrypting the secret data; then it hides the result in a cover image using 2D-DWT-1L or 2D-DWT-2L. T. Alladi *et al.* [34] reviewed existing blockchain applications in Industry 4.0 and IoT settings. Specifically, this paper discussed the current research trends in each of the related industrial sectors, as well as successful commercial implementations of blockchain in these relevant sectors. Wei liang *et al.* [35] proposed a secure FaBric blockchain-based data transmission technique for industrial IoT. This technique uses the blockchain-based dynamic secret sharing mechanism.

4.3 Problem Domain

There are different types of challenges in an IoT-based healthcare system. Different types of attacks or malicious activity may degrade activity of the medical devices and disrupt the healthcare communication system. There are two types of attacks, namely Active Attack and Passive Attack. An active attack attempts to alter system resources or affect their operation. A passive attack does not affect system resources but attempts to steal vital information from the system. An attack can be occurred by an insider or from outside of the health organization. Based on the target of the attack, there are three types of attacks against the Internet of Things.

- Attacks against medical devices.
- Attacks against the communication between devices and masters.
- Attacks against the masters.

A common method of attack involves tampering or altering of messages. The medical data and information which are transmitted through an IoT environment is very sensitive and vital for treatment. So any changes on these data or information causes risk for patients.

4.4 Solution Domain and Objectives

In this article we have emphasized attacks which destroy the data or information in a communication network. Here we provide some security algorithms that protect different attacks in the communication network of an IoT-based healthcare system. We focus on two basic things related to message communication, i.e., authentication and encryption-decryption. For authentication we have used hash function and a key, named intermediate key which is generated by using the two public keys of sender and receiver. For encryption-decryption, two keys (session key and intermediate key) are used which are generated by using the concept of dynamic problem such as subset sum problem, linear congruence and Pell's method. To get the better non-linearity in encryption we have used linear and non-linear functions. A rigorous frame structure is used for message transmission in a wireless network. Different types of information are accumulated in this structure and this information is used for identity verification, key generation and encryption-decryption. The main objective is to enhance the life quality for people or patients who need support of IoT-based healthcare by avoiding unnecessary healthcare costs and efforts, and to provide the proper medical support and treatment at the right time.

4.5   Proposed Work

4.5.1   Methodology

Our model is composed of five algorithms: (i) Intermediate key generation for authentication and encryption, (ii) Session key generation for encryption, (iii) Encryption, (iv) Authentication realization, (v) Decryption process. Our protocol is described below by a compact algorithm with some modules.

ALGORITHM

Input: - plaintext.

Output: - encrypted file.

Methods:

Step 1. Call SSKG ( )	// session key generation using two public keys of two patients.
Step 2. Call INTMKG ( )	// intermediate key generation for file encryption.
Step 3. Call ENCYP ( )	// file encryption process for generating cipher text for secure transmission.
Step 4. Call AUTH_ CHK ( )	// Authentication check.
Step 5. Call DECYP ( )	// decryption process for generating plain text.

All the steps are given below in detail. Here public key of patient means the patient-id provided by the hospital or clinic.

4.5.2   Session Key Generation

Session key is a secret key for symmetric encryption which is used for a particular transaction or session and is valid for a small period of time. In our scheme particularly subset sum problem of approximation algorithm is used to create session key. At first the user chooses the range of numbers and these numbers are used as input to the approximation algorithm. A particular output of the subset sum problem is the required session key.

ALGORITHM-1 (SSKG ())

Input: upper limit (U), lower limit (L) and key length.

Output: session key.

Methods:

Step 1. Set sum, i, n, tot, v as integer and w [] as integer array.

Step 2. v←user chosen. //v is the length of the key.

Step 3. L← lower limit, U← upper limit, and $tot \leftarrow 0$, $n \leftarrow (U - L) + 1$. // $5 \leq n \leq 100$.

Step 4. For i=0 to n

Step 5. w [i]← value between U and L.

   end for

Step 6. *Set sum $\leftarrow L + (L + 1) + (L + 2) + \cdots + (L + v)$.* // v is any integer chosen by user which provides length of session key.

Step 7. *For $i = 0$ to n*

Step 8. *$tot \leftarrow tot + w[i]$*

   end for

Step 9. Call subsum(0,0,tot)

Step 10. End

Sub Procedure:

sub_sum( ) : cs, k, r as integer   // sub_sum() is a function and cs, k, r are parameters.

Step 1. Set i, x[] as integer.

Step 2. x [k]←1

Step 3. if $((cs + w[k]) > sum)$ then

Step 4. *For $i = 0$ to less than or equal to k*

Step 5.   if $(x[i] == 1)$ then

Step 6.   print $w[i]$ // the values in w[i] represents session key.

   endif

   end for

   end if

Step 7. if $((cs + w[k] + w[k + 1]) <= sum)$

Step 8. Call subsum$(cs + w[k], k + 1, r - w[k])$

   end if

Step 9. if $((cs + r - w[k]) >= sum)$ *and* $((cs + w[k + 1]) <= sum))$

Step 10. $x[k] \leftarrow 0$

Step 11. Call sub_sum$(cs, k + 1, r - w[k])$

Step 12. end if

Step 13. end Sub Procedure

This session key is used to generate cipher text from plain text and vice versa. This established session key provides confidentiality for subsequent communication and for each session the session key will fresh. This key is sent to recipient end through a frame structure which is described below.

4.5.3   Intermediate Key Generation

In our scheme we have used the intermediate key for the authentication check between two patients and also for the encryption process. Here the intermediate key is generated by using two public keys of two patients. So the intermediate key may vary for different pair of patients and also by session. To generate intermediate key we have used the concept of linear congruence in number theory, three variables linear function and Pell's formula. The details of the algorithm are given below.

ALGORITHM-2 (INTMKG ( ))

Input: Two public keys of two patients and four constants.

Output: Intermediate key.

Methods:

Step 1. Set d, i, len, fval as integer (as global variable).

Step 2. Set imk q[], ps[], pr[] as integer array.

Step 3. Set fval ← *key_fn( ).*   {/* the *key_fn( ) is a module which provides a value in key generation.*/}

Step 4. pr []←public key of receiver.

Step 5. ps[]← public key of sender.

Step 6. len← get_length (receiver's or sender's public key).

Step 7. For i=0 to len

Step 8. ps[i] ← ps[i] XOR d and pr[i] ← pr[i] XOR d. /* d is a random value between the lowest ascii value of sender and highest ascii value of receiver.

Step 9. if (gcd(ps[i], fval)= = 1) then

Step 10. imk[i]← call linear_congr (ps[i], pr[i],fval)   {/* linear congruence, the equation ps[i]x≡pr[i] (mod fval) provides unique solution (Theorem1) which is stored in imk[]. This is the required intermediate key.*/}

Step 11. else imk[i] ← call linear_congr (ps[i]+1,pr[i],fval)

Step 12. End if

Step 13. End for

Step 14. Stop

Sub Procedure:

key_fn ( ): public key of sender, public key of receiver.

Step 1. Set n_1, n_3, n_4 , d_1, d_2 as integer variable.

Step 2. d_1 ← Value chosen by user and d_2← value chosen by user.

Step 3. n_1 & n_2← randomChar (public key of sender) such that $(n_1 \sim n_2)$ ≥d_1. If it is not possible to get such numbers n_1 and n_2 with said condition then we take n_1 and n_2 such that $(n_1 \sim n_2)$ nearest to d_1.

Step 4. n_3 & n_4← randomChar (public key of receiver) such that $(n_3 \sim n_4)$ ≥d_2. If it is not possible to get such numbers n_1 and n_2 with said condition then we take n_1 and n_2 such that $(n_1 \sim n_2)$ nearest to d_2.

Step 5. We get two numbers for each n_1, n_2, n_3, n_4 respectively using the Pell's equation ($x^2-ny^2=1$). Thus we get 8 numbers in total.

Step 6. The modulus operation is done on 8 numbers by a meanOf (d_1, d_2).

Step 7. Variable number of times the shuffle operation is done on 8 numbers.

Step 8. First three or four numbers are used for constant terms in a three variable linear function $f(x,y,z)$ and again after shuffle operation remaining numbers are used for values of x, y and z in the function. This module returns the functional value which is used for key generation.

Step 9. End sub procedure.

This intermediate key is transmitted to the recipient end through a secured channel before encryption. At the recipient end this key is used for authentication purpose and encryption purpose.

4.5.4   Encryption Process

In this phase the intermediate key and session key take part in the encryption process. To provide non-linearity in encryption process we use circular left shift (CLS) operation in encryption process. A two variable non-linear function (*fn_enc (session key, intermediate key)*) is used where the ascii value of each character of session key and intermediate key and their difference is used to calculate functional value. The functional value is used as the number of times the circular left shift occurs. Since we use a non-linear function the output of the function is not linear with input and this provides an extra non-linearity in cipher text. This type of double encryption with session key and intermediate key provides extra robustness in our technique. In both cases *XOR* [9] the operation is done with a CLS operation at the end. An example is given below.

Example: let $fn\_enc(x,y) = \dfrac{x^2}{y} + y^3$ be a non-linear function.

Where y=ascii value of each character of session key, x=ascii value of each character of intermediate key. Now $m = fn\_enc(x,y)\%$ (*ascii_diff*), where *ascii_diff*= the ascii difference between each character of intermediate key and session key. The functional value m is used as the number of times the circular left shift occurs in each character of partial cipher text to generate final cipher text.

The encryption algorithm is given below.

ALGORITHM-3: (ENCYP ( ))

Input: plain text, intermediate key, session key.

Output: encrypted file.

Method:

Step 1. *Set* m as integer, *plain_file* as plain text file and *cipher_file, cipher_final* as cipher text file.

Step 2. *Set* output_file as temporary file.

Step 3. *if* (!*eof*) then

Step 4. output_file=*bit_XOROP* (*plain_file, sessionkey*)

Step 5. cipher_file = *bit_XOROP* (*output$_{file}$, intermediatekey*)

Step 6. m= fn_enc (session key, intermediate key)   /* one example is given above.*/

Step 7. Cipher_final= *cipher_file*≪*m*.   // circular left shift operation.

Step 8. end if

Step 9. Stop

4.5.5   Generation of Authentication Code and Transmission File

After finishing the encryption process we have created a rigorous frame structure (transmission file) with four attributes, Header, Cipher text [13], Tail_msg and Pading using the module AUTH_CHK (). MD5 hash function is used to generate hash value of intermediate key. The module provides a compact frame format which is ready for transmission to the receiver end.

ALGORITHM-4: (AUTHEN_TRANS ( ))

Input: intermediate key, session key, cipher text and d_1, d_2 chosen by user.

Output: transmission file (trans_file).

Methods:

Step 1. Set imk [ ], ssk [ ], Padding [ ], Header_msg [ ], Tail_msg[],enc_val[] as integer array.

Step 2. Set trans_file as a file.   {/* this file is transmitted to the receiver end */}

Step 3. imk [ ] ← intermediate key and ssk[ ]← session key.

Step 4. Padding [] ← hash_ValOf(imk[]).

Step 5. Header_msg [ ] ← hash_ValOf ($imk[] \ll ((d_1 + d_2)/4))$ XOR ssk [].

Step 6. Tail_msg[ ]← enc_val[ ]   {/* enc_val[] contains encrypted value of d_1 and d.*/}

Step 7. trans_file←Call concate_text (Header_msg [ ], cipher text, Tail_msg[], Padding[]).

Step 8. Stop.

If the key size is 16 byte then total frame structure for transmission is given below which is created by the function AUTHEN_TRANS ( ).

HEADER_MSG (32 BYTE)	CIPHER TEXT	TAIL_MSG	PADDING (32 BYTE)

The Tail_msg part of transmission file contains encrypted value of two constants (d_1, d_2). This encryption is done by RSA technique. Padding field contains hash value of intermediate key. This padding field is used for authentication purpose. The session key is recovered from header part using CLS operation and the intermediate key.

4.5.6 Decryption Phase

In decryption phase, at first receiver generates intermediate key by calling IMKG ( ) and then checks authentication using hash value of intermediate key from padding field. After finishing authentication check, the session key is generated from HEADER_MSG of transmission file and then the decryption process is started using two keys. The entire decryption process is given below by a compact algorithm.

ALGORITHM-5: (DECYP ( ))

Input: Intermediate key, cipher text.

Output: plain text.

Methods:

Step 1. Set a, n, i as integer and ssk [ ], imk [ ] as integer array.

Step 2. Retrieve d_1 and d_2 from TAIL_MSG of transmission file or frame structure.

Step 3. imk [ ] ← intermediate key.

Step 4. Call AUTHEN_CHK (imk [ ], trans_file).

Step 5. if (true) then

Step 6. ssk [ ] ← get_SessionKey(Header_msg of trans_file, d_1, d_2).
/* session key generation*/

Step 7. Decryption process is done with two keys which is reverse of encryption process.

Step 8. else   Print *Authentication fails.*

     end if

Step 9. Stop.

4.6 Results and Discussion

The above algorithms are implemented in the latest version of TURBO C interface in a PC of Intel Core i3 (sixth generation or newer) processor, operating system Microsoft Windows 10 x64, 8GB RAM and 500GB internal storage device. In the following sections, simulated results of the proposed scheme are presented. In our experiments, several sizes of different type files are used as plain text.

A good encryption technique should be robust against different types of cryptanalytic, statistical and brute-force attacks. In this section, we discuss different types of security analysis like key space analysis, dictionary analysis, etc., different types of randomness analysis, sensitivity analysis, statistical analysis and functionality analysis on our proposed encryption scheme [11].

4.6.1   Statistical Analysis

Nowadays different types of statistical attacks and statistical analysis are used by intruders or hackers to analyze the cipher text for decryption. Therefore, an ideal cipher text should be robust against any statistical attacks. To prove the robustness of our proposed encryption scheme, we have performed statistical analysis by calculating the histogram, avalanche effect and randomness by calculating serial test.

(a) HISTOGRAM ANALYSIS: A text-histogram illustrates [10] how characters in a text are distributed by graphing the number of characters at each level. Here histogram analysis is done on the several encrypted as well as its original text files that have widely different content. We have shown the encrypted files of the original files (plain text) using the secret keys 'crypto@12375' and *AmMn3459AB81* (in decimal) in Figure 4.1.

Observations: It is clear from Figure 4.1 that the histograms of the encrypted files are fairly uniform and significantly different from the

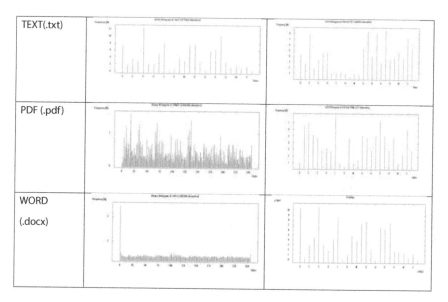

Figure 4.1 Histogram analysis.

respective histograms of the original files (plain text) and hence do not provide any clue to employ any statistical attack on the proposed encryption procedure.

Correlation analysis: Here we calculate the correlation [4] between ascii difference and total number of changed characters. A secure encryption scheme should transform a text file (.docx, .txt) into a random like encrypted file with low correlation. The formula for Pearson correlation coefficient is given below.

$$r = \frac{n\sum xy - \sum x \sum y}{\sqrt{[n\sum x^2 - (\sum x)^2][n\sum y^2 - (\sum y)^2]}}$$

The correlation values are given below through Table 4.1.

The Pearson correlation coefficient provides the strength and direction of the linear relationship between two variables. From the Table 4.1 it is seen that the value of correlation coefficient between X and Y is -0.426<0. This indicates that there is a strong negative relationship between the variables or the variables may have a non-linear relationship. The relationship is negative because, as one variable increases, the other decreases. But from the scatter plot (Figure 4.2) it is seen that a non-linear relationship exists between two variables (X, Y).

4.6.2   Randomness Analysis of Key

Randomness means all elements of the sequence are generated independently of each other, and the value of the next element in the sequence cannot be predicted, regardless of how many elements have already been produced. Random and pseudorandom numbers generated for cryptographic applications should be unpredictable (forward and backward). The outputs of a PRNG are deterministic functions of the seed; i.e., all true randomness is dependent on seed generation [28]. An RNG uses a non-deterministic source, i.e., the entropy source. Here we have used RNG and

Table 4.1 Data analysis on correlation.

SD of X values	SD of Y values	Correlation coefficient (r)	Coefficient of determination	Significance of test value	Standard error slope values
45.89	200.05	-0.426	18.15%	-1.33	1.394

(X values: No. of changed characters, Y values: ascii difference)

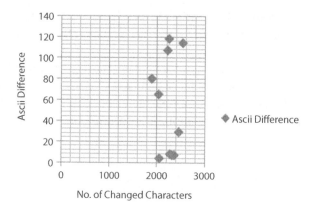

Figure 4.2 Graph on correlation analysis.

approximation algorithm for generating numbers with true randomness. These random numbers are used for generation of session key. To prove the randomness of our session key we have used serial test [3, 10]. The following statics is used for serial test.

$$X = \frac{4}{(n-1)}\left(n_{00}^2 + n_{01}^2 + n_{10}^2 + n_{11}^2\right) - \frac{2}{n}\left(n_0^2 + n_1^2\right) + 1$$

Which approximately follows a χ^2 distribution with 2 degrees of freedom if $n \geq 21$. Table 4.2 is given below.

Table 4.2 Serial test.

Key size (byte)	Result of proposed tech.	Result of only PRNG()[3]	Result of only RNG()[10]
16	1.12	1.09	1.08
24	1.2	1	1.01
36	1.26	1.26	1.2
48	2.12	2.11	2.13
56	11	8.98	10
64	19	17	18.03

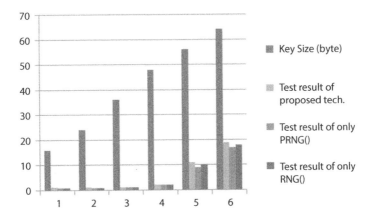

Figure 4.3 Graph of above table.

Observation: For a significance level of α = 0.05, the threshold values of X for serial test are 1.12, 1.2, 1.26, 2.12, 11, 19 respectively. Thus the sequence generated by the above algorithm passes serial test. The above Table 4.2 and graph (Figure 4.3) prove that our proposed technique is secure against different statistical attacks and differential attacks [30].

4.6.3   Key Sensitivity Analysis

An ideal encryption technique should be sensitive with respect to the secret key, i.e., a single bit change in the secret key should produce a completely different cipher text. For testing the key sensitivity of the proposed encryption procedure, we have performed the encryption process in the files (.txt) with slight changes in the secret key. The avalanche effect is shown below only for changed session key and with fixed intermediate key. The following Table 4.3 and graph (Figure 4.4) show the total scenario.

Observation: we have shown the results of some attempts to decrypt an encrypted file with slightly different secret keys than the one used for the encryption of the original file. The above Table 4.3 shows the added characters, deleted characters and changed characters with slight change (one byte) in session key, and the above graph (Figure 4.4) also shows the increasing and decreasing performance among added characters, deleted characters and changed characters for one byte change in key. It is clear that the decryption with a slightly different key fails completely and hence the proposed encryption procedure is highly key sensitive [35].

Table 4.3 Avalanche effect: change in session key.

Key	Ascii difference	Total number of added characters	Total number of deleted characters	Total number of changed characters
crypto@12345	0	3526	3545	2540
cyypto@12345	7	3716	3710	2362
cryptq@12345	8	3860	3838	2271
crypto@12346	107	3928	3876	2217
crypto#12345	29	3615	3610	2458
crysto@12345	80	4262	4245	1892
crypto@1234z	7	3795	3778	2314
crypto@12445	118	3868	3845	2245
crypto@02345	4	4105	4081	2049
Arypto@12345	65	4091	4088	2032

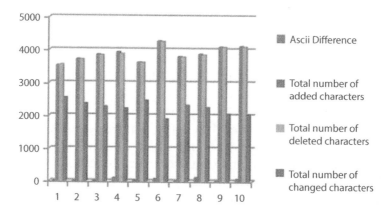

Figure 4.4 Graph of above table.

4.6.4 Security Analysis

4.6.4.1 Key Space Analysis

The required property of a good encryption algorithm is the large key space by which algorithm can resist different types of attacks. The total number of different keys in the encryption process indicates the size of the key space. The brute-force attack is impractical in such crypto systems where key space is large. Now we consider a general case where the size of the secret key is k bits i.e., k is the length of key in bits. There are two keys in our proposed scheme, one of which is the intermediate key with size k bits and other is the session key whose size is k bits also. Now for the intermediate key, the key space is 2^k and for session key, the key space is 2^k and total key space is 2^{2k}. In this large key space platform we discuss the following attacks.

4.6.4.2   Brute-Force Attack

The large key space makes the brute- force attack [18] infeasible. In this attack, the attacker tries to translate the cipher text into plain text using every possible key. On average, half of all possible keys are enough for achieving success. Algorithms are known to all in most networking systems but a brute-force attack will be impossible if the algorithm uses large key space. At present the fastest super computer is Tianhe-2 having speeded *33.86 petaflops i.e., $33.86x10^{15}$* floating point operations per second. Let us consider each trial requires 2000 FLOPS to complete one check. So the number of trials complete per second is: *$16.93x10^{12}$*. The number of seconds in a year is: *365 * 24 * 60 * 60 = 3153600 sec*.

Now from the above key space the formula for break the key is *$2^{2k}/$ (16.93 * 10^{12} * 3153600) = Y*, Y denotes number of years. So if k increases then Y increases ($k \infty Y$) thus for large key length it is difficult to break the key. A cipher text with such a long key space is sufficient for reliable practical use. This proves that a key with large enough space is sufficient to overcome the brute-force attack.

4.6.4.3   Dictionary Attack

A dictionary attack [19] may uncover an available list of words or using this attack a password can be found from online. Thus the attacker may get a password using a dictionary attack. The traditional dictionaries are not the only ones used to find a password; online dictionaries of words from foreign languages, or on specialized topics such as music, film, sports, etc., are also used. For repeated use of these words in encryption process an opponent may create an "encrypted" (hashed) list of dictionary or high-probability passwords. This dictionary may be used by an attacker in guessing the right encryption key for decryption. Dictionary attacks are more efficient than brute-force attacks, which cannot try nearly as many combinations. If the key is not contained in the dictionary, the attacker will never successfully find it.

In our proposed methodology, the above different algorithms have used random number generation functions, linear congruential function, etc., and as a result the intermediate key or session key generated in this way not only contains English words or variations or phrases but also contains different ascii characters, numbers, and special characters. This would exhaust the attacker's dictionary without a positive match.

4.6.4.4   Impersonation Attack

Impersonation [20] means an act of pretending to be another person for purpose of fraud. This type of attack involves a message or email that seems to come from a trusted one. If an attacker intends to get another user's information then the attacker sends a message or email to another user and forges valid information. An impersonation attack can be done when an attacker can successfully forge valid data.

Strong security policies and vigilance on communication media are required to stop an impersonation attack. Here we have used intermediate key for message authentication and RSA technique for user authentication. After authentication we can generate session key which is used for encryption. Thus our technique provides security against an impersonation attack.

4.6.4.5   Replay Attack

A replay attack [21] is a type of network attack in which an attacker detects a data transmission and has it delayed or repeated fraudulently. As a result the attacker can gain access to a network, gain vital information from another or complete a duplicate transaction. An attacker may launch a replay attack to delay or even stop the response to any request message [23]. To defend against a replay attack, in this article the concept of session key is used and in every session the session key is fresh. Thus when an attacker retransmits or has delayed to send message then the previous key may not work.

4.6.4.6   Tampering Attack

An attacker tampers [27] other users' information or data using a tampering attack. An attacker may launch a tampering attack on a smart system if it intends to change data illegally.

In our proposed methodology, we have introduced a rigorous frame structure with multiple attributes. Among the multiple attributes the cipher text is one, so it is hard to detect the range of cipher text. Thus the attacker cannot launch a tampering attack easily [31].

4.6.5   Comparative Analysis

In this section the functionality of our scheme is done by comparing our proposed technology with different standard cryptographic algorithms, different existing schemes and different IoT attacks. The following Table 4.4 shows comparison among different standard algorithms and our proposed scheme. The following Table 4.5 shows the pertinence of our methodology compared to other existing techniques.

The above comparative study shows strength, and acceptance of our scheme. The proposed protocol provides more functionality such as strong user authentication and mutual authentication between the two patients, and it establishes a secure session key for the user i.e., patients. These are the paramount requirements for wireless healthcare applications. It is worth noting that our proposed protocol provides indispensable security features.

4.6.5.1   Comparative Analysis Related to IoT Attacks

The following Table 4.6 comparative analyses are related to IoT attacks, and it also proves the efficiency of our proposed scheme with respect to different types of parameters.

We compare three attacks with the parameters such as damage level, existing proposal and detection chances, vulnerability, etc., in IoT devices. A sinkhole attack is done at the network layer and in this attack the routing information is attracted by the node which is near the base station. A worm attack takes place at the application layer by inserting malicious code, and a side channel attack occurs at both application layer and physical layer. In this attack, the attacker uses the side channel information to generate encryption key. All these attacks except side channel attack are active attacks and can modify the information. All these attacks can modify the data or message, drop the packets, steal private information and encryption key, etc. At the time of computation each IoT device sends some side channel information to crack the encryption key. Many solutions are provided for each attack but they have some limitations. In our paper, we have emphasized only side channel attacks with respect to a healthcare system. Different algorithms defined above are used to prevent the leakage of private information and encryption key.

Table 4.4 Comparison between proposed algorithm and standard algorithms.

Algorithms	Important features	Important features of our proposed algorithm
IDEA	i) IDEA encrypts 64-bit plaintext to 64-bit cipher text blocks, using a 128-bit input key. ii) It uses both confusion and diffusion technique. iii) A dominant design concept in IDEA is mixing operations from three different algebraic groups of 2^n elements. iv) The security of IDEA currently seems that it is bounded only by the weaknesses arising from the relatively small (compared to its key length) block length of 64 bits [1, 3].	i) Our technique encrypts plaintext to cipher text bit by bit, using m-bit input key. ii) The main design concept of our technique (a) intermediate key generation using the concept of linear congruence. (b) Session key generation using approximation algorithm. (c) Circular left shift is used to produce non-linearity in encryption process.
RC5	i) The RC5 block cipher maintains word-oriented architecture for variable word sizes w = 16, 32, or 64 bits. ii) The number of rounds r and the length of key byte is b byte which is variable. iii) For encryption, there are two steps in each round, (a) bit-wise XOR operation, (b) circular left shift. (c) Addition with the next sub key [4, 10].	i) Our proposed scheme is stream cipher–based. Here two keys are used for encryption/ decryption. ii) Key length is variable. iii) For encryption, there are two steps: (a) bit-wise XOR operation (b) Circular left shift with a linear function. It provides number of times CLS occurs.

(Continued)

Table 4.4 Comparison between proposed algorithm and standard algorithms. (*Continued*)

Algorithms	Important features	Important features of our proposed algorithm
BLOWFISH	i) This technique is based on stream cipher. It uses addition, XOR operation for encryption. ii) It has a variable key length up to a maximum of 448 bits long which ensures security. iii) Blowfish suits applications where the key remains constant for a long time and it is not suitable for packet switching [1, 4].	i) Our scheme is also based on steam cipher. It uses XOR, CLS operations to impose more non linearity in cipher text. ii) The use of double keys and one of this key is changeable by nature which provides robustness in our technique. iii) Suitable for packet switching.
DES	i) Linear cryptanalysis provides the most powerful attack on DES to date where enormous number of known plain text pairs is feasible. ii) Differential cryptanalysis is one of the most general cryptanalytic tools to date against modern iterated block ciphers, including DES. It is primarily a chosen-plaintext attack. iii) Storage complexity, both linear and differential cryptanalysis requires only negligible storage. iv) Due to its short key size, the DES algorithm is now considered insecure and should not be used. However, a strengthened version of DES called Triple-DES is used [3, 10].	i) Our algorithm is based on stream cipher with two keys one is session key which is changeable in nature. So it protects linear cryptanalysis as well as differential cryptanalysis. ii) Our algorithm takes negligible storage for linear and differential cryptanalysis. iii) Our algorithm is secure with respect to key size, because we have used two keys with variable length.

Table 4.5 Comparison between some existing algorithm and proposed algorithm.

Schemes→ Security properties↓	Ref [8]	Ref [12]	Ref [15]	Ref [24]	Ref [25]	Ref [26]	Proposed technique
Confidentiality	Yes	No	No	No	Yes	Yes	Yes
Integrity	No	No	No	No	Yes	Yes	Yes
Authenticity (message authentication and user authentication)	Yes	No	No	Yes	No	Yes	Message authentication using intermediate key & user authentication by RSA.
Freshness Protection	No	No	Yes	Yes	No	No	Yes
Privacy Protection	No	Yes	No	Yes	Yes	Yes	Yes
Defend against Man-in-middle attack	No	No	No	No	No	No	Yes
Defend against replay attack	No	No	No	No	No	No	Yes
Defend against tampering attack	No	No	No	No	Yes	Yes	Yes

(Continued)

Table 4.5 Comparison between some existing algorithm and proposed algorithm. (*Continued*)

Schemes→ Security properties↓	Ref [8]	Ref [12]	Ref [15]	Ref [24]	Ref [25]	Ref [26]	Proposed technique
Vulnerability	No	No	No	Yes	Yes	Yes	Yes
Defend against Impersonation attack	No	Yes	No	Yes	Yes	No	Yes
Cryptanalysis (linear and differential)	No	No	No	Yes	Yes	Yes	Yes
Session key establishment	No	No	No	No	Yes	Yes	Yes
Secure against Information-leakage attack	Yes	No	No	Yes	Yes	Yes	Yes

Table 4.6 Different IoT attacks.

Classification/parameters	Sinkhole attack	Worm attack	Side-channel attack
OSI Layers	Network	Application	Application
Attack Type	Active. It provides the wrong information which results in packet dropping [9].	Active. It modifies the files [6].	Passive. here the attacker can find Encryption key by using the side-channel information [1].
Attack Threat	Availability, Confidentiality-As all the data is attracted to the compromised node.	Availability, Integrity, Authenticity-As it can delete, modify the data [6].	Confidentiality, Integrity-by using side channel Information it can find the encryption key [1].
Damage Level	High - As all data is flowing through compromised node the attacker can do anything with packet	High - As it can delete files, mail documents [6].	High - As the attacker can obtains the secret key without detecting [1]
Prevention	Yes - if node authentication is provided [6].	Yes - by avoiding suspicious sites, files [14].	Yes - By using preventive Methods [22].
Attacks based on	Routing [25].	Malicious Code	Side Channel Information [22]
Vulnerability	Node Authentication is not provided [6].	Not Following Security Policies	Side-channel information [22].

Our proposed algorithm works on the application layer. In our proposed algorithm different types of complex and strong mathematical function from Integer theory and linear function are used, and as a result the algorithms when running provide minimum side channel information so that the attacker cannot guess the encryption key. Our scheme also provides confidentiality and integrity by checking authentication on both sender and recipient side.

4.6.6   Significance of Authentication in Our Proposed Scheme

The identity proof is done by Authentication mechanisms [8]. The authentication process ensures the originality of document, that is, whether the document is coming from the right person or not. In a secure system mainly in medical IoT domain the user must identify himself/herself, and then the system will authenticate the identity before using the system, because without proper authentication medical data transmission may occur and cause severe damage in the patient party. The authentication process can be professionally seen as: 1) SMS-based authentication, 2) Intermediate key–based authentication, 3) Public key authentication. The intermediate key–based authentication and public key–based authenticity are used in our proposed system; the user shares a single session key with an algorithm named RSA which provides public key authentication. The hash value of amalgamation of two keys, i.e., 1st part of intermediate key and 2nd part of session key is concatenated with the plain text. On the recipient side, the receiver gets session key using RSA technique and generates intermediate key using algorithm-2 and after checking the hash value using Algorithm-4 of our scheme, the sender decides whether the message has come from the right person or not.

4.7   Conclusion

There are different types of challenges in healthcare systems at the present time. Many possibilities are growing using medical information technologies, but these also pose challenges. Trends in health sensing and application of IoT in healthcare system show interesting new developments. They can enhance and improve healthcare abilities, boost preventive care and foster collaborative healthcare. An integral approach is necessary for a healthcare system which safeguards important aspects such as security and privacy protection. In this paper, we have developed a cryptosystem where an encryption technique is presented based on intermediate key and session key. The session key generation is done by using public key of sender (patient or hospital staff) and receiver (patient or hospital staff) and concept of approximation algorithm, linear congruence and linear function. To provide more non-linearity in cipher text we have used circular left shift operation with a non-linear function in the encryption technique. Our technique also provides the authentications which enrich the robustness as well as beauty of encryption technique. Different experimental results prove the feasibility and efficiency of the proposed scheme. Comparative analysis among proposed technique and standard techniques, exhaustive key search analysis, and cryptanalysis shows the acceptability of our technique. To the best of our knowledge our proposed technique is the simplest one, having minimal computational overhead during encryption and decryption.

References

1. A. Das and C. E. Veni Madhavan, *Public-key Cryptography: Theory and Practice*, Pearson Education, in press.
2. D. Boneh, M. Franklin, Identity-based encryption from the Weil pairing, in Kilian, J. (ed.) CRYPTO2001. LNCS, vol. 2139, Springer, Heidelberg, 2001, pp. 213–229.
3. W. Stallings, *Cryptography and Network Security: Principles and Practice*, third edition, Prentice Hall, 2003.
4. Atul Kahate, *Cryptography and Network Security*, Tata McGraw-Hill publishing company, New Delhi, 2008.
5. E.T. Oladipupo, O.A. Alade, "An Approach to Improve Data Security using Modified XOR Encryption Algorithm", 2014, *International Journal of Core Research in Communication Engineering*, Volume No. 1, Issue No. 2.
6. D. Stinson, *Cryptography: Theory and Practice*, third edition, Chapman & Hall/CRC, 2006.
7. A. Agrawal, S. Gorbunov, V. Vaikuntanathan, H. Wee, Functional encryption: New perspectives and lower bounds, in R. Canetti, J.A. Garay, (eds.) *CRYPTO 2013, Part II*. LNCS, vol. 8043. Springer, Heidelberg, 2013, pp. 500–518.
8. Kumar, V. (2015). Ontology Based Public Healthcare System in Internet of Things (IoT). *Procedia Computer Science, 50*, 99–102. doi:10.1016/j.procs.2015.04.067.
9. S. A. Chaudhry et al. An improved and provably secure privacy preserving authentication protocol for SIP. *Peer-to-Peer Networking and Applications.* 2017; 10(1): 1-15.
10. A. Kak, "Lecture Notes on Computer and Network Security", 2015, Purdue University [Online] Available: https://engineering.purdue.edu/kak/compsec/Lectures.html.

11. Zaidan B, Zaidan A, Al-Frajat A, Jalab H. On the differences between hiding information and cryptography techniques: An overview. *Journal of Applied Sciences.* 2010; 10:1650–5.
12. Maia, P., Batista, T., Cavalcante, E., Baffa, A., Delicato, F. C., Pires, P. F., & Zomaya,A. (2014). A web platform for interconnecting body sensors and improving health care. *Procedia Computer Science,* 40, 135–142. doi:10.1016/j. procs.2014.10.041.
13. C. Joshi, and U.K. Singh, "A Review on Taxonomies of Attacks and Vulnerability in Computer and Network System". *International Journal of Advanced Research in Computer Science and Software Engineering (IJRCSSE)* Volume 5, Issue 1, January 2015, pp 742-747.
14. Siddharth Ghansela "Network Security: Attacks, Tools and Techniques", *ijarcsse* Volume 3, Issue 6, June 2013.
15. Mohan V. Pawer, Anuradha J, "Network Security and Types of Attacks in Network", *In proceedings International Conference on Intelligent Computing, Communication & Convergence (ICCC-2015), Procedia Computer Science* 48 (2015) 503–506. DOI: 10.1016/j.procs.2015.04.126.
16. Olivier, F., Carlos, G., & Florent, N. (2015). New Security Architecture for IoT Network.*Procedia Computer Science,* 52, 1028–1033. doi:10.1016/j. procs.2015.05.099
17. J.G. Chakravorty, P.R. Ghosh, *Advanced Higher Algebra,* U.N. Dhur and Sons Private Ltd., 2018. ISBN 978-3- 80673-67-7.
18. Hong Yaling. Research on computer network security analysis model [J]. *Computer CD Software and Applications,* 2013(z): 1-152.
19. M.-C. Chuang and M. C. Chen, "An anonymous multi-server authenticated key agreement scheme based on trust computting using smart cards and biometrics," *Expert Systems with Applications,* vol. 41, no. 4, pp. 1411–1418, 2014.
20. J. S. Kumar and D. R. Patel, "A survey on internet of things: Security and privacy issues," *International Journal of Computer Applications,* vol. 90, no. 11, 2014.
21. Y. H. Hwang, "Iot security & privacy: threats and challenges," in *Proceedings of the 1st ACM Workshop on IoT Privacy, Trust and Security.* ACM, 2015, pp. 1–1.
22. M. M. Hossain, M. Fotouhi, and R. Hasan, "Towards an analysis of security issues, challenges, and open problems in the Internet of things," in *Services (SERVICES), 2015 IEEE World Congress on. IEEE,* 2015, pp. 21–28.
23. L. Da Xu, W. He, and S. Li, "Internet of things in industries: A survey," *IEEE Transactions on industrial informatics,* vol. 10, no. 4, pp. 2233–2243, 2014.
24. L. M. R. Tarouco, L. M. Bertholdo, L. Z. Granville, L. M. R. Arbiza, F. Carbone, M. Marotta, and J. J. C. de Santanna, "Internet of things in healthcare: Interoperability and security issues," in *Communications (ICC), IEEE International Conference on. IEEE,* 2012, pp. 6121–6125.

25. A. Mohan, "Cyber security for personal medical devices internet of things," in Distributed Computing in Sensor Systems (DCOSS), *2014 IEEE International Conference on. IEEE*, 2014, pp. 372–374.
26. M. Abomhara and G. M. Køien, "Security and privacy in the internet of things: Current status and open issues," in *Privacy and Security in Mobile Systems (PRISMS), International Conference on. IEEE*, 2014, pp. 1–8.
27. Liu, X. & Ma, W. "CDAKA: A Provably-Secure Heterogeneous Cross-Domain Authenticated Key Agreement Protocol with Symptoms-Matching in TMIS", *J Med Syst* (2018) 42: 135. https://doi.org/10.1007/s10916-018-0985-7.
28. Al Ameen, Moshaddique & Liu, Jingwei & Kwak, Kyung. (2012). Security and Privacy Issues in Wireless Sensor Networks for Healthcare Applications. *Journal of medical systems*. 36. 93-101. 10.1007/s10916-010-9449-4.
29. Kruse, C.S., Smith, B., Vanderlinden, H. et al." Security Techniques for the Electronic Health Records", *J Med Syst* (2017) 41: 127. https://doi.org/10.1007/s10916-017-0778-4.
30. J. E. Shockley, *Introduction to Number Theory*, Holt, Rinehart and Winston, New York, 1967.
31. Kurt Mehlhorn, Peter Sanders, *Algorithms and Data Structure*, Springer, Berlin, Heidelberg, 2008. Online ISBN 978-3-540-77978-3.
32. H. Tao, M. Z. A. Bhuiyan, A. N. Abdalla, M. M. Hassan, J. M. Zain and T. Hayajneh, "Secured Data Collection With Hardware-Based Ciphers for IoT-Based Healthcare," in *IEEE Internet of Things Journal*, vol. 6, no. 1, pp. 410-420, Feb. 2019, doi: 10.1109/JIOT.2018.2854714.
33. M. Elhoseny, G. Ramírez-González, O. M. Abu-Elnasr, S. A. Shawkat, N. Arunkumar and A. Farouk, "Secure Medical Data Transmission Model for IoT-Based Healthcare Systems," in *IEEE Access*, vol. 6, pp. 20596-20608, 2018, doi: 10.1109/ACCESS.2018.2817615.
34. T. Alladi, V. Chamola, R. M. Parizi and K. R. Choo, "Blockchain Applications for Industry 4.0 and Industrial IoT: A Review," in *IEEE Access*, vol. 7, pp. 176935-176951, 2019, doi: 10.1109/ACCESS.2019.2956748.
35. W. Liang, M. Tang, J. Long, X. Peng, J. Xu and K. Li, "A Secure FaBric Blockchain-Based Data Transmission Technique for Industrial Internet-of-Things," in *IEEE Transactions on Industrial Informatics*, vol. 15, no. 6, pp. 3582-3592, June 2019, doi: 10.1109/TII.2019.2907092.

5

A Hybrid Method for Fake Profile Detection in Social Network Using Artificial Intelligence

Ajesh F¹*, Aswathy S U², Felix M Philip³ and Jeyakrishnan V⁴

¹*Research Scholar, Department of Computer Science and Engineering, Anna University, Chennai, Tamilnadu, India*
²*Professor, Department of Computer Science and Engineering, Jyothi Engineering College, Thrissur, Kerala, India*
³*Professor, Department of Computer Science and Information Technology, Jain (Deemed-to-be University), Kochi Campus, Kerala, India*
⁴*Professor, Department of Computer Science and Engineering, Saintgits College of Engineering, Kottayam, Kerala, India*

Abstract

Social life for everyone in the present generation has become synonymous with online social networks or social relationships between people who share their interests, activities, experiences or real-life interrelationships. Such media created a drastic shift in how we view our social lives. Making friends and keeping in touch and receiving their messages has become much easier. Yet the rapid development of social networks has led to many problems, such as fake accounts and online impersonation. Controlling these problems is unfeasible. To detect fake profiles, we use an artificial learning technique based on a hybrid model. The research process clearly illustrated the power of the proposed scheme to detect fake profiles with high accuracy. Traditionally, we have different classification methods in place to recognize fake accounts in social networks. Nonetheless, we will increase the accuracy rate of social network fake profile recognition. In this paper, we suggest techniques for Artificial Intelligence and Natural Language Processing (NLP) techniques to increase accuracy of fake profile recognition. We use the Random Forest

Corresponding author: ajeshf@gmail.com

Shibin David, R. S. Anand, V. Jeyakrishnan, and M. Niranjanamurthy (eds.) Security Issues and Privacy Concerns in Industry 4.0 Applications, (89–112) © 2021 Scrivener Publishing LLC

Classifier, Support Vector Machine (SVM) and Optimized Naïve Bayes algorithm to categorize profiles into fake or genuine classes. Since this is an automated recognition tool, an online social network that has large amounts of accounts that cannot be verified manually can easily expand. These three algorithms were used to determine the true or false identity of the target accounts. This algorithm uses less features, but about 98% of our training dataset accounts can still be correctly defined.

Keywords: Artificial intelligence, Facebook, fake profiles, privacy, social media, social network analysis

5.1   Introduction

Social networking has become a well-known leisure activity on the Internet, attracting billions of active users who spend every second on these services. Online Social Network (OSN) services range from social experiences such as Facebook-like sites, YouTube-like distributions including focused social media platforms such as Twitter or Google Buzz, to typical social networking brought to existing systems such as Flickr [1]. On the other hand, the most important bottleneck is the need for improvement of security issues and the protection of OSN information [2–4]. People exchange large amounts of their private knowledge with the general public while using social networks. That makes them good targets for different types of attacks, but the worst thing is the theft of identification.

Theft of online identification seems to have been a major issue over the years, given that it has an impact on millions of people around the world. Victims of identity theft may be subject to specific types of damages, such as loss of time/cash, damage to the public profile or damage to relationships with partners and loved ones. At present, most social networks no longer check for ordinary users. This has produced very weak privacy and protection policies. Indeed, most social networks tend to reduce anonymity, making it the best platform for fraud and violence.

Like innocent attackers, social networking offers have contributed to the theft of serious identity and impersonality. To make matters worse, users need to have a proper understanding of how to make an account on social network websites. Easily tracking what users share online can lead to huge losses if bills are hacked. Account info on social networks can be either static or dynamic. Details that can be added or implemented as part of an account creation with individual support are known as static knowledge, and small illustrations are explained in the network as dynamic knowledge using this technique. Static knowledge involves the personal statistical features and importance of a person, while dynamic knowledge involves people's run-time patterns as well as the location of the platform. Many of the actual work focuses on static data and dynamic data.

Problems surrounding social networking, including anonymity, cyber-bullying, abuse and harassment, are just a few examples of instances of fraudulent identity misuse of social networking sites. Fake accounts are the accounts of misidentified males and females. Fake Facebook accounts engage in malicious and undesirable behavior that puts social community users at risk. In order to defame a man or a woman in order to encourage a person or a person to spread, people are building fake accounts for digital manipulation, virtual impersonation. Facebook has its own security framework that protects users' credentials from deletion and spoofing. Generally, the analog is referred to as the Facebook Immune System (FIS). FIS can no longer monitor a large number of user-created fake Facebook profiles.

5.2   Literature Survey

Various false detection strategies are focused on the study of individual social network profiles in order to recognise characteristics that could lead to a distinction between real and fake accounts. Classifiers are developed and used for extracted characteristics in order to detect false accounts.

Detection and prevention of false accounts is a demanding field of study for the time being. Studies with many promising results have been conducted in the field. The paper by Nazir *et al.* elaborates on the detection and characterization of phantom profiles on online gaming platforms. "Fighters Club," a Facebook application that allows users to give incentives to invite peers, has been analyzed and is believed to encourage users to create fake incentive accounts. Support Vector Machines (SVMs) were used for classification with the help of 13 features of each user of the game. The authors have found that the method does not provide any means of discriminating against false users.

Despite this negative result, Adikari and Dutta talk about fake detection as about 84% accurate and false results down to 2.44% [3]. The work used limited profile data available from LinkedIn and SVMs, main component analysis, neural networks were used for detection in Figure 5.1. Other

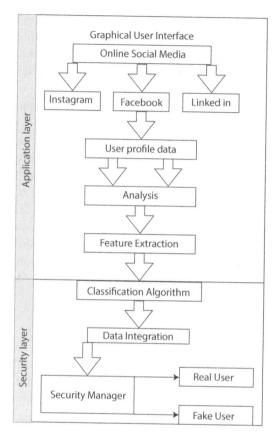

Figure 5.1 Architecture of fake profile detection.

features such as skills and interests, spoken languages, recommendations and awards have also been used, and the features of known fake accounts posted on special websites have been considered ground-based.

Different recognition methods can be divided into two groups in OSMs: feature-based approach and social-graph-based approach. In the first approach, researchers concentrate on extracting user profile features and analyzing user behaviour patterns to generate a machine learning classification to classify fake user accounts [24–32]. Researchers use community-based detection algorithms in social-graphic approaches to detect and group sockets that share the same interest.

For fake profiles managed by humans, apps, and (bots and humans involved), Orthogonal Sparse Bigram (OSB) was used to identify spam accounts using a pair of words used [7]. Bots and human accounts were differentiated using URLs, APIs and the regularity of tweets as features.

Wang *et al*'s paper discusses crowd-turfing and its operational structure by grubbing up such websites coordinating the crowd-turfing campaign and also by launching a campaign by the like but mild authors [6]. The study found that the campaigns could be effective in hiring users and pose a serious threat to security due to their high popularity.

Liu *et al.* has studied the detection of similarities or differences in user traits, focusing more on e-mail correspondence than on social networks [5]. An attempt has been made to identify spear phishing. The method used was to profile individual e-mail writers and identify the source of new incoming e-mails that would identify whether they were from the same source. Creating fake social network accounts causes more harm than any other cybercrime [10].

Kharaji *et al.* compared a simple prototype approach to a fully developed menu procedure and found that users, especially beginners, opt for a common dialog-based approach rather than a prototype approach that provides efficient ordinary systems with normal simple language processing and human-pc interfaces [11–20]. The authors also acknowledged that the refinement of dialog management in e-commerce platforms has a high priority over managing typical language sentences. Moreover, NL's dialog-based navigation and menu-based navigation designed to meet individual needs could ensure ease of access to knowledge on e-commerce websites. They recently developed a new iteration methodology that involves improved language analysis, dialog and data management. Informal interfaces using average languages were found to be effective, as opposed to traditional menus or search-based interfaces.

The social network, which is undergoing almost exponential growth, is prone to unethical and illegal activities using fake profiles, infringing personal data [8, 9]. These fake profiles are often difficult to identify and detect using current solutions. LinkedIn is often chosen by a majority of people in the real sector of work. In LinkedIn, the individual data with public access is limited and insufficient to identify false profiles. This gives rise to a huge demand for systems capable of false profile identification in LinkedIn [21–23]. A study conducted by Shakinda Adikari and Kaushik Dutta found a set of minimum data and mining procedures that could be used to detect fake profiles in LinkedIn. Z. Halim *et al.* proposed a procedure based on spatial-temporal mining and latent semantics analysis. The group of customers concerned with identified malicious events is compared with the result of spatial-temporal coincidence with that of the initial accounts on the platform.

5.3   Methodology

Social media accounting involves a lot of information like position, number of contacts, number of posts, jobs, etc. Some of them may be personal, and the others are open. Since personal information is not available, we just used a shared method to evaluate a fake ID. However, if social networking companies then use our proposed system, they could use personal information to identify false identities despite infringements of any privacy concerns. This knowledge is considered to be account features to confirm false and actual accounts.

5.3.1   Datasets

We need a dataset of real and fake profiles labelled accordingly. Algorithms must be trained using the training dataset and tested using the testing dataset. Since there is no regular dataset, we need to plan the dataset by scrapping Facebook profiles, Instagram and LinkedIn. But no such databases are available due to privacy concerns [30].

5.3.2   Detection of Fake Account

The following are the steps we have taken to recognize fake accounts:

1) All the characteristics on which the classification model is based are chosen as described in section 5.3.3. Relay attributes should not be based on some other factors, and all those characteristics that can improve the efficiency of classification should be selected.
2) After an appropriate feature selection method, a data collection of previously identified fake and actual profiles is required once again for the model training of the classification algorithm.
3) The selected attributes in Step 1 must be collected from the fake and actual profile pages. The online social media organizations that want our proposal to be applied will easily remove the functionality from existing servers. We have adapted the scrapping of profiles as no social network dataset is openly capable of detecting false profiles accurately.
4) Following this, the data collection of false and actual profiles is compiled, and 80% of real and fake profiles can be used to prepare a test dataset. The efficiency of the classification

method is calculated using the training dataset comprising 922 profiles and 240 profile test datasets.

5) After the preparation of the test and training dataset, the training dataset shall be fed into the classification model. It is based on a training algorithm and is intended to give the test data set the correctly predicted rates.

6) Tariffs are excluded from the validation dataset and left to the qualified classifier for confirmation. The efficiency of the classification shall be determined by measuring the number of correct observations divided by the total number of observations. Classification findings are set out in section 5.4.4. We used three different classifiers and evaluated the efficiency of the classification of these algorithms.

5.3.3 Suggested Framework

The suggested structure in Figure 5.2 shows the step-by-step process to be followed in order to start identifying a fake account. The figure shows the successful learning from the reviews of the results of the classification algorithm. Online social media organizations can integrate this structure easily.

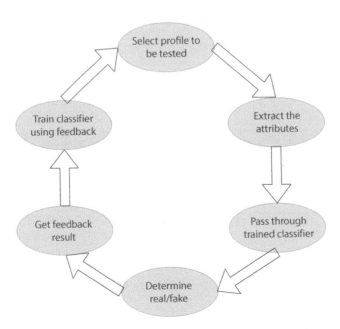

Figure 5.2 Schema for identifying and understanding the fraudulent profiles.

1) The detection method begins with the selection of a user account to be checked for fake/true.
2) After the account is identified, the correct features or features of the user profile for which the classification algorithm is to be applied are selected.
3) The features retrieved in step 2 shall be transferred to the qualified classifier. The classifier is properly trained as new training data is fed into another classifier.
4) The trained model shall decide whether the profile is true or false.
5) If the profile page is labeled, the classifier may not be 100% correct, so the output feedback is returned to the classifier. For example, if the profile is recognized as fake, the social media site may send a notification of the profile for

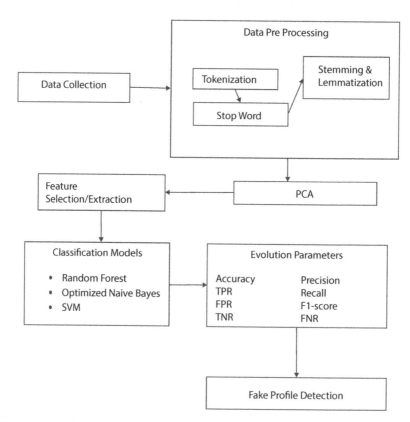

Figure 5.3 Working procedure for proposed system.

identification. If the relevant recognition is given, the reply would be sent to the classifier that the profile was not false. Otherwise, it is assumed to be fake.

6) This pattern repeats and, as time passes, this leads to an increase in training data, thus trying to make the classifier more reliable in assessing false profiles.

Figure 5.3 explains the computational modeling and NLP program for the recognition of incorrect accounts on social network sites in this paper. We also implement the SVM classifier model, the Optimized Naïve Bayes algorithm and the Random Forest algorithm to improve fake account prediction. The proposed technique consists of three main steps. Initially with the pre-processing of the NLP, the second stage is the principal component analysis (PCA) and finally the algorithms used for learning. The three sections will be discussed below.

5.3.3.1   Pre-Processing

Pre-processing text is an important part of the natural language processing method. The following shows the significance of the NLP pre-processing;

1. To minimize the dimensions of indexing records obtained from the textual content records.
   i.   Stop words bills.
   ii.   Stemming diminishes indexing size.
2. To make the IR method more powerful and reliable.
   i.   Stop words aren't useful for mining textual content, so the recovery method can be confused
   ii.   Stemming used in a text record for matching the similar words.

5.3.3.1.1   Tokenization

Tokenization is defined as the method by which the actual content of the text is broken into phrases or tokens. This results in an examination of the phrases in a sentence. The generated tokens become input for future parsing processing, where the tokenization of records is the main requirement for the parser. Tokenization is important in both linguistics and laptop science. However, some of the problems faced here are the removal of punctuation marks.

5.3.3.1.2   Stop Word Removal

Stop phrases are not useful for the classification of records. They have to be eliminated, therefore. However, the development of such a recording of stop words is inconsistent between textual sources. Stop the removal of words helps to reduce text knowledge and also improves performance.

5.3.3.1.3   Stemming and Lemmatization

Stemming and lemming are used to scale down inflectional types as well as phrase varieties associated with derivation into a fashioned base form. Stemming is typically a simple heuristic method that cuts off the ends of words. It involves removing by-product affixes. Lemmatization uses vocabulary and morphological analysis of phrases, with the aim of eliminating only inflective endings and returning to lemma.

5.3.3.2   *Principal Component Analysis (PCA)*

Multivariate classical method is the basic concept behind PCA. Multiple dataset has several variables to remember. If there are n variables with multiple dimensions in a data set, multidimensional space is difficult to realize. Figure 5.4 shows that the PCA method reduces dimensions by combining the index and the similar observation that is classified. The PCA method has been widely used in analytical forms. PCA is a method of extracting the relevant information in the absence of parameters from a large data set. In this process, the variables are summed up in the multi-state space to obtain a set of unconnected components. Each of these components is a linear combination of the major variables. The main components derived from the special covariance matrices are the non-correlated components achieved. This method is mainly used to reduce the number of attributes and to find a structure of

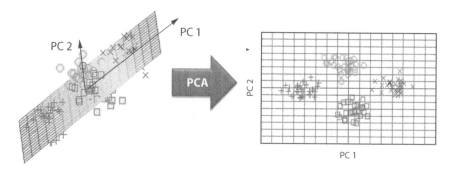

Figure 5.4 Dimensionality reduction using PCA.

communication between attributes. Several criteria have been proposed for the selection of the number of core components that is an important issue. These criteria can be categorized as formal and informal. While considering an informal approach, first the correct precision is determined and then the total number of variations selected. Another method is used by Eigen.

5.3.3.3 Learning Algorithms

Classification algorithms are the learning algorithms used. Classification comes under a supervised approach to machine learning. By definition a classification can be explained as a process of learning the target function say 'F' which is used to map each record to say 'X' to 'Y' which is a set of features to one of the class labels predefined by constructing a classification model from the input data set. Here, we 're using three learning algorithms. This helps us identify the right fit for the training set's feature set and class labels. The model obtained by using the learning algorithm will correctly predict the class label with high accuracy from the input data set. Figure 5.5 shows how the classification model is produced. The classifiers that we used are mentioned below:

- Support Vector Machine (SVM)
- Random Forest Classifier
- Optimized Naïve Bayes algorithm

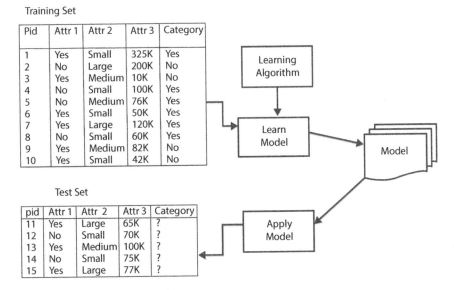

Figure 5.5 A classification model.

These three standard algorithms are widely used for many issues such as spam email detection, galaxy classification, malignant cell classification, and so on.

A. Support Vector Machine (SVM)

The SVM uses hyperplanes to classify data points into different classes. SVM's best hyperplane is the flat with the highest gap between two classes. Help vectors are points near the hyperplane that establish plane boundaries. Support vectors have an influence on the position and direction of the hyperplane. We maximize the range of the classifiers by changing the position of the hyperplane to find the best one that fits. Figure 5.6 shows the linear classification. The '+' mark indicates the data point of type 1 and the '-' mark indicates the data points of type 0. The SVM will be implemented using Matlab.

B. The Random Forest Classifier

The Random Forest Classifier is a group of individual decision trees, Figure 5.7, which operates as a single unit. The technique of training each tree using different random sample is called bagging or bootstrap aggregation. Each decision tree in this classifier defines class prediction, and most votes are our model's prediction. This classifier classifies the decision tree collection to the subset of the generated training sets. Trees defend each other from mistakes. Trees may be wrong or right, but trees should push in the right direction. This also helps solve outliers issues in the data collection. To improve the accuracy of the broad dataset, it generates missing values for the profile attributes.

C. Optimized Naïve Bayes Algorithm

The principle behind the Naïve Bayes Algorithm is the Bayes Theorem, which is used to model the probabilistic relationship between the class

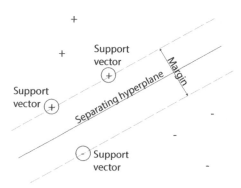

Figure 5.6 SVM classification for 2-Dimensional data.

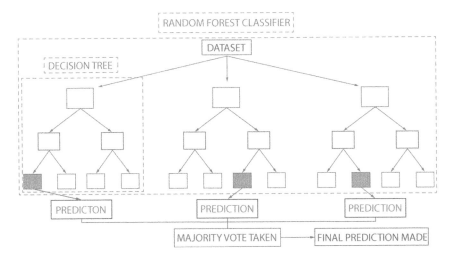

Figure 5.7 Random forest classifier.

labels and the feature matrix. The theorem uses and combines prior knowledge. To understand the theorem in detail, consider the data of a particular
class and we calculate the probability that it will be true. The frequency
table is based on the data set used for training and the probability calculation. This classifier is easy to implement with Bayes Theorem:

$$P(A|B) = \frac{P(B|A).P(A)}{P(B)} \quad (5.1)$$

Where P(A) refers to the probability of event A occurring, and P(A)
refers to the probability of event A occurring if event B occurred.

For increasing the accuracy in Naïve Bayes Algorithm a bag-of-token
model was developed. For each feature k the value is obtained on the basis
of the number of occurrence of the token k. The probability is measured by:

$$P(\text{token} = k \,|\, class = l) = \frac{1+\beta 1}{N+\beta 2} \quad (5.2)$$

By considering the class l we define β_1 refers to the weighted number of
appearance of token k and β_2 represents the weighted number of appearance of all the tokens. Within the training set the number of instances is
represented using N.

5.3.3.4   Feature or Attribute Selection

Feature selection is an important concept that is the basis for increasing the performance and accuracy of the classifier. We always use attributes that directly affect our results. Consider Table 5.1, which provides some of the

Table 5.1 Initial features from profiles.

Features	Description of the characteristics
Social_Id	User ID
Social_Uname	User name
Social_dp	Profile of default
Social_Screen_name	Screen Name
Social_fo_count	Counting Followers
Social_fr_count	Counting Friends
Social_fa_count	Favourite Count
Social_created_at	Creation of account date at
Social_Ptd	Protection Status
Social_up	Update Date
Social_url	AccountUrl
Social_pbt	Profile Background Title
Social_L	Language
Social_tz	Time zone
Social_location	Geographical location
Social_Ge	Géo localisation
Social_PiU	Url Profile Image
Social_Txc	Profile Text Color
Social_phttps	Profile Image Url Https
Social_vfd	Verification Status
Social_Despt	Account description

initial features. Not all of these features are necessary, so we need to select the appropriate features that are important.

There are also many other features, such as gender, count of friends, count of photos uploaded to profiles, education information, work, relationship status, number of photos uploaded, number of groups, number of likes, and so on.

5.4   Result Analysis

Here we use machine learning to test the proposed process. For classifier training, we use the 10-fold cross-validation method, see Figure 5.8, from which we get efficiency matrices.

5.4.1   Cross-Validation

Predictive models are tested using methods such as cross-validation, splitting the real data set into two, the training set, and the other set as a test set. Model testing is performed using the first set called the training set, and model I d is tested using the test set. For k-fold cross-validation, the k-sample validation process is performed k-1 times.

This allows all samples to be used only once for testing purposes and all samples to be used for training and testing. The data is divided into k-folds and 10-folds. Instead use 9-folds and check the pattern using the 10th fold. The assessment process is replicated as many times as possible, rendering each fold as a test set once. The score is recorded and the average of the score is calculated.

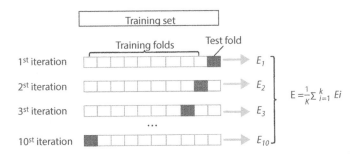

Figure 5.8 10-fold cross-validation for a dataset.

5.4.2   Analysis of Metrics

The calculation takes into account the confusion matrix shown in Table 5.2 where w represents the total number of normal profiles correctly classified by the model, x refers to the number of fake profiles misclassified, y refers to the number of normal profiles incorrectly classified and z refers to the number of fake profiles correctly classified.

The three classifiers of the learning algorithms are evaluated using AUC and Accuracy. The AUC is the area under the curve and is used as performance metrics for the classifier; when the AUC is close, the final performance of the classification will be good. In AUC, we get the ROC curves and calculate them using the following metrics.

$$\text{True Positive Rate (TPR)} = \frac{w}{w+x} \tag{5.3}$$

$$\text{True Negative Rate (TNR)} = \frac{z}{z+y} \tag{5.4}$$

$$\text{False Positive Rate (FPR)} = \frac{z}{z+w} \tag{5.5}$$

$$\text{False Negative Rate (FNR)} = \frac{x}{x+w} \tag{5.6}$$

$$\text{Accuracy (Acc)} = \frac{w+z}{w+x+Y+Z} \tag{5.7}$$

Table 5.2 Confusion matrix for fake profile detection testing data set.

Classification models	TP	FN	FP	TN
Random Forest	67	6	3	24
Naïve Bayes	57	16	15	12
SVM	71	2	1	26

$$\text{Precision (Pr)} = \frac{z}{y+z} \qquad (5.8)$$

$$\text{Recall (Re)} = \frac{z}{z+x} \qquad (5.9)$$

$$\text{F} - \text{Score (FS)} = \frac{2*Pr*Re}{Pr+Re} \qquad (5.10)$$

5.4.3   Performance Evaluation of Proposed Model

Here we use a dataset to evaluate the proposed method. We have 5,000,000 user data with 16,000,000 connections between these data. While considering 1,000 nodes in the dataset we get the result 990 of them were true nodes and 10 were fake nodes. The ratio of the false nodes to the true node is 1:100. We get the matrix from the graph, then measure and quantify the similarities between these nodes. PCA techniques were then used to extract features from this node and generate artificial data.

The actual outcome of 99% real users and 1% false profiles is changed to 75% real profiles and 25% fake profiles. This data is given to the next stage as an input and cross-validation technique used to find out from data the TPR, FPR, Accuracy, and AUC. Comparing this result, we can classify the AUC with the highest sublevel and the most accurate classifier.

5.4.4   Performance Analysis of Classifiers

Among the three chosen classifiers, SVM obtained the best 97% accuracy scores. Table 5.3 displays the confusion matrix derived by the SVM classifier, with 100% of the original and 97% of the falsely classified profiles, with a very small percentage of the original profiles misidentified.

Table 5.4 contains both the original and the fake profiles calculated from the confusion matrix created by Random Forest, Optimized Naive Bayes and SVM. Efficiency vs. the number of profiles in the training data set and Efficiency vs. the number of attributes selected from the profile are shown in Figures 5.9 and 5.10, respectively.

Table 5.3 Performance analysis of Random Forest, Optimized Naive Bayes and SVM.

Classification models	Accuracy	TPR	FPR	TNR	FNR
Random Forest	91	91.78082192	11.11111111	88.88889	7.63904058
Optimized Naïve Bayes	69	78.08219178	55.55555556	44.44444	21.6258761
SVM	97	97.26027397	3.703703704	96.2963	2.76134122

Table 5.4 Evaluation metrics (Precision, Recall and F-Score) of Random Forest, Optimized Naive Bayes and SVM.

Classification models	Pr	Re	FS
Random Forest (RF)	95.71428571	80	93.70629
Optimized Naïve Bayes (ONB)	79.16666667	42.857143	78.62069
SVM	98.61111111	92.857143	97.93103

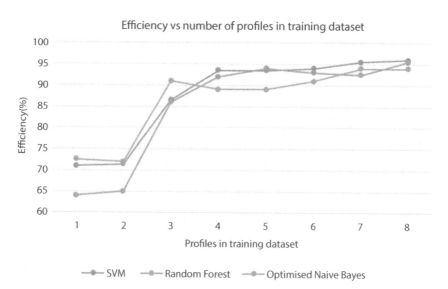

Figure 5.9 Efficiency vs. the number of profiles belonging to the training data set.

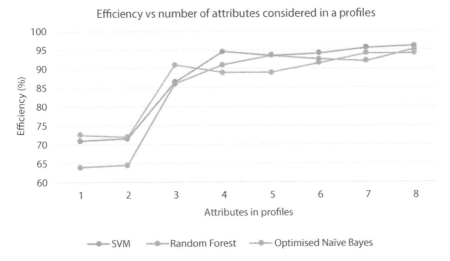

Figure 5.10 Efficiency vs. the number of attributes selected from the profile.

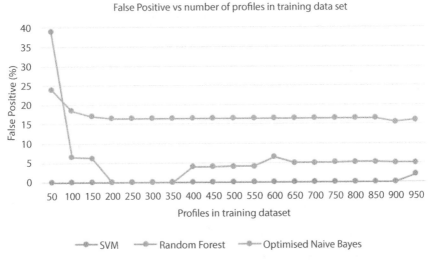

Figure 5.11 FP (False Positive) versus the number of profiles belonging to training dataset.

Figure 5.11 shows that the FPR (False Positive Rate) for the SVM classifier is the least one that implies that if the social network profile is predicted to be fake using the SVM classifier, the chances for this profile to be fake are very high.

Figure 5.12 shows that the False Negative rate with SVM has an average rate. It is clear, therefore, that SVM is the best method used to classify fake accounts on social networks.

It is understood from the above graphs that SVM has the highest efficiency. Also, from Figure 5.13 and Figure 5.14, we can conclude that when the number of attributes selected increases, the efficiency of the algorithm will also increase. The SVM classifier algorithm provides TPR = 97%, FPR = 2%, Accuracy = 97.6%, and AUC = 1.

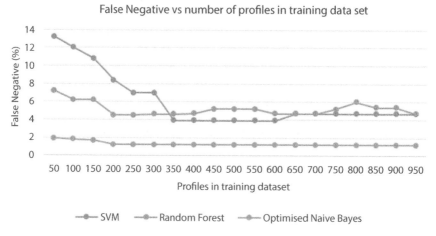

Figure 5.12 FN (False Negative) versus the number of profiles belonging to training dataset.

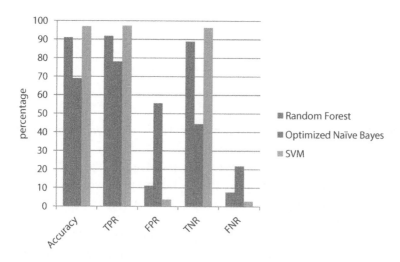

Figure 5.13 Performance analysis of different classifiers.

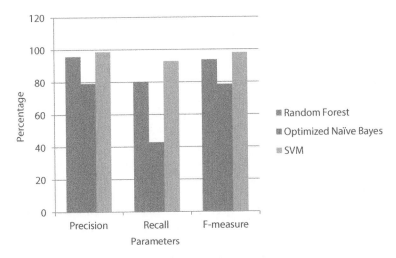

Figure 5.14 Evaluation metrics (Precision, Recall and F-Score) of Random Forest, Optimized Naive Bayes and SVM.

5.5 Conclusion

Fake social media profiles are created by people and their groups. These profiles should be detected from a wide, high-efficiency social network. Many techniques have been used to detect these profiles, but they have ended up being less accurate. Analyzing the findings of this paper, it is clear that by implementing Natural Language Processing techniques, methods for identifying fake profiles can be enhanced to some degree. As a result, we obtain a high accuracy of about 97% when it comes to finding such fake profiles on social networks. Here, we have proposed NLP techniques with machine learning algorithms. This helps to detect fake social media profiles. We use SVM, Random Forest Algorithms and Optimized Naïve Bayes Algorithms as learning algorithms. These learning algorithms have just increased the accuracy of detection. The SVM algorithm provides TPR = 97%, FPR = 2%, Accuracy = 97.6% and AUC = 1.

References

1. S. Kannan, Vairaprakash Gurusamy, Preprocessing Techniques for Text Mining, 05 March 2015.
2. Devadhas G. Glan, and S. S. Kumar. "An improved tumor segmentation algorithm from T2 and FLAIR multimodality MRI brain images by support

vector machine and genetic algorithm." *Cogent Engineering* 5, no. 1 (2018): 1470915.

3. Shalinda Adikari and Kaushik Dutta, Identifying Fake Profiles in LinkedIn, PACIS 2014 Proceedings, AISeL.

4. Z. Halim, M. Gul, N. ul Hassan, R. Baig, S. Rehman, and F. Naz, "Malicious users' circle detection in social network based on spatiotemporal co-occurrence," in *Computer Networks and Information Technology (ICCNIT)*, 2011 International Conference, July, pp. 35–390.

5. Liu Y, Gummadi K, Krishnamurthy B, Mislove A," Analyzing Facebook privacy settings: User expectations vs. reality", in: *Proceedings of the 2011 ACM SIGCOMM conference on Internet measurement conference, ACM*, pp. 61–70.

6. Mahmood S, Desmedt Y, "Poster: preliminary analysis of google's privacy." In: *Proceedings of the 18th ACM conference on computer and communications security*, ACM 2011, pp. 809–812.

7. Ajesh F, Dr R Ravi, "Hybrid features and optimization-driven recurrent neural network for Glaucoma detection" *International Journal of Imaging Systems and Technology*, Wiley, May 2020.

8. Devadhas G. Glan, and S. S. Kumar "Brain Tumor Detection and Segmentation Using A Wrapper Based Genetic Algorithm For Optimized Feature Set", Cluster computing pp pages Issue: 22, 13369–13380 (2018).

9. Ajesh F, Dr R Ravi, Early diagnosis of glaucoma using multi-feature analysis and DBN based classification," In *Journal of Ambient Intelligence and Humanized Computing*, February 2020.

10. D. Kagan, Y. Elovichi, and M. Fire, "Generic anomalous vertices detection utilizing a link prediction algorithm," *Social Network Analysis and Mining*, vol. 8, no. 1, 27 pages, 2018.

11. Kharaji MY, Rizi FS. An IAC approach for detecting profile cloning in online social networks. 2014 March 8. arXiv preprint arXiv:1403.2006.

12. Ji Y, He Y, Jiang X, Cao J, Li Q. Combating the evasion mechanisms of social bots. *Comput Secur* 2016; 58:230–49 Elsevier.

13. Beatriche, G.: Detection of fake profiles in Online Social Networks (OSNs), Master's degree in Applied Telecommunications and Engineering Management (MASTEAM), 2018.

14. Romanov, A., Semenov, A., Veijalainen, J.: Revealing fake profiles in social networks by longitudinal data analysis. In: *13th International Conference on Web Information Systems and Technologies, January 2017.*

15. Granik, M., Mesyura, V.: Fake news detection using naive Bayes classifier. In: Conference: *IEEE First Ukraine Conference on Electrical and Computer Engineering (UKRCON)*, May 2017.

16. B. Gonen, M. A. Canbaz, "User characterization for online social networks," *Social Network Analysis and Mining*, 2016.

17. M. Conti, R. Poovendran, and M. Secchiero, "FakeBook: Detecting fake profiles in on-line social networks," in *Proceedings of the 2012 IEEE/ACM International Conference on Advances in Social Networks Analysis and Mining, ASONAM 2012*, pp. 1071–1078, Turkey, August 2012.

18. Z. Shan, H. Cao, J. Lv, C. Yan, and A. Liu, "Enhancing and identifying cloning attacks in online social networks," in *Proceedings of the the 7th International Conference*, pp. 1–6, Kota Kinabalu, Malaysia, January 2013.

19. Y. Boshmaf, D. Logothetis, G. Siganos et al., "Íntegro: Leveraging victim prediction for robust fake account detection in large scale OSNs," *Computers & Security*, vol. 61, pp. 142–168, 2016.

20. Elyusufi, Y., Seghiouer, H., Alimam, M.A.: Building profiles based on ontology for recommendation custom interfaces. In: *International Conference on Multimedia Computing and Systems (ICMCS) Anonymous IEEE*, pp. 558–562 (2014).

21. L. Sadowski, M. Nikoo, andM. Nikoo, "Principal Component Analysis combined with a Self Organization Feature Map to determine the pull-off adhesion between concrete layers," *Construction and Building Materials*, vol. 78, pp. 386–396, 2015.

22. S. Gurajala, J.White, B. Hudson, and J. Matthews, "profile characteristic of fake Twitter accounts," *Big Data Society*, pp. 1–13, 2016.

23. Boshmaf Y, Logothetis D, Siganos G, Lería J, Lorenzo J, Ripeanu M, et al. Íntegro: leveraging victim prediction for robust fake account detection in large scale OSNs. *Comput Secur* 2016;61:142–68. Elsevier https://doi.org/10.1016/j.cose.2016.05.005.

24. Yang Z, Xue J, Yang X, Wang X, Dai Y. VoteTrust: leveraging friend invitation graph to defend against social network sybils. *IEEE Trans Dependable Secure Comput* 2016;13(4):488–501. https://doi.org/10.1109/TDSC.2015.2410792

25. D. Ramalingam, V. Chinnaiah, Fake profile detection techniques in large- scale online social networks: A comprehensive review, *Computers and Electrical Engineering* (2017), http://dx.doi.org/10.1016/j.compeleceng.2017.05.020

26. F. A. Ozbay and B. Alatas, "Fake news detection within online social media using supervised artificial intelligence algorithms," *Phys. A Stat. Mech. its Appl.*, no. xxxx, p. 123174, 2019.

27. S. F. Sabbeh and S. Y. Baatwah, "Arabic news credibility on twitter: An enhanced model using hybrid features," *J. Theor. Appl. Inf. Technol.*, vol. 96, no. 8, pp. 2327–2338, 2018.

28. S. Kwon, M. Cha, K. Jung, W. Chen, and Y. Wang, "Prominent features of rumor propagation in online social media," *Proc. - IEEE Int. Conf. Data Mining, ICDM*, pp. 1103–1108, 2013.

29. A. El Azab, A. M. Idrees, M. A. Mahmoud, and H. Hefny, "Fake Account Detection in Twitter Based on Minimum Weighted Feature set," *Int. J. Comput. Electr. Autom. Control Inf. Eng.*, vol. 10, no. 1, pp. 13–18, 2016.

30. N. Manju, B. S. Harish, and V. Prajwal, "Ensemble Feature Selection and Classification of Internet Traffic using XGBoost Classifier," *International Journal of Computer Network and Information Security*, vol. 11, no. 7, pp. 37–44, July 2019.
31. Y. Yuan, L. Huo, Y. Yuan, and Z. Wang, "Semi-supervised tri-Adaboost algorithm for network intrusion detection," *Int. J. Distrib. Sens. Networks*, vol. 15, no. 6, 2019.
32. B. Markines, C. Cattuto, and F. Menczer, "Social spam detection," ACM Int. Conf. Proceeding Ser., pp. 41–48, 2009.

6

Packet Drop Detection in Agricultural-Based Internet of Things Platform

Sebastian Terence[1] and Geethanjali Purushothaman[2*]

[1]Department of Computer Science, Karunya Institute of Technology and Sciences, Coimbatore, India
[2]School of Electrical Engineering, VIT, Vellore, India

Abstract

The Internet of Things (IoT) is an evolving technology that has been used in a number of applications such as agriculture, education, smart cities and industry. It has few disadvantages, even though IoT technologies are used in various fields. One of IoT's big disadvantages is the security issue. IoT network is vulnerable to numerous attacks; one of IoT's most damaging attacks is a packet dropping attack. The adversaries compromise the IoT portion in packet dropping attacks to disrupt the network output by dropping packets. In this paper, we detect the packet dropping attack in the IoT platform focused on agriculture. We used thirty indoor plants, and each plant is equipped with a sensor for soil moisture. There are three sensors connected to one gateway, so that a total of ten gateways are used. For storage purposes the sensor data is moved to the ThingSpeak cloud platform. Any of the gateways acted as the node of malice. The result analysis shows that, in various circumstances, our algorithm successfully detects the malicious node with high precision and less false detection.

Keywords: Internet of Things, packet drop, agriculture, security attack, plant monitoring

6.1 Introduction

The Internet of Things (IoT) is one of science and research societies' emerging phenomena. IoT is applicable to different applications in the

---

Corresponding author: pgeethanjali@vit.ac.in

Shibin David, R. S. Anand, V. Jeyakrishnan, and M. Niranjanamurthy (eds.) Security Issues and Privacy Concerns in Industry 4.0 Applications, (113–130) © 2021 Scrivener Publishing LLC

real world. By 2025, the potential economic effect of IoT is expected to be between $2.7 and $6.2 trillion for every year through increased operating efficiencies [1]. IoT is considered to be the expansion of internet technologies which comprise various components such as sensors, actuators, smart objects, gateways, etc. IoT allows things, items to be smarter, and they can be accessed from anywhere and at any time. IoT is used in many applications, such as agriculture, smart cities, smart houses, manufacturing systems, food supplies, etc.

IoT is applied in various areas, and security is one of its major limitations. Various research results show that IoT applications are suffering from various security problems [3]. Some conventional wireless networks like sensor networks and mobile ad-hoc networks are suffering as a result of many attacks like wormhole attack, selfish node, packet dropping attacks, etc. Among these, packet dropping attack is a vital attack, where malicious node may drop all data packet or partial data packets. This sort of packet drops occurred because of adversaries' hateful behavior. The opponent feed wireless node with fake details then the wireless node begin to drop the data packet to disturb the flow of the network [4]. Since IoT consists of numerous wireless tools, such as gateways, actuators, and sensors, there are plenty of opportunities to conduct packet drop attacks in IoT.

We used a novel algorithm in our previous research to identify a packet dropping attack on a farm IoT network. We used nine indoor plants for our previous research for experiment. Each plant is outfitted with a sensor. These sensors are capable of measuring the moisture of the soil. There are three sensors associated with one gateway (NodeMCU), and a total of three gateways have been used. We detect a malicious drop in packets between three gateways [5]. In this paper we expanded our previous work by using thirty indoor plants, where each plant is fitted with a sensor of soil moisture and ten gateways. Periodically sensors send data to the gateway. Gateways are connected to the internet by Wi-Fi module. The gateway forwards collected data to ThinkSpeak cloud. We accessed data from ThinkSpeak cloud and processed it on the Java platform. To detect malicious gateways we proposed our algorithm and it detects malicious packet dropping nodes. The results show that our algorithm in the IoT platform is able to detect multiple malicious nodes.

6.2   Problem Statement and Related Work

Wireless networks such as ad-hoc network, vehicular ad-hoc network, wireless sensor network and delay tolerant network suffered due to packet dropping attacks. The adversary caught wireless node in these attacks and corrupted wireless node with data from fault. The malicious node behaves similar to a legitimate node but it interrupts network traffic by dropping data packet [6, 7]. The wireless node that is an open network is exploited the most by attackers. The adversaries are also targeting the IoT network for packet dropping attacks. The attackers can target an IoT gateway which is located in open atmosphere and feed gateway with harmful code such that the malicious gateway can require malicious behavior such as selectively dropping data from sensor or dropping all packets obtained. To observe the physical phenomenon, generally IoT gadgets are placed in an open atmosphere. It offers a way for attackers to target and exploit the IoT systems for various malicious activities. Many approaches in a wireless network are used to detect malicious activities such as sensor network, ad-hoc network, vehicular ad-hoc network, IoT, etc. Sequence number and time stamp were used by the authors to identify packet dropping attacks in the medical IoT system [8]. In [9], the authors used an instruction detection system to handle packet dropping attacks but it is lacking in the autonomous discovery procedure [9]. The authors also implemented a fingerprint authentication system to avoid IoT blackhole attacks [10]. Intrusion detection technology was implemented in 6LoWPAN-based IoT program to detect malicious activities [11]. In [12], the authors detected selfish node in an IoT platform using game theory technique. Dual link techniques and machine learning algorithms were applied to detect malicious node in IoT network [13]. All these techniques have their own advantages and disadvantages. The system structure and detection technique is explained in the next section. Many of these strategies have their own inconveniences and advantages. The layout of the system and the method of detection is also explained in the next section.

6.3   Implementation of Packet Dropping Detection in IoT Platform

An IoT network includes sensor group, actuator group, and gateway. IoT techniques are used in different applications related to farming in real time, as stated in the previous section. Yet most of these strategies are not effective against a malicious packet drop attack. We have projected packet drop detection in the agriculture-based IoT systems. We used REES52 soil moisture in this work to measure soil moisture; received analog data are converted into digital form using ADC and collected data is sent into NodeMCU (gateway). Gateway transmits the data to ThingSpeak, an open-source free cloud storage. The IoT setup is designed to evaluate plant moisture in the soil. The objective of this work is to discover the packet dropping attacks in a smart farming IoT network. The arrangement of sensors and gateways are shown in **Figure 6.1**. Here NM is NodeMCU and S indicates sensors. Every NodeMCU is connected with three sensors and it forwards data to cloud storage. Every sensor equipped with analog to digital converter (ADC), which helps to convert analog values into digital values. The converted digital values are transferred to NodeMCU. The NodeMCU is connected to internet by Wi-Fi. Periodically NodeMCU transferred received data to ThinkSpeak cloud platform.

In this work we used ten different varieties of succulents. Succulents are semi-shade plants and highly sensitive to water and climate. We analysed the water-absorbing nature of succulents by measuring soil moisture of these plants. Interestingly, the result shows that the soil moisture of

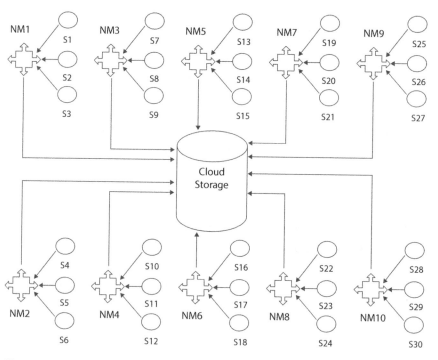

Figure 6.1 Arrangement of sensors and Gateways in IoT-based system.

these plants are not the same. The soil-absorbing capacity of these plants differs based on their nature and structure such as leaf thickness, colour and so on.

As shown in Figure 6.2, the experiment was carried out with thirty plants of ten different varieties. These plants are semi-shaded plants; each plant is positioned with a sensor to identify the soil's wetness content. There are three sensors which are attached to one NodeMCU. A total of ten NodeMCUs were used in the experiment. NodeMCU gathers sensor data and sends data to open-source cloud platform ThinkSpeak. The data processing at ThinkSpeak cloud platform is shown in Figures 6.3 and 6.4. We have conducted this experiment for thirty days and periodically data were stored in ThinkSpeak open-source cloud platform. To test the proposed algorithm, up to 30% of NodeMCU acts as malicious nodes. It drops the data packet selectively. In Java platform, the proposed detection algorithm called behavior-based detection (BBD) is implemented for detection of the malicious node. The data obtained from the cloud platform ThingSpeak was read using Java application Apache POI. The proposed technique was able to identify multiple packet dropping node in the network. The packet dropping behavior of malicious node varies from 10% to 30%. For experiment nature, malicious node malicious node drops data packet 20% and 30%.

The proposed algorithm BBD detect malicious node based on number of packet drop ratio. If node drops more number of data packets then it

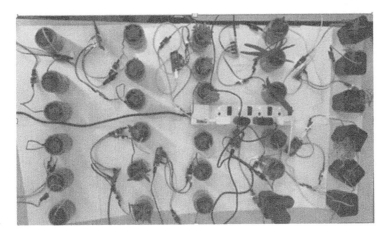

Figure 6.2 Plant monitoring using IoT.

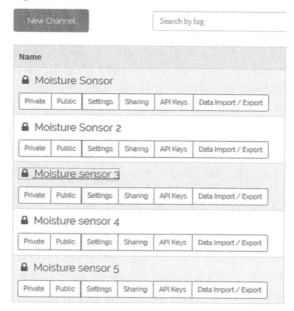

Figure 6.3 ThinkSpeak dashboard.

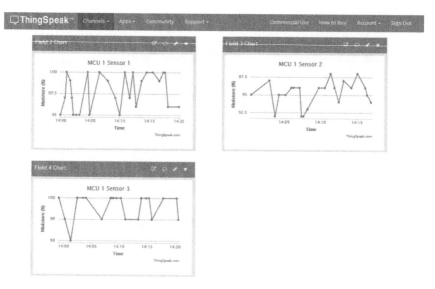

Figure 6.4 Sensor's Reading in ThinkSpeak.

would be considered as suspicious node. Then based on number of packet drop, the nodes are considered as suspicious node malicious node. Here we used two thresholds, namely threshold1 and threshold2.

Algorithm

1. for i=1 to n
1. if data from gateway then
2. NPR [gateway] then
3. end if.
4. if NPR [gateway$_i$]>λ2 then
5. gateway$_i$=suspicious

Multiple thresholds help to classify the malicious node into two categories, namely suspicious node and malicious node. So the node which drops less would be considered as suspicious node and a node which drops more data packet would be identified as malicious node. The algorithm and detailed description of this algorithm is given blow. The malicious node detection algorithm is given below. This algorithm detects malicious node based on number of packet transferring characteristics of gateway. In this technique, periodically gateway sends received data packet to ThinkSpeak cloud platform. We accessed data from ThinkSpeak cloud platform. Java language was used to obtain data from ThinkSpeak cloud platform. After data was obtained, we calculated cumulative packet received from each gateway. Then cumulative gateway data transferred values are compared with the threshold values. To detect malicious node we used two thresholds, namely threshold1 (λ1) and threshold2 (λ2). Threshold1 and threshold2 were calculated based on statistical calculation such as mean and standard deviation. The number of packet received (NPR) of malicious node was compared with λ1 and λ2. If NPR of particular NodeMCU is smaller than λ1, then it would be assumed as malicious node. If NPR of NodeMCU is larger than λ1 and smaller than λ2, the gateway would be assumed as suspicious node. The computation cost of proposed algorithm is $O(n)$, where n is number of gateway in the network. The performance analysis of our technique is explained in the next section.

6.4   Performance Analysis

To analyse the performance of the proposed technique, a real-time IoT-based smart farming system was used. IoT data are stored on ThingSpeak cloud platform. The stored data is accessed and fed into Java system for malicious packet drop detection. The various hardware and software components are shown in Table 6.1.

From the result analysis it is evident that the detection algorithm detects malicious nodes, thus helping to remove malicious nodes from the IoT network. The proposed technique's efficiency is calculated using the following network parameters, such as accuracy, false negative and false positive.

Figures 6.5 and 6.7 show the accuracy of the detection algorithm. Figure 6.5 shows the detection algorithm accuracy where the malicious node packet drop ratio (PDR) is 10%. Figures 6.6 and 6.7 display the accuracy of detection where malicious node PDR is 20%, and 30% respectively. From this

Table 6.1 Hardware and software components.

S. No	Hardware and software components	Purpose
1.	NodeMCU	Gateway
2.	REES52 soil moisture	To measure soil moisture
3.	ThinkSpeak Cloud	Storage
4.	Java Application	Malicious detation

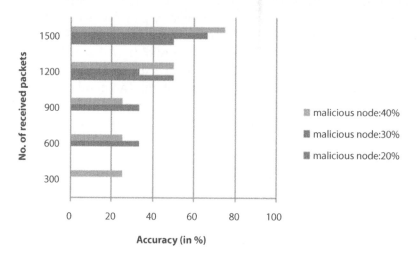

Figure 6.5 Number of reached packets vs. accuracy (PDR:10%).

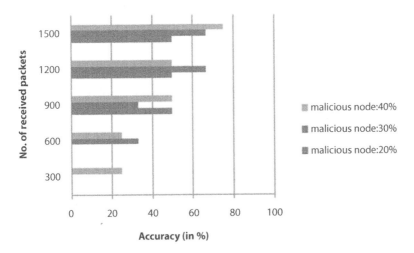

Figure 6.6 Number of reached packets vs accuracy (PDR:20%).

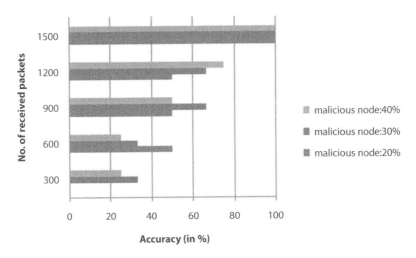

Figure 6.7 Number of reached packets vs. accuracy (PDR: 30%).

study it is clear that when packet drop is heavy (PDR: 30%), the proposed algorithm is 100% accurate.

The reason is the algorithm is able to detect all the packet dropping gateways when PDR is 30%. But its detection accuracy is reduced when PDR is less than 30%. Its detection accuracy falls below 50% when PDR is less, number of malicious node is less and number of packet transmission is less.

The false negative of the detection algorithm is displayed in Figures 6.8–6.10. From these figures we understand the following points: i) False negative

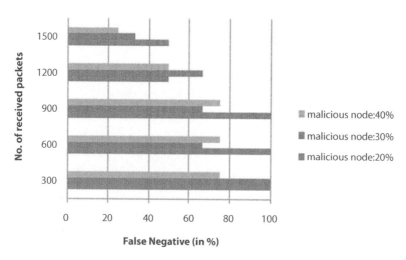

Figure 6.8 Number of received packets vs. FN (PDR:10%).

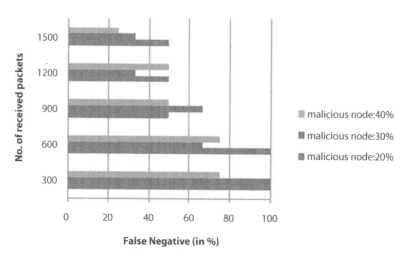

Figure 6.9 Number of received packets vs. FN (PDR:20%).

is high when packet transmission is low (300 packets are received); ii) false negative is decreased when packet transmission is high (1,500 packets are received). The reason is when packet transmission is low, the algorithm is unable to identify the malicious node, but when packet transmission rate high, it able to detect the packet dropping nodes. It's also interesting to note that the detection algorithm gives 0% of false positive. The reason is

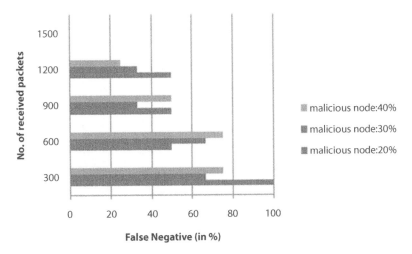

Figure 6.10 Number of received packets vs. FN (PDR: 30%).

the detection algorithm detects the malicious based on packet dropping behaviour; since genuine nodes didn't drop more number of packets, these nodes are not considered as malicious node.

To assess the efficiency of the BBD, its performance is correlated with detecting forwarding misbehaviour (DFM) [14]. The result shows that the BBD very reliably detects malicious node, and it also produces less false alarms. Figures 6.11–6.16 indicate accuracy of IoT devices. It is evident

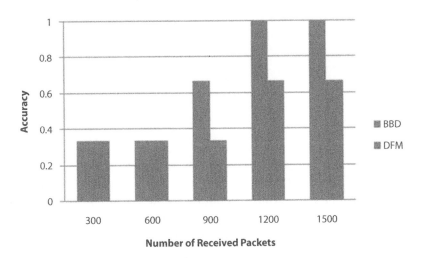

Figure 6.11 Accuracy vs no. of received packets (M.N:30%) [PDR: 30%].

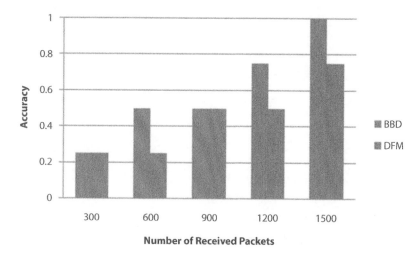

Figure 6.12 Accuracy vs. no. of received packets (M.N:20%) [PDR: 30%].

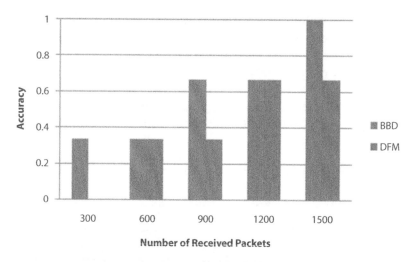

Figure 6.13 Accuracy vs no. of received packets (M.N:30%) [PDR: 20%].

from the experiment that the proposed BBD technique achieves high accuracy as compared with DFM. The experiment is performed in different scenarios such as different packet dropout rates and different malicious node rates. The BBD yields higher accuracy in all such situations.

False alarm levels of ten gateway devices are shown in Figures 6.17–6.22. The result shows the BBD yielding less false alarm rates than DFM. Usually

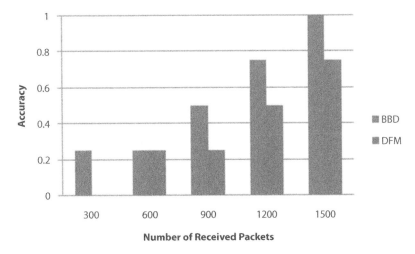

Figure 6.14 Accuracy vs. no. of received packets (M.N:20%) [PDR:20%].

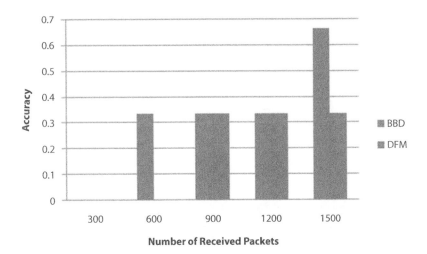

Figure 6.15 Accuracy vs. no. of received packets (M.N:30%) [PDR: 10%].

malicious node can drop up to 30% of packets, but the proposed technique can provide higher precision and false alarm rate. It is evident from the performance analysis that the proposed BBD algorithm can identify packet drop in the IoT-based smart farming. From the results it is clear that detection algorithm increases throughput, PDR and decreases end-to-end delay in the presence of malicious node.

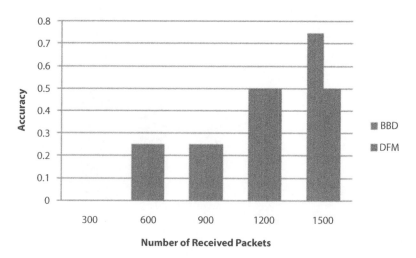

Figure 6.16 Accuracy vs. no. of received packets (M.N:20%) [PDR: 10%].

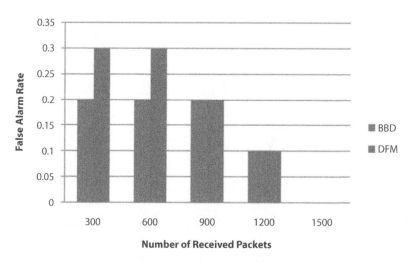

Figure 6.17 False alarm rate vs. no. of received packets (M.N:30%) [PDR: 30%].

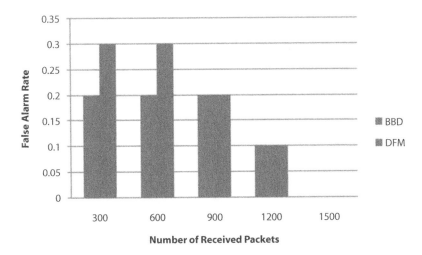

Figure 6.18 False alarm rate vs. no. of received packets (M.N:30%) [PDR: 20%].

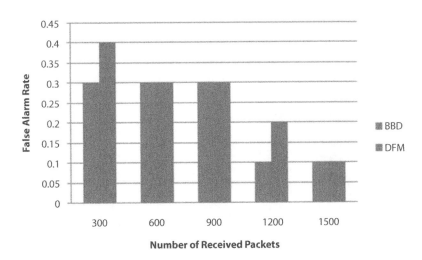

Figure 6.19 False alarm rate vs. no. of received packets (20%) [PDR: 30%].

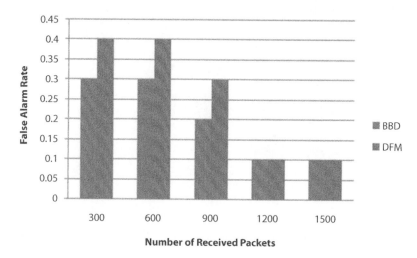

Figure 6.20 False alarm rate vs. no. of received packets (M.N:20%) [PDR: 20%].

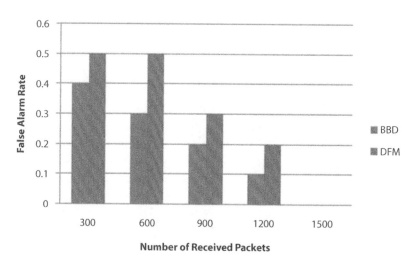

Figure 6.21 False alarm rate vs. no. of received packets (M.N:10%) [PDR:30%].

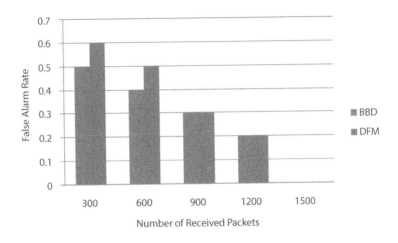

Figure 6.22 False alarm rate vs. no. of received packets (M.N:10%) [PDR: 20%].

6.5   Conclusion

IoT has been used in many applications. IoT decreases human involvement and simplifies human life. Various devices such as sensors, actuaries, gateways, and so on are used in IoT. Security risks are one of the key concerns in IoT. Opponents can compromise any of the IoT tools, and launch any form of security threats. In an IoT-based smart farming system, we researched packet dropping attacks. We used behavior-based malicious detection technique to identify the IoT platform falling of malicious packets. To assess our algorithm's efficiency, we used thirty sensors and ten gateways. Many gateways acted as the node of malice. Our algorithm successfully detects nodes falling multiple packets in IoT framework. It gives good detection accuracy when packet drop is good, and less false negatives. Our algorithm also does not give false positives. We will use several parameters in future work to detect the malicious node, and will compare the performance of the proposed work with other malicious detection techniques.

References

1. International Communication Union (ITU), Fact an Figures for ICT Revolution and Remaining Gaps, available at: www.itu,int/ict.
2. Asghari, P., Rahmani, A.M. and Javadi, H.H.S., Internet of Things applications: A systematic review, *Computer Networks*, 148, pp. 241-261, 2019.

3. Tzounis, A., Katsoulas, N., Bartzanas, T. and Kittas, C., Internet of Things in agriculture, recent advances and future challenges, *Biosystems Engineering*, 164, pp. 31-48, 2017.
4. Terence, J. S, and Geethanjali P, A Novel Technique to Detect Malicious Packet Dropping Attacks in Wireless Sensor Networks, *Journal of Information Processing* Systems, 15, no. 1, 2019.
5. Terence, J.S. and Purushothaman, G., Low Cost Real Time Implementation of Malicious Packet Dropping Detection in IoT Platform, in *Proceedings of the 1st International Conference on Advances in Distributed Computing and Machine Learning*, pp. 230-241, 2020.
6. Mathew, Annie, and J. Sebastian Terence, A survey on various detection techniques of sinkhole attacks in WSN, In *2017 International Conference on Communication and Signal Processing (ICCSP)*, pp. 1115-1119. IEEE, 2017.
7. Sebastian Terence and Geethanjali Purushothaman, Behavior based Routing Misbehavior Detection in Wireless Sensor Networks, *KSII Transactions on Internet and Information Systems*, vol. 13, no. 11, pp. 5354-5469, 2019.
8. Mathur, A., Newe, T., Rao, M., Defence against Blackhole and Selective Forwarding Attacks for Medical WSNs in the IoT, *Sensors*, 16, 118, 2016.
9. R. de, A.C. Mello, R.L. Ribeiro, Almedia, E.D. Moreno, Mitigating Attacks in the Internet of Things with a Self-protecting Architecture, *AICT2017: The Thirteen Advanced International Conference on Telecommunications*, pp. 14-19, 2017.
10. Kumar R., Internet of Things for the Prevention of Black Hole Using Fingerprint Authentication and Genetic Algorithm Optimization, *International Journal of Computer Network and Information Security*, Aug 1;9(8):17, 2018.
11. Ahmed, F. and Ko, Y.B., Mitigation of black hole attacks in Routing Protocol for Low Power and Lossy Networks, *Security and Communication Networks*, 9(18), pp.5143-5154, 2016.
12. Nobahary, S., Garakani, H.G., Khademzadeh, A. and Rahmani, A.M., Selfish node detection based on hierarchical game theory in IoT. *EURASIP Journal on Wireless Communications and Networking, 2019*(1), p. 255, 2019.
13. Liu, X., Abdelhakim, M., Krishnamurthy, P. and Tipper, D., Identifying malicious nodes in multihop iot networks using dual link technologies and unsupervised learning. *Open Journal of Internet Of Things (OJIOT)*, 4(1), pp.109-125, 2018.
14. Venkata Abhishek, V., Tandon, A., Lim, Joon., & Sikdar, B., Detecting Forwarding Misbehavior in Clustered IoT Networks. In *Proceedings of the 14th ACM International Symposium on QoS and Security for Wireless and Mobile Networks*, pp.1-6, 2018.

7

Smart Drone with Open CV to Clean the Railway Track

Sujaritha M¹ and Sujatha R²*

¹*Professor, Sri Krishna College of Engineering & Technology, Coimbatore, Tamilnadu, India*
²*Assistant Professor, Sri Krishna College of Technology, Coimbatore, Tamilnadu, India*

Abstract

India has the second-largest railway system, and the wastage in the rail tracks is arduous to clean manually. Manual Scavengers collect the solid and liquid waste through sacks, buckets, etc. Due to some production of gases from those waste materials, it affects the respiratory system of the manual scavengers. A better solution is to stop manual work through use of a Drone. Using the drones with a single-man control and also with the sensor control for each station will be more proficient. Technically it will result in a more cost-efficient system. A drone is a more accessible tool that could eventually be put into the hands of a human to clean up the entire mess in a railway station. Manually controlled drones must be made to clean the railway tracks once in every estimated hour. The drone will we embedded with a powerful suction motor which is strapped to an air bag on the other side. It will have a frequently chargeable battery, or a solar cell which can be used to charge the drone periodically. Without human intervention, the idea will be making use of a Line Follower sensor to trace the rail tracks. The line follower sensor is embedded with drones; as a result it will follow the rail tracks and will not get out of the tracks. Open CV (Open Source) is a computer vision and a freeware that is used in image processing. It is installed in a host and is programmed to identify obstacles in a track using a camera attached to a drone. Since the railway tracks are fully magnetized, metal content must be reduced to the maximum to avoid the magnetism. By this method, railway tracks will cleaned up by using the drones efficiently, which will reduce the need for manpower too.

Keywords: Drone, Indian Railways, automation, Internet of Things

---

*Corresponding author: sujamole@gmail.com

Shibin David, R. S. Anand, V. Jeyakrishnan, and M. Niranjanamurthy (eds.) Security Issues and Privacy Concerns in Industry 4.0 Applications, (131–140) © 2021 Scrivener Publishing LLC

7.1   Introduction

Drone technology is a kind of emerging technology, and its real-time application is explored in limited domains. Drones offer the extension of society's scope, the overthrow of physical space, the ability to locate any place or object and view anything. Drones have been one of the most exciting class of gadgets on display for the past few years. They became more powerful in addition to their cheaper, lighter, and easier to use versions as well.

Considering that India has the second-largest railway system, the wastage in the rail tracks is arduous to clean manually. Our idea is to clean the tracks, using the drones with a single operator for each station [10]. Technically it results in a cost-efficient system. Therefore, in this paper, drones with raspberry Pi are used to trace the garbage in the track and clean it by putting it in the bags which are attached with the drone. It is a more accessible tool that could eventually be put into the hands of a human to clean up the entire mess in a railway station.

7.2   Related Work

The Indian railway network connects people from every nook and corner of the country. It is one of the world's biggest networks and it offers jobs to the majority of the people of different classes in India. Recently there were so many advancements and improvements in the infrastructure development of the railways through which it progresses as a fund-raising organization. The oldest method was proposed as a trajectory with the dynamics and kinematics of the robot manipulator with the help of a nozzle, water throw or spread to clean the track. Railway transport has been used by low to high society and the sophisticated features offered by the system has made people willing to pay the ticket price and enjoy the classy travel. Therefore, the railway system is in a position to provide complete sanitation. A solution through technology and automation is required to remove litter on the railway tracks and clean the grubby toilets and clogged basins in order to maintain the hygienic condition of India's railways [1]. This paper proposes robotics and control technology to solve the prevailing condition to a considerable extent. A massive exercise has been undertaken by the Northern Railway to check the cleanliness with the help of track cleaning machines [2]. The team of Northern Railway Diesel Loco Shed, located at Shakurbasti, New Delhi, has developed tools made up of heavy-duty materials to clean the track. Another machine called ballast cleaner was introduced in Network Rail (UK), to ballast the impurities in the railway track [3]. The drawback of these machines is that they are massive. Major railway stations are only ones that can benefit from using these machines.

Hiroshi Murase *et al.* [4], anticipated a method for detecting obstacles by using the input and trained front view images. Using the machine learning approach, obstacle detection has been employed, so pedestrian, bicycle, etc., can be pretrained. The drawback of the system is comprised of unknown classes of obstacles that cannot be detected. To overcome this problem, a system is proposed of background subtraction method that can be applied to moving cameras. First, the proposed method computes frame-by-frame correspondences between the current and the reference (database) image sequences. By applying the subtraction of images in each frame, obstacles are detected.

Jesin James [5] and Jesse Wilso implemented an intelligent machine specially designed for the Indian railways which can clean the railway tracks in a systematic manner. This system comprises a four-wheel running robot and specially with a cleaning unit, suction unit, an intelligent train sensing unit, an intelligent control system, power unit and automatic displacement unit. Also, the railways can save a lot of money on labour charges and water charges.

Nagla *et al.* [6], state the methods of dynamics, kinematics, and trajectory planning of a robot for cleaning the railway tracks mainly below the surface of the platform. Generally they mention the properties of the service robot and clearly explain about the variations among the service and industrial robots. The objectives of the system also include the identification of preferable trajectory planning and scheduling algorithm for effective cleaning of tracks and to reduce the water wastage.

Malini *et al.*, designed an enhanced quadcopter to clean the track by adding features such as outdoor cleaning, gathering and storing GPS data, and performing auto commands, such as collecting waste from rough terrain, by using image processing techniques [7]. This enhanced quadcopter contains a frame, motors, electronic speed controllers, Raspberry-Pi development board, and sensor boards. The GPS used in this system helps the quadcopter to properly determine its location, send the data captured by the camera and store and log data. This solution also describes the auto-commands, to detect and collect the waste on the rough terrain automatically by using an image processing technique.

Yuan *et al.* [8] devised a double round, three point and bilinear positioning method and also vector path tracing and cubic interpolation algorithms.

Distance detection is mainly by using infrared and ultrasonic waves. In addition, a smart obstacle-avoidance algorithm has been applied to avoid the obstacles. The overall main goal is to achieve stability, reliability, and high efficiency in avoidance of obstacles through image processing techniques.

Gibert *et al.* [9] proposed three different methods for fast detection: i) reducing the class variation, ii) alignment of training data, and iii) improving the classifications margin of the difficult samples using a bootstrap method. Defective rail problems were detected by SVM classifier and gradient features, with the probability of 98% and 1.23% of false alarm rate. A dataset of 85 miles of concrete tie images was taken for the implementation of the above methodology.

7.3   Problem Definition

The Indian Railways (IR) is a massive enterprise in India and connects all over the country. The main drawback and biggest problems in railways are the amount of solid waste like plastics and paper material left by train passengers every day across the country. Probably solid waste generated in trains can be classified as biodegradable, non-biodegradable and slow degradable. Biodegradable means the food which is left over by the passengers, non-biodegradable means plastic such as bottle cups, bottle lids, and carry bags, as of now. Slow degradable means newspapers, food containers, and disposable cups, etc. No better system has been introduced to collect and manage this expansive amount of waste. Here we have a solution for this problem by the use of drone. This solution uses a drone system for detecting and cleaning wastes that are deposited by the passengers.

7.4   The Proposed System

7.4.1   Drones with Human Intervention

Manually controlled drones must be made to clean the railway tracks once every estimated hour [11]. The proposed drone is embedded with a powerful suction motor which is strapped to an air bag on the other side. The air bag will be kept in the platforms connected to the drones via tubes with a maximum length depending upon the interspace between the platforms and tracks. The proposed drone has a frequently chargeable battery, or a solar cell which can be used to charge the drone periodically.

7.4.2   Drones without Human Intervention

A Line Follower sensor is used to trace the rail tracks. The line follower sensor is embedded with drones; as a result it will follow the rail tracks and does not get out of the tracks. The hooks are connected to the tubes and the same air bag is used with a suction motor to suck the wastage. The drone will move to and fro through the tracks and clean up the mess. Open CV (Open Source) is a computer vision and a freeware that is used for image processing. It is installed in the host and programmed to identify obstacles in the track using a camera attached to a drone.

The train tracks are magnetized. The tracks have some electric charge; whenever the vibration is produced by the train from such a distance, the charges in the track will flow quickly and it forms a magnetic field around it.

Since the railway tracks are fully magnetized, metal content must be reduced to the minimum to avoid the magnetism. For that purpose, we are replacing the metals with Ferritic metal, even the small screwings. In this way we can clean up the mess in the railway tracks using the drones efficiently, which will lead to less manpower, etc.

Figure 7.1 shows that the Raspberry PI comes with pre-built USB ports which provides room for a Wi-Fi adapter. The Wi-Fi adapters on both the raspberry PIs are connected through a secured tunnel. Without the Raspberri Pi, the drone emerges to follow the certain points and return

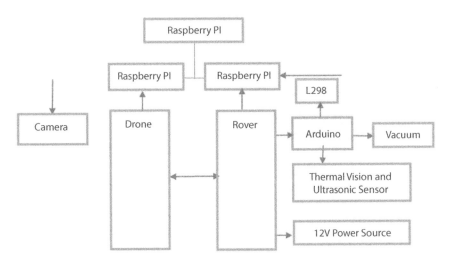

Figure 7.1 Proposed architecture.

back with some other information, but when the Raspberry Pi is linked with the drone, it provides the way point information to the drone; that is, where to go, where the dust is placed; like that, much information will be given to the drone. A rover is connected with the drone, and data from the drone is passed to the rover simultaneously. The drone transmits the data with the help of RF transmission. This transmission will transmit and receive the information from UAV. Most of the rover's commands are programmed in the drone's Raspberry PI. The camera is attached to the Raspberry PI on the drone using USB and is driven by Open CV. Raspberry

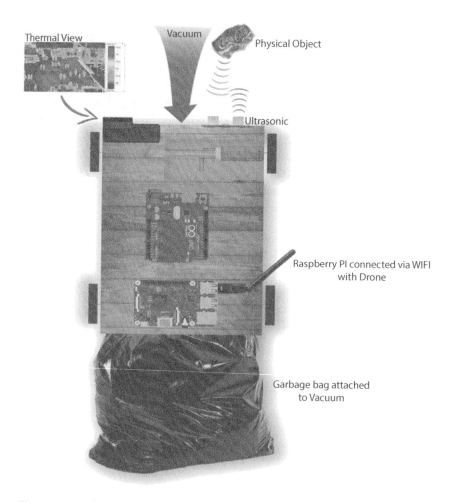

Figure 7.2 Working model of the system.

PI, Camera and the drone run on the same battery source. The 12V power source is attached to the rover and is connected to the rover's Raspberry PI. Arduino on the other hand is connected to the Raspberry PI and uses its power. Arduino IDE is installed on the PI and is programmed to control the wheels, vacuum, sensor and the thermal vision camera. L298 is connected to the Arduino using jumper wires, which is applied for other devices also.

7.4.3   Working Model

Initial work started with a wooden plank attached to the wheels. Next came the Arduino which drove the rover structure with L298 driver. The next idea was to detect obstacles in the track. An ultrasonic sensor was used to overcome that and for more advanced observation, thermal cameras were used along with Open CV (Computer vision) shown in Figure 7.2. To collect the unwanted obstacles from the track, a powerful vacuum cleaner connected to the Arduino sucks them in and throws them into the disposable garbage bag attached to the end. When the bag is full, the rover detaches the bag. The railway maintenance staff collect the bag filled with garbage and dispose of it in a safe environment. The rover is attached with a garden sprayer which sprays the disinfectant liquid all over the tracks for additional hygiene. The drone flies above the rover in sync. It is equipped with a camera and raspberry PI. The drone uses Open CV to detect obstacles using image.

7.5   Experimental Results

In Figure 7.3 a drone is flying above the railway track to mark the coordinates of the garbage. Figure 7.4 shows the railway track with lot of garbage and waste materials.

Figure 7.5 explains the scanning process that helps to count the number of waste materials in the track using open CV which is embedded in the drone. In Figure 7.6 the drone counts the number of waste materials as a coordinate in the track and sends the message to the rover.

In Figure 7.7, the rover will move to collect the garbage by using coordinates which have been marked previously. In Figure 7.8, the rover will spray sanitary lotion wherever it moves and finally the track is fully cleaned.

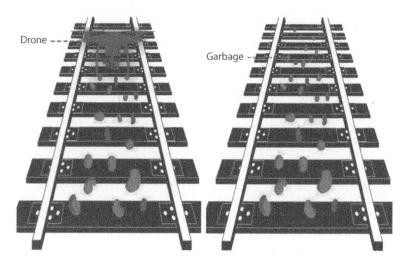

Figure 7.3 Drone in track.   **Figure 7.4** Track with garbage.

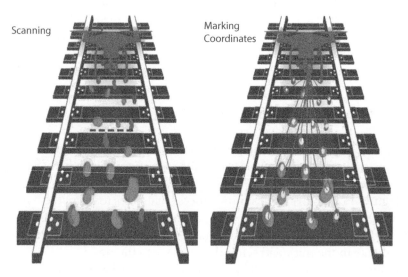

Figure 7.5 Open CV with drone to scan.   **Figure 7.6** Working of rover in track.

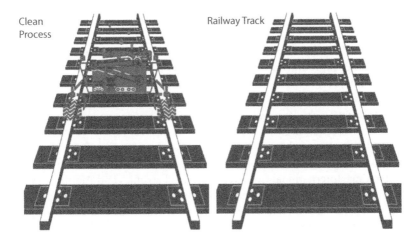

Figure 7.7 Collection of garbage.

Figure 7.8 Spraying of sanitary lotion cleaned the railway track.

7.6 Conclusion

Manual cleaning of a railway track was a very arduous process. Therefore, with the help of the drone and image processing technology and open CV tool a system has been designed and developed to clean the railway track automatically. The presented system can save manpower, energy and clean the tracks and stations in an automated way. The proposed Intelligent system for Track Cleaning delivers a well-organized cleaning process and also offers clean and dirt-free railway tracks in the railway stations without involving human labor. The proposed drone can also be utilized for removing unexpected interventions. It saves time and destroys the litter completely and provides a hygienic environment. The proposed robotic application avoids manual scavenging, which is unhealthy and harmful to humans. The proposed system facilitates the user with sophisticated features and so the system is user friendly and also replaces the multiple users.

References

1. Manoj Hedaoo, Dr. Suchita Hirde, Ms. Arshi Khan, "Sanitation in indian railway premises: a great cause of concern", *International Journal of Advanced Engineering Technology*, (2015).
2. http://www.nr.indianrailways.gov.in/view_detail.jsp?lang =0&dcd= 3591&id=0,4,268.

3. http://www.railwaystrategies.co.uk/articlepage.php?contentid=2196 &issueid=103.

4. Hiroshi Murase, Masato Ukai, Nozomi Nagamine, Ryuta Nakasone "Moving Camera Background Substraction for Obstacle Detection on Railway Tracks" *IEEE*, pp. 3967-3971.

5. Jesin James, Jesse Wilson, Jovna Jetto, Alna Thomas, Dhahabiya V K, "Intelligent Track Cleaning Robot", International Conference on Mechatronics and Automation August 7 - 10, Harbin, China.

6. K.S. Nagla, MoinUddin, R. Jha, Akshay Mathur, "Service Robot for Indian Railway Tracks at Platforms: Feasibility, Kinematics, Dynamics and Trajectory planning" International Conference on Mechatronics and Automation, June 25 - 28, 2006, Luoyang, China, *IOSR Journal of VLSI and Signal Processing* (IOSR-JVSP) Volume 6, Issue 3, Ver. I (May-Jun. 2016), PP 78-81 e-ISSN: 2319 – 4200, p-ISSN No. : 2319 – 4197.

7. Malini K V, Asha K, Hithesh Choudry, Mubarak S, Kishore Kumar K, "Cleaning of Vernacular Railway Tracks Using Drone", *International Journal of Engineering Research in Electrical and Electronic Engineering*, Volume 5, Issue 2, ISSN 2395-2717, pp. 4-7, February (2019).

8. Wen-Yuan Chen, Shih-Sung Cheng, Ching-Te Wang, ChinFu Tsai and Chiou-Kou Tung, "The Cleaning Machine Path Design Using Image Recognition Techniques" *IEEE*, 2014, pp. 439-442.

9. Prakruti Bhatt, Sanat Sarangi, Srinivasu Pappula, "Comparison of CNN models for application in crop health assessment with participatory sensing", 2017 IEEEGlobal Humanitarian Technology Conference (GHTC), Oct (2017).

10. Xavier Gibert, Vishal M. Patel, and Rama Chellappa "Robust Fastener Detection for Autonomous Visual Railway Track Inspection" Winter Conference on Applications of Computer Vision, *IEEE*, pp. 694-701, (2015).

11. Zhang X, Li X, Wang K, and Lu Y, "A Survey of Modelling and Identification of Quadrotor Robot," in *Abstract and Applied Analysis*, vol. 2014, pp. 16 (2014).

8

Blockchain and Big Data: Supportive Aid for Daily Life

Awais Khan Jumani[1], Asif Ali Laghari[2]* and Abdullah Ayub Khan[2]

[1]Department of Computer Science, ILMA University Karachi, Sindh, Pakistan
[2]Department of Computer Science, Sindh Madressatul Islam University, Karachi, Sindh, Pakistan

Abstract

This Chapter studied both Blockchain and Big data which brings innovative opportunities around the world by changing businesses operations. There is no doubt that this technology has revolutionized finance and many other fields. It places Bitcoin transaction in blocks, and then connects them in chronological order, because each block has the hash value of the previous block. These all blocks use time-stamps and cryptographic techniques to record data in blocks. In order to add a block to the chain, a transaction must be made, verified and stored in the block. After adding a new block to the blockchain, it will automatically update like news feed of Facebook and the block will be publically available to anyone. The purpose of this chapter is to understand the current research challenges, and future directions of blockchain from technical perspective. In this chapter, we will have analyzed the current quality concerns in blockchain implementation (scalability, usability, data privacy, data security, lack of interoperability, lack of understanding and implementation costs), determined the attributes (anonymity, reliability, transparency, autonomy, immutability, data integrity and security), and also defines the concepts of blockchain, smart contracts in industries and type of blockchain (public, private, hybrid and consortium blockchain).

Keywords: Blockchain, big data, big data supportive, blockchain applications, cryptocurrency, distributed ledger, protocols, blockchain in industries

*Corresponding author: asif.laghari@smiu.edu.pk

Shibin David, R. S. Anand, V. Jeyakrishnan, and M. Niranjanamurthy (eds.) Security Issues and Privacy Concerns in Industry 4.0 Applications, (141–178) © 2021 Scrivener Publishing LLC

8.1   Introduction

Blockchain was initially developed for Bitcoin infrastructure to order Bitcoin's transactions by placing them in blocks and then connect them in chronological order because each block has the hash value of the previous block [1]. Now recent hypes of Blockchain technology brings hope of its use in different fields such as education, government, agriculture, tourism, healthcare, IOT, supply chain, finance, digital advertising, digital marketing, and data management, etc. But the adoption of disruptive technology by any field will bring various problems or challenges to technology, regulations, society and adoption related fields, such as data integrity difficulties, data security and privacy issues, lack of skilled employees or staff and sufficient resources [2]. It also transforms our society and the way of businesses, as the smart contracts and other Blockchain concepts are quite different from other legal objects and cannot easily fit in the traditional legal concepts.

This research is to analyze the current quality challenges of blockchain implementations, such as scalability, usability, data privacy, security, lack of interoperability, lack of understanding, and implementation costs and also study the key concepts and characteristics to identify the key challenges affecting the large-scale adoption of blockchain.

The blockchain has proposed a new paradigm for businesses [3]. This decentralized, distributed record-keeping technology was originally developed for Bitcoin Cryptocurrency in 2008. Now the interest of different industries in blockchain technology is gradually increasing. Blockchain is a decentralized distributed digital ledger technology that uses cryptographic techniques and protocols to keep records and control transactions [4]. It is a series of blocks that use time stamps to record data and use hash function to link a new block to the previous blocks in the chain, because all the blocks have the hash of the previous block. The Blockchain is used to order the transactions by placing the transactions in each block and then connecting them in order. In a Bitcoin blockchain, a block can store up to 1 megabyte of data, depending on the size of the transaction, which means that a block can hold thousands of transactions under one roof. In the blockchain, digital information (block) is stored in a distributed database (chain). These blocks store three types of information:

1. Information about transaction, such as time, date and amount.

2. Information about participants, such as username instead of real name of participant and a unique digital signature.
3. Stores a unique hash code (cryptographic code) that distinguishes it from other blocks, and connects a new block to previous blocks in a blockchain.

The blockchain consists of several blocks connected together. Fig. 8.1 shows the work of blockchain technology; if one block stores a new transaction it will be added to the blockchain. In order to add block to the blockchain, a transaction must be made, verified and stored in a block with unique identity "Hash" code. After verifying all transaction in the block, they will get the hash value, and will also get the hash value of the previous block [5]. When a new block is added to the blockchain successfully, the block will be publically available to anyone. For instance, we can access information about transaction and time, and when and by whom data was added to the blockchain [6].

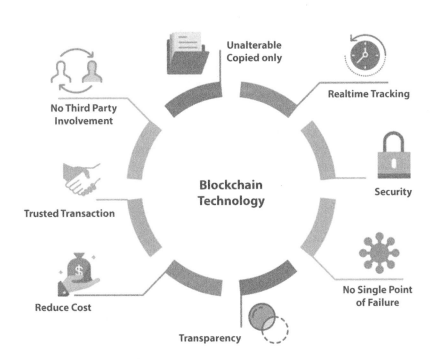

Fig. 8.1 Blockchain technology.

8.1.1 Steps of Blockchain Technology Works

1. Requested a transaction. For example, sending money.
2. Transaction broadcast on the network.
3. Through cryptography transaction verified by the network.
4. Transactions expressed online in book form.
5. Transaction block added to the blockchain.
6. Transaction is completed (as shown in Fig. 8.2).

8.1.2 Blockchain Private

Private blockchain shows the integrated service where all network can easily connect with each other and more important they will see their own content expect others. In this manner, blockchains create facility of ledger so user will receive their own ledger which will automatically be updated when blocks are added. Many of the social media networks provide real-time facility in which the user can easily read and post their updated activity.

In the blockchain, each node has its own network and its copy ledger, so every ledger can create their own copy and it is very difficult to manipulate each copy of ledger information. That's why blockchain is more private and secure. After that, blockchains have a distributed ledger system so no account will have compromised their security and no one can hack the blockchain account. If a hacker wants to hack blockchain then he will gain the information regarding every ledger, so it is impossible to collect every ledger information. However, as can be seen in the bitcoin blockchain, no one has a right to identify the user who conducts a transaction, even though such type of information is not completely anonymous because every participant information is limited to their username and digital signature [7].

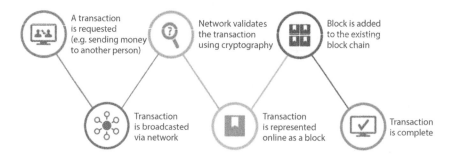

Fig. 8.2 Works timeline of blockchain technology.

8.1.3   Blockchain Security

Blockchain security and privacy provides many facilities to its users and it has become popular in the limited time it has been available. Meanwhile blocks are stored in sequential order; all new blocks are always added to the end on the chain. Hence, block of the blockchain contains hash value and their previous has value too, so it is very difficult to modify or manipulate every single block of the blockchain. If a hacker wants to edit any information in block then their hash value will also be changed. So, in the transaction, if the hacker wants to change the value, then their hash code will be changed. After that, blockchain next code will contain the old hash value so the hacker will change each block of that transaction and he will need to update every block for compromising the transaction of any victim. For changing and calculating of the hash values it needs a high-power computing machine. If a hacker has such a machine then it's still difficult to compromise any victim's transaction. To improve the trust issue, the blockchain implements an agreement for their nodes or blocks of that chain before any type of transactions. Mainly, the Proof of Work (POW) is used in Bitcoin blockchain for improving the users' trust. Blockchain is one of the best security systems because it confuses hackers while they are making any kind of suspicious activity. So POW does not completely stop hackers but usually it confuses the hacker and it needs to solve 50% any transaction of work. But they need more powerful computing machines [8].

8.2   Blockchain vs. Bitcoin

Blockchain and Bitcoin are two completely independent things [9]:

1. Bitcoin is a Cryptocurrency, and blockchain is a distributed database.
2. Bitcoin is powered by blockchain, but blockchain has discovered various usages beyond Bitcoin.
3. Bitcoin approves anonymity, while blockchain is about transparency. To be applied in certain areas (especially in the banking sector), blockchain must meet strict "know your customer" rules.
4. Bitcoin transfers money between users, and the blockchain can be used to transfer several types of information, including information or ownership.

8.2.1   Blockchain Applications

Digital currency data is stored on a blockchain and it is more secure and reliable for storing the data; for example, it can be used in supply chain management, real estate transaction, and even for voting [10]. As a professional services network, Deloitte surveyed in seven countries to study the integration of blockchain into business operations, and found that 34% of people were already using blockchain systems, while many other people will join the blockchain application, and it is nearly about 41% ratios which will catch into 12 months. After that, a lot of industries are investing money into blockchain currency and nearly 40% of industries will invest $5 million in the future. The most popular blockchain applications are used in Internet of Things, finance, cryptocurrencies, healthcare, supply chains, smart contracts, and voting, etc. Table 8.1 shows the pros and cons of blockchain technology [11].

8.2.2   Next Level of Blockchain

In 1991, the blockchain was proposed as a research project and it has now attracted widespread attention. Companies around the world are considering the capabilities of this technology and the direction of development in the coming years [13]. After implementing and exploring many applications of the technology, blockchain has become more popular due to Bitcoin and cryptocurrencies [14, 15].

In 2008, the Blockchain and Bitcoin cash system were introduced using cryptographic techniques and protocols. Blockchain and Bitcoin are two complex interconnected notions, and outside the digital currency domain the technology is meaningless [16]. Moreover, it is known as a decentralized database where all transactions have been recorded on multiple nodes. By placing them in time-stamped blocks and connecting them in sequential order with hash, as well as, in blockchain every block contains its own hash value, which is connected with previous hash value [17]. Initially, it was invented for the financial transaction system. At the time, the idea was to trade without any intermediaries, but now, it is not only applicable to the finance sector, but is also used in different business areas, because it uses a distributed node network that can provide a level of trust – consensus rather than using a third party to verify transactions. The structure of the technology also supports data anonymity, data integrity, data transparency and data security [18]. Blockchain has changed our social and business methods, because smart contracts and other blockchain concepts are quite different from other legal objects that cannot easily fit in the traditional legal concepts. This is why people are increasingly interested in blockchain. As we all know,

Table 8.1 Shows the blockchain pros and cons [12].

Blockchain		
Pros		Cons
1	**Improved accuracy by eliminating manual participation verification** – In this security, blockchain is connected through the thousands of computer networks. As well as, their transaction system also connected with many computer nodes; if someone wants to change anything in any block than he may change thousands of blocks and their hash code. So it is impossible to connect and make changes into the thousands of computers.	**Technology cost** – The blockchain system saves the user transactions cost, but it cannot be free. For example: transaction verification system used in bitcoin by the proof of work, so it consumes lot of electricity power during the transaction. Because, the functions of millions of computers on the Bitcoin network are close to the annual electricity consumption of Denmark. Even though usage of bitcoin is high cost many users easily continue to increase the electricity bills for ensuring the completion of transactions.
2	**The transaction is efficient, private and secure** - it may take lot of time to resolve transaction through bank system. Blochain have the facility to work 24/7 in a week. The main important thing about blockchain is that it completes any transaction in 10 minutes. After some hours it shows the completely safe. Due to time zone issues and the need for enhanced payment processing by all parties, cross-border transactions take a long time to process and this is useful in this manner.	**Low efficiency** – we have noticed that bitcoin takes 10 minutes to add blocks into the blockchain. If this rating point can be estimated that bitcoin blockchain only works on 7 TPS, on the other hand, some other cryptocurrencies, like Ethereum, can take 20 TPS; after that the last bitcoin cash system can handle 60 TPS so it works better than the bitcoin blockchain system.

(Continued)

Table 8.1 Shows the blockchain pros and cons [12]. (*Continued*)

Blockchain		
Pros		Cons
3	**Transparency** – in the blockchain, even if personal information is private, the technology itself is almost always open source. Moreover, in this system modification of any code needs high computational power of the network. Furthermore, it is more difficult to track any data which is processed by the blockchain technology. Because, blockchain technology is not only connected with one computer, it is connected to millions of computer networks and one of the best things is that it whenever there are any changes inside any network then it may notify the other networks that it means suspicious activity.	**Illegal activities** – on the blockchain network confidentiality can protect users from hacker attacks and protect privacy, while also allowing illegal activities. The most cited example of illegal transactions for blockchain may be the Silk Road, an online dark-web market, which allows users to browse the website without tracking and illegally buying Bitcoin. Current US regulations prohibit users of online transactions such as blockchain-based transactions from becoming completely anonymous.
4	**Reduce cost by eliminating third-party authentications** – usually, the consumer pays the bank to verify the transaction, and the document is signed by a notary. With the help of blockchain, there is no need for third-party involvement as well as their extra costs. For example, every time a business owner uses a credit card to accept a payment, a small fee is incurred because the bank has to process these transactions. Furthermore, bitcoin cannot be controlled by the central authority, and also, it has no transaction fees.	Hacks Vulnerability – The innovative blockchain network is vulnerable to 51% attacks. Many of the hackers have problems in hacking a blockchain account because it needs huge computational power and many other expensive devices. So inside the blockchain mechanism it verified that the majority of the system is controlled by the blockchain network. But Joseph Bonanau, a computer science researcher at New York University, said this situation may change and estimated that 49% attacks may increase because a hacker can now simply rent computing power without having to buy all the equipment.

modern blockchain are designed to ensure privacy, security, bandwidth, size, throughput, performance, data integrity, usability and scalability, but these quality features pose many challenges that require improvement.

8.2.3   Blockchain Architecture's Basic Components

The Blockchain architecture consists of blocks, nodes, transactions, miners, consensus and contracts [18]. Fig. 8.3 shows the basic components of Blockchain.

- **Block** – a Blockchain block is known as data structure, which is used to store every transaction. Where every block contains data, hash value and previous hash value inside the block.
- **Chain** – a series of sequential stored blocks.
- **Node** – computers or users within the blockchain or the connection points between participants.
- **Transaction** – a small exchange of data works inside the blockchain and is stored.
- **Hash** – blockchain depends upon the hash value and it is the main part of the cryptocurrency.
- **Miner** – a specific node that performs the block's validation process.

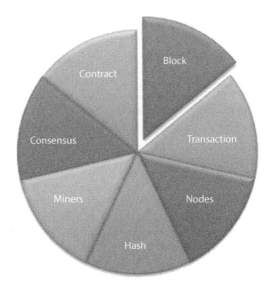

Fig. 8.3 Blockchain architecture's basic components.

- **Consensus** – defined protocols that are used to perform operations of blockchain.
- **Contract** – contract occurs when consensus is fulfilled and the nodes validate the transaction.

8.2.4 Blockchain Architecture

An architecture of blockchain depends upon the nodes. Every node contains different information which is related to the previous node. After that, this information can be stored in a hash function because every hash value has its own unique address. Whenever any changes are required into the block then it may change into the hash function [19]. Fig. 8.4 shows the block of the blockchain includes three parts:

- ❖ Data: It contains information about transaction that took place.
- ❖ Hash: A unique identification of the blocks.
- ❖ Previous Hash: It is related to the previous hash value which is inside the block.

8.2.5 Blockchain Characteristics

Blockchain tries to solve the problems of distributed database synchronization with distributed consensus [20]. Blockchain technology contains many characteristics: Fig. 8.5 shows the key features of blockchain.

- **Anonymity** – in the transaction sender and receiver cannot be identified.
- **Confidentiality** – only the sender and receiver can know the transaction amount.
- **Autonomy** – blockchain devices have ability to interact with each other without any external source.
- **Cryptography** – cryptography has an encryption mechanism, where public and private keys are used for the digital

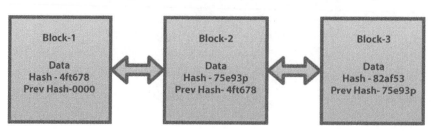

Fig. 8.4 Blockchain architecture.

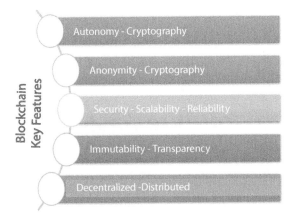

Fig. 8.5 Blockchain key features.

signature. Also, hash function can protect information and verify its authenticated users.

- **Distributed** – a distributed database shared and synchronized across multiple nodes on the network.
- **Immutability** – the data cannot be changed easily because each transaction block uses the principle of cryptography.
- **Decentralized** – the system does not rely on acentral control point, and can eliminate any single point failures to improve fault tolerance.
- **Scalability** – the ability to handle a growing transaction volume.
- **Security** – all records are protected by cryptography and because of smart contracts, information exchange is considered as a transaction that can provide secure communication between users.
- **Transparency** – it provides fully auditable and valid transaction ledger by recording the history of all transaction changes.
- **Reliability** – blockchain is reliable because all nodes keep complete copy of ledger. Therefore, if one node is disconnected, the system is always available to all other participants in the network.

8.3 Blockchain Components

Blockchain is a combination of multiple concepts, e.g., cryptography, distributed ledger, smart contracts and consensus mechanisms [21]. Fig. 8.6 shows the blockchain components.

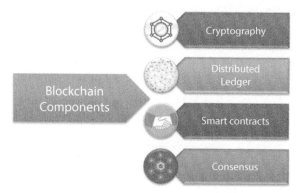

Fig. 8.6 Blockchain components.

8.3.1   Cryptography

Cryptography occupies the core position in the blockchain. It is mainly used to protect information of transaction, user privacy and ensure data consistency [22]. Blockchain technology relies on cryptographic encryption protocols and transactions processing techniques. All blocks in the blockchain are connected to each other with security through cryptographic techniques, such as hash algorithms, consensus mechanisms (a set of rules that allows network nodes to reach shared contracts), digital signatures, timestamps, and asymmetric encryption algorithms [23]. Cryptography or encryption technology proposes a new transaction and value exchange paradigm; it has a strong protection mechanism where all data has been protected with cryptographic encryption. So, it only allows authorized users to decrypt the data. After that, it verifies all the transactions because cryptocurrency is

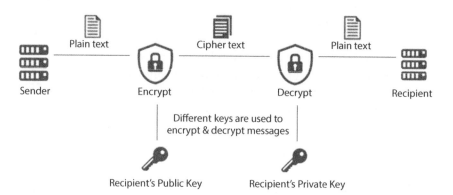

Fig. 8.7 How blockchain cryptography works.

known as digital currency [24]. In this system digital signatures are used to prove identity, so transaction can be traced back to the theoretical anonymous password identity, but can be linked back to the actual identity. Fig. 8.7 shows how the blockchain works with cryptography [25].

8.3.2   Distributed Ledger

Blockchain is a distributed ledger technology that contains information about the participants and all transactions executed on different nodes of the network. It forms the foundation of how to collect and transfer information among users. It concerns both data and transactions and allows all participants to use database, update, manipulate and storage of records and also allows value extraction from database [26]. Because it is a decentralized distributed system, where data is stored on different nodes, it provides immutability, efficiency, security, accountability and also ensures transparency. Once the information is stored in the system, no one can easily modify or delete it because the information is controlled and maintained by all other nodes on the system. That is why it is considered a key feature of blockchain, but it also has a security risk as it is controlled and accessed by multiple nodes, or there are several backdoors that can be used to attack the system, so if a hacker finds vulnerability the entire system can be affected [27].

8.3.3   Smart Contracts

Smart contracts are computerized transactions rules designed to facilitate the implementation, validation, and execution of digital contracts or agreements. It does not require a third party to perform reliable and irreversible transactions, and is implemented in a distributed environment. According to [28, 29], smart contracts are computer codes, executed when conditions are fulfilled. Fig. 8.8 shows the working of smart contracts.

In blockchain smart contracts are used to create a contract between two or more participants. In addition, the contract can also be used for different purposes in various industries and environments. Simply, they are considered as script stored on the blockchain, which can perform certain operations when certain conditions are met, such as information transfer, fund release and product purchase. This event-driven program executes on a shared ledger and protects ledger resources. Once the information has been added and the conditions of consensus of all parties met, the contract will be automatically executed, and because the contract exists in the distributed ledger, participants cannot modify the consensus by themselves [30].

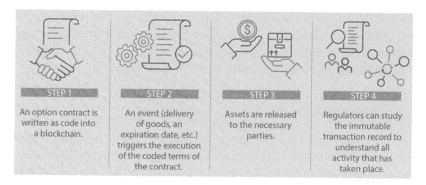

STEP 1	STEP 2	STEP 3	STEP 4
An option contract is written as code into a blockchain.	An event (delivery of goods, an expiration date, etc.) triggers the execution of the coded terms of the contract.	Assets are released to the necessary parties.	Regulators can study the immutable transaction record to understand all activity that has taken place.

Fig. 8.8 Working of smart contracts.

Smart contracts bring a number of benefits to the participants such as accuracy, autonomy, speed, saving, transparency, security, trust and backup of storage, etc. Implementing it ensures proper authorization and grants access to the authorized network. They are also used for validation and verification of network participants. It is quite different from other legal objects that cannot be easily fitted with traditional legal concepts. There are many risks in using smart contracts such as lack of controls and regulation, and the irreversibility of contracts [31]. In contrast, because the smart contracts are autonomous, self-sufficient and decentralized compared to traditional contracts, their risks are greatly reduced. Since smart contracts are still in their infancy, their pros and cons may not be clearly defined [32].

8.3.4   Consensus Mechanism

The method of achieving consensus decision-making is called consensus mechanism. It is used to verify transaction and to keep records. This fault-tolerant tool is used in blockchain to provide the necessary contract between distributed systems (for example, using cryptocurrency) for a single data value or single state of the network. These rules allow network nodes to reach an agreement. When a transaction is initialized, these rules are followed, based on validation, security, and P2P consensus to ensure authenticity of the transactions [33] and the implementation of distributed consensus in blockchain. So, it is very difficult to damage any record. One of the best things is that it has the ability to prevent malicious activities like hacking [34, 35].

In the distributed consensus of the blockchain, miners verify transactions, so fraudulent transactions cannot be collectively verified and validated. All network nodes are monitoring the blockchain activities, especially malicious activities. No external or internal users have access to enter malicious or fake data into the blocks without alerting the other receiver. Therefore, the integrity of the records will not be compromised. If the general ledgers are hacked then blockchain improves the hacked copies with other networks and replaces it [36].

In the blockchain, there are different types of consensus mechanism, such as Proof of Work (PoW), Proof of Capacity (PoC), Proof of Stake (PoS), etc. The fully decentralized blockchain system is based on proof of work and proof of stake for the purpose of validation.

8.3.4.1   Proof of Work (PoW)

Proof of Work (PoW) is the first consensus mechanism introduced by Bitcoin to ensure authentication and verifiability of transactions and eliminate the need for centralization. This protocol requires nodes (miner) to provide Proof of Work (mining) by solving a complex computational problem, and requires a huge computing power. The function of this protocol is to verify all network operations required to manage a single miner node in the whole blockchain network. It manipulates the history of transactions and ensures the security of data in blockchain [37]. Through Proof of Work, the node permanently adds a block to the blockchain that keeps the data secure by linking and hashing (a non-reversible process to encrypt information of block).

8.3.4.2   Proof of Stake (PoS)

The Proof of Stake (PoS) protocol is different from Proof of Work, which involves a combination of a participant's stake in the network and an algorithm that randomly assigns verification task to nodes. Given that the participants are not required to solve complex problems, this mechanism can significantly reduce energy consumption. Therefore, many blockchains (such as Ethereum) have gradually turned to Proof of Stake and improved scalability [38].

8.4   Categories of Blockchain

All structures of blockchain are divided into three categories: public, private and hybrid.

8.4.1 Public Blockchain

The public blockchain is open source and there are absolutely no access restrictions. It allows anyone to participate as a user, miner, developer or community member. All transactions conducted on the public blockchain are completely transparent, which means that anyone can become a validator by participating in consensus implementation [39]. Such networks usually provide financial incentives to those who protect them. The Public blockchain uses Proof of Work and Proof of Stake consensus mechanisms and Bitcoin, Litecoin and Ethereum are the most famous examples of public blockchain. Anyone can start mining here, conduct transaction in the chain and can review or audit the blockchain.

8.4.2 Private Blockchain

A private blockchain is permissioned [40] and centralized. No one can join unless invited by the network administrator. Participants and validators have limited access rights. These features are very valuable for companies that want to collaborate and share information, but don't want to display their sensitive business information in a public blockchain, such as Bankchain. In this type of blockchain, anyone unauthorized cannot start mining, cannot make a transaction, and cannot review or audit the blockchain.

8.4.3 Consortium Blockchain

These blockchains are different from private blockchains and are considered as their subcategory because they have all the same features of private blockchains. The consortium blockchain is managed and controlled by a selected group of members rather than a single entity. Users of a consortium blockchain can run a complete node and start mining, can conduct transaction or decision making on the chain and also can audit or review the blockchain [41]. The consortium blockchain will be more beneficial to industries and organizations where multiple organizations operate in the same industry and need to have a common basis for transaction or relaying information, as this will enable them to share their industry insights with other participants.

8.4.4 Hybrid Blockchain

A hybrid blockchain has both centralized and decentralized features [42]. It combines the security and transparency features of a public blockchain with privacy features of a private blockchain. This provides the company with great flexibility in choosing between open and transparent data and private data. This feature makes it easy for companies to achieve the transparency they need without sacrificing security and privacy. Table 8.2 shows a comparison between private, public and consortium blockchain.

Table 8.2 A comparison between private, public and consortium blockchain.

Property	Public	Private	Consortium
Structure	Decentralized	Centralized	Partially decentralized
Ownership	Public/ decentralized	Centralized	Semi centralized
Identity	Anonymous	Identified users	Identified users
Access	Public (Open Read/write)	Both public/ private	Both public/ private
Consensus	PoW and PoS	Pre-approved	Pre-approved
Consensus mechanisms	All miners	One organization	Selects set of nodes
Efficiency	Low	High	High
Consumption	High Energy	Low Energy	Low Energy
Immutability	Impossible to tamper	Could be tampered	Could be tampered
Protocol efficiency	Low	High	High
Speed	Slower (10 minutes)	Faster (as a transactional system)	Vary by number of nodes
Use - cases	Crypto – economy	Reference data management	Secure data sharing
Examples	Ethereum, Bitcoin, Lite-coin	Multi-chain, MONAX	EWF (Energy), R3 (Banks)

8.5   Blockchain Applications

As mentioned earlier, Blockchain is a decentralized distributed database [43]. Here are some blockchain applications that are active today. Fig. 8.9 shows the Blockchain applications.

8.5.1   Financial Application

8.5.1.1   Bitcoin

Blockchain and Bitcoin are two complicated interconnected concepts that use cryptographic techniques and protocols to conduct financial transactions with virtual currencies and to have an audit mechanism [44]. This is a decentralized p2p cryptocurrency system that uses a blockchain to place Bitcoin transactions in blocks with time-stamps and connect them in chronological order because each Block has previous block hashes [45]. Bitbond, BTC Jam, DeBuNe (Decentralized Business Network), and BitnPlay are active examples of Bitcoin.

8.5.1.2   Ripple

Ripple is a decentralized currency exchange and remittance system. It was released in 2012 and mainly used by banks or market makers [46]. It relies on a shared ledger and uses distributed open source protocols to store information about all Ripple accounts. The network is managed and controlled by an independent server network, which constantly verifies transaction records. The server can be owned by anyone, including banks or market makers [47]. Ripple will immediately verify the account

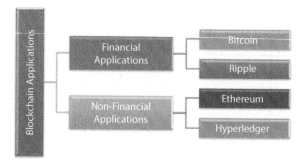

Fig. 8.9 Blockchain applications.

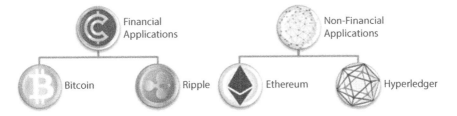

Financial
Applications

Non-Financial
Applications

Bitcoin

Ripple

Ethereum

Hyperledger

Fig. 8.10 Blockchain financial and non-financial applications.

and balance for payment transfer and issue a payment notification within a few seconds. The payment is irreversible and will not be refunded. The ledger uses a decentralized native cryptocurrency called XRP. As of April 2020, it is the third-largest coin by market value of digital coins. Fig. 8.10 shows the Financial and Non-Financial Applications [48].

8.5.2 Non-Financial Applications

8.5.2.1 Ethereum

VitalikButerin a cryptocurrency programmer created an open source and decentralized application platform known as Ethereum [49]. He developed a system where he mixed the distributed computing techniques which is totally based on Turing scripting language. Also, it can perform on the smart contract processing of blockchain. Moreover, the modified version of Satoshi Nakamoto support the consensus through blockchain transactions. Ethereum has been updated with the passage of time and shifted with Proof of Stake [50].

8.5.2.2 Hyperledger

Linux foundation introduced the Hyperledger in 2015. It is known as an open source technology where it helps the cross-industry blockchain technology. After that, it developed the blockchain enterprise where all registered members can access their account [51]. Also, it is known as a global partnership hosted by the Linux Foundation and can include leaders in IoT such as Banking, Financing, Supply Chain, Technology and Manufacturing. Furthermore, blockchain technology is well known and is used almost everywhere, such as supply chain management, smart contract, identity management, voting, healthcare, Filament IoT, and e-plug IoT, etc.

8.6   Blockchain in Different Sectors

Blockchain and other emerging technologies are bringing innovative opportunities worldwide by changing the way businesses operate. In a digital world Blockchain is one of the fastest-growing technologies and has received a lot of attention in recent years. There is no doubt that this technology has revolutionized finance and many other sectors.

As we know, it was invented for the financial sector; the idea was to trade without any intermediaries. It is a distributed network of nodes that use consensus instead of intermediaries to verify transactions and supports anonymity, integrity, transparency and security of data in the network. But now, it is not only used in the financial field, but has also been adopted by many other industries. It has changed our social and business methods, because smart contracts and other Blockchain concepts are quite different from other legal objects that cannot easily fit in the traditional legal concepts, which is why people are increasingly interested in blockchain.

Blockchain is gaining huge interest among different sectors such as the cryptocurrency exchange, gaming world, supply chain management, healthcare, legal industries, real estate, banking and finance, restaurant industry, closing statements, internet of things, music industry, voting mechanism, advertising and energy, and it facilitates the development of these industries and business areas. However, due to some unexplained challenges, it is still far from mass implementation.

8.7   Blockchain Implementation Challenges

Blockchain has the potential to design interactive systems, but still faces many technical challenges [52] and limitations to adopting it. Scalability, interoperability, data integrity, privacy, security, usability, throughput and performance are some of the key attributes required for high-quality implementation of blockchain. Blockchain applications use unique technology features, but these quality features bring many challenges; improvements need to be made not only to make these applications more scalable and efficient, but also more durable [53]. There are some unsolved challenges in blockchain implementation.

- **Scalability** - Blockchain faces scalability issues as it cannot provide services to many users because Bitcoin blockchain only processes nearly 7 TPS (Transaction per second), while Ethereum has processed around 20 TPS, which cannot meet the real-time processing requirements of millions of transactions. According to International Data Corporation (IDC), global spending on blockchain solution is increasing, and by 2022, it is expected to reach US$11.7 billion [54]. In order to achieve widespread adoption of this technology, there must be sufficient throughput and businesses with large numbers of customers must consider the technology to achieve scalability.

- **Usability** - It is still difficult to buy and sell cryptocurrencies. Participation in the cryptocurrency ecosystem requires a certain level of verification, and most users are not attractive. Complex security processes have become barriers to blockchain adoption and creating a more user-friendly process to securely purchase and store cryptocurrencies remains a serious challenge in the industry.

- **Data privacy** - The implementation of blockchain technology brings various challenges, such as data integrity difficulties, data security and privacy issues, and lack of skilled staff or sufficient resources [55]. Because it is a distributed ledger, all nodes can access the data on the platform. Therefore, without data privacy, companies will not be able to maintain their influence over competitors. Subsequently, many potential users avoided the technology because of fear of losing their competitive advantages.

- **Security** - Due to some immature processes, the blockchain still faces security issues. There are many loopholes that make users vulnerable to cybercrime attacks, and there are many malwares in the industry that pose a serious risk to users. Because the blockchain has no central authority, no one can secretly modify the ledger. Each node must verify the entry in the record to modify the ledger. There may be security issues in the case of a 51% attack. According to Satoshi Nakamoto, "when a person or a group's mining capacity exceeds 50%, the attack power will be 51%. This attack can prevent other miners from creating blocks or making any transactions." To avoid this, it is necessary to continuously monitor the mining pool.

- **Lack of interoperability** - Lack of interoperability is another challenge for large-scale blockchain implementation, as users of a blockchain platform cannot fully interact with users of other blockchain platforms. No standard allows transparent interaction between these platforms. For example, Hyperledger Fabric of IBM is excellent in supply chain management, while R3s Corda is the most suitable for financial solutions [56]. There is clearly no connection between these platforms, which makes cross-platform navigation difficult. But over time, there are many projects that provide interoperability between different blockchain networks. For example, the Ethereum Alliance and Hyperledger held a meeting on this issue in 2019. It is worth noting that these projects are designed to work together to try to solve this issue. And the cosmos also uses IBC (Inter-Blockchain communication) protocols to allow blockchain economies to operate outside silos and transfer files between them.

- **Lack of understanding** - As there is no clear roadmap for implementing blockchain, it is difficult to get the most useful solution. Because most of the upcoming blockchain solutions are novel, and for most people in the industry, they are mostly technical. Similarly, most organizations lack sufficient knowledge about the use of blockchain. In other words, no one in the organization has a clear understanding of the concept of blockchain. Therefore, it is difficult to formulate a solid technology-centric business strategy. Many sources have reiterated the lack of understanding from consumers, businesses and authorities about the potential blockchain use-cases, how it works and what the technology can actually do [57]. In addition, technology creates potential decentralized transparency and accountability that can create new regulations that allow individuals to reduce their dependence on controlled (sometimes inefficient) services provided by connected and intermediary service providers [58]. Therefore, it is essential to understand how to integrate this technology into business strategy and personal activities to understand its social impact.

- **Implementation cost** - Finding the most suitable block-chain application is not easy, as most of them are not yet fully developed. In addition, the most suitable platforms pay a cost huge cost in terms of implementation and even energy costs. For example, Bitcoin blockchain can process only 7 TPS and consumes a lot of energy in this process. Ethereum can manage 20 TPS. Unfortunately, as compared to VISA, which can complete 24,000 TPS, none of these are satisfactory. So, it is clear that while Bitcoin has completed very few transactions per second, it takes a lot of energy in a year.
- **Finding the right partner** - This blockchain implementation challenge arises when an organization wants to implement this technology, but the cost of blockchain is too high, and there is no clear roadmap for implementing blockchain. Therefore, to understand the basic principles, they need experienced partners, who already have knowledge about it, and can help to find the best blockchain implementation roadmap. But finding the right partner is problematic because of the lack of talent that can fully meet the needs. Therefore, it may be difficult to obtain the correct solution.

8.8   Revolutionized Challenges in Industries

Blockchain technology has revolutionized the financial industry as well as many other industries in different fields. However, industries that want to adopt it still face many challenges, such as data integrity difficulties, scalability, data security and privacy issues, lack of interoperability, lack of skilled staff or sufficient resources, and technology cost. Table 8.3 summarizes the blockchain implementation challenges that affect technical, institutional, and marketing factors, and gives references to overcome these challenges and constraints. As we all know, blockchain applications are used in the financial field and also in different industries and fields [91]. Therefore, Table 8.4 summarizes the sector-wide applications and uses of blockchain. Innovative blockchain technology aims to ensure the quality features of participants or organizations that want to adopt it, such as decentralization, transparency, security, reliability, etc. Fig. 8.11 shows how the uses

Table 8.3 Factors affecting the implementation of blockchain technology.

Factors affecting blockchain implementation	Challenges	References
Technical Factors		
Distributed ledger	~ Newness ~ Lack of Standardization ~ Leads to data integrity and security risks ~ Cybercrime	[59] [60] [61] [62]
Information exchange/ Transactions	~ Block size ~ Standardization ~ Time to process transactions ~ Scalability ~ Data privacy ~ Data security	[63] [64] [65] [66] [67] [68]
Shared infrastructure	~ Development of standard infrastructure components ~ Lack of standardization ~ Lack of interoperability	[69] [70] [71]
Institutional Factors		
Norms and Cultures	~ Lack of understanding blockchain ~ Need to overcome cultural resistance ~ Resistance to change of customers and companies.	[72] [73] [74]
Regulation and Legislation	~ The need to introduce new laws and regulations ~ Capacity of law enforcement agencies to deal with fraudulent activities. ~ Decision makers confused about Bitcoin and Blockchain. ~ The law must consider the nature of blockchain. ~ Need to deal with Taxation.	[75] [76] [77] [78] [79]
Governance	~ Government out of control ~ Risk of market manipulation and unfair practices. ~ Use a suitable governance framework	[80] [81] [82]

(Continued)

Table 8.3 Factors affecting the implementation of blockchain technology. (*Continued*)

Factors affecting blockchain implementation	Challenges	References
Market Factors		
Market Structure	~ Requires high degree of computerization ~ Interconnectedness increased between participants	[83] [84]
Agreements and contracts	~ Transferring existing contracts to new blockchain methodology ~ Smart contracts are not clear enough ~ Confusion between smart contracts and e-contracts. ~ Pose programming challenges	[85] [86] [87] [88]
Business process	~ Cost of blockchain adoption and implementation very high for business ~ Unable to use traditional business process to use blockchain technology	[89] [90]

of these quality features can benefit blockchain implementation in different industries, but these quality features pose many challenges that require improvement. Fig. 8.12 and Fig. 8.13 show the limitations and barriers to large-scale implementation of blockchain technology. And Fig. 8.14 shows how much these blockchain adoption barriers will increase by 2020. Fig. 8.15 shows the percentage of industries that global executives believe is the most advanced development of blockchain to successfully conduct business. Blockchain has revolutionized finance and other fields and gained huge interest in the fields of healthcare, cryptocurrency exchange, gaming world, supply chain management, legal industries, banking and finance, music and advertising industries, internet of things, etc. Fig. 8.16 shows how these sectors are currently using blockchain applications. And Fig. 8.17 shows how the blockchain adoption rate has gradually increased from 2009 [92].

Table 8.4 Sector-wide uses and application areas of blockchain technology.

Sectors	Application areas and uses
Agriculture	Soil data, shipping of agro-products, processing records related to agricultural data, sales and market data of agricultural products, production, etc.
Distribution	Records of sales, market, storage, digital currencies, transport, mining chips, secondhand goods and so on.
Energy sector	Resource availability, energy generation data, energy suppliers and demand data records, electricity price data, maintenance of utility condition records, on demand supply, resource tracking etc.
Food industry	Records information about food packing, online ordering, delivery, shipping, online ordering and transactions, quality assurance data, etc.
Finance	Social banking, digital trading assets, cryptocurrencies. Currency exchange, currency deposits, remittances, crowd funding, smart securities, smart contracts.
Healthcare	Digitized medical records, digital case reports, prescription records, vital signs, hospital information systems, medical expenses.
Industrial	Store data about product production, assurance, warranty info, guarantee info, delivery and transaction, supplies, components, raw materials, manufacturing management, packaging data, sensors and actuators, and robotics, etc.
Smart city	Records digital data, digital transactions, pollution control data, water and power management data, smart services products, smart data maintenance, smart transactions data, etc.
Trade	Records import and export data, digital data by software industries, transaction processing data, and all other data of financial value.
Transportation and logistics	Records data of goods delivery and transportation, vehicle tracking, shipping container tracking, logistics service identifiers, and toll data maintenance, etc.
Others	Artwork, digital content, economic sharing, government and voting, jewelry and precious metals, ownership, space development, virtual countries.

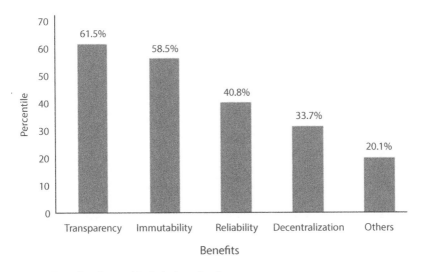

Fig. 8.11 Benefits of using blockchain technology.

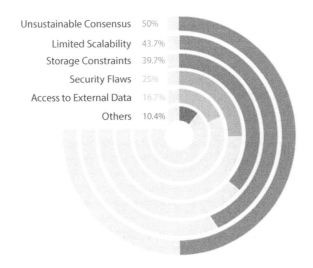

Fig. 8.12 Limitations of implementing blockchain.

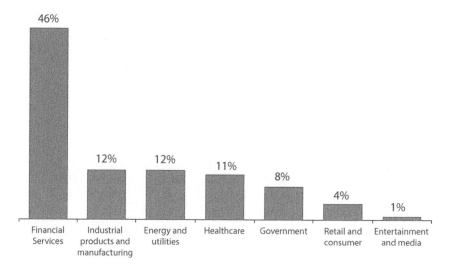

Fig. 8.13 Industries that global executives believe are most advanced in blockchain development.

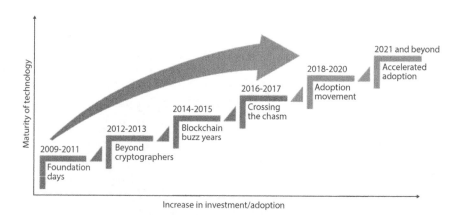

Fig. 8.14 Blockchain adoption rate is gradually increasing.

7% Others
3% Manufacturing
30% Banking & Finance
3% Energy & Utilities
4% Professional Services
6% Technology Services
6% Generic
8% Media, Entertainment & Gaming
8% Healthcare
13% Government & Public Goods
12% Insurance

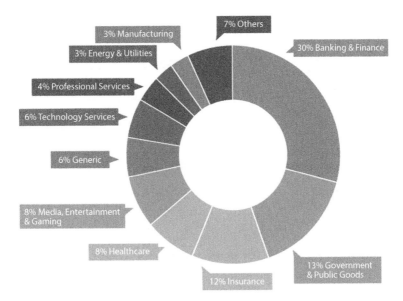

Fig. 8.15 Sectors currently using blockchain technology.

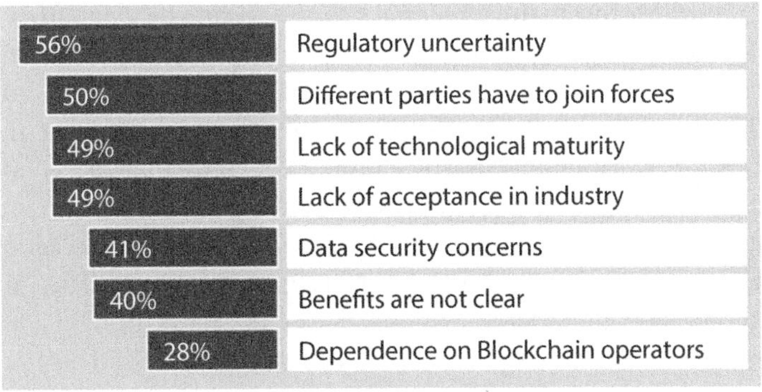

56% Regulatory uncertainty
50% Different parties have to join forces
49% Lack of technological maturity
49% Lack of acceptance in industry
41% Data security concerns
40% Benefits are not clear
28% Dependence on Blockchain operators

Fig. 8.16 Barriers to large-scale adoption of blockchain.

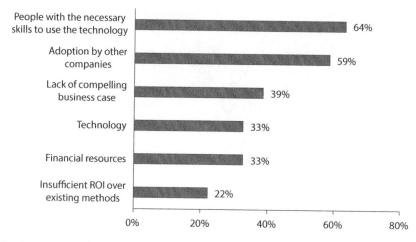

Fig. 8.17 Barriers for blockchain adoptions by 2020.

8.9   Conclusion

There is no doubt that innovative blockchain has revolutionized finance, education, government, healthcare, supply chain, Internet of Things, digital marketing, and other fields. However, the adoption of destructive technology will bring many challenges to the technical, regulatory, social and adoption-related fields. The purpose of this research is to recognize the existing blockchain technology's research topics, challenges, and the future directions from a technical perspective. In this study, we analyzed the current quality issues in blockchain implementation (scalability, usability, data privacy, security, lack of interoperability, lack of understanding and implementation costs), and determined the blockchain implementation quality attributes (security, anonymity and data integrity) and also defined the concept of blockchain, smart contracts, cryptography, consensus mechanism, functions, advantages and disadvantages, and the categories of blockchain (such as public, private hybrid and consortium). Blockchain has changed our social and business methods, because smart contracts and other blockchain concepts are very different from other legal objects; they cannot easily fit in the traditional legal objects, which is why the interest in blockchain is increasing. The result indicated that research on blockchain implementation's quality requirements is still in its infancy. Advanced blockchain technology rapidly reshapes the organizations, affecting basic aspects of its daily business processes and activities. Before successfully implementing blockchain, any organization must be modified, and the system also needs to take organizational measure to meet the conditions.

- The implementation of blockchain technology brings various challenges, such as data integrity difficulties, data security and privacy issues, and lack of skilled staff or sufficient resources.
- As blockchain is distributed ledger technology, all nodes can access the data on the platform. Therefore, without the right to data privacy, the company will not be able to maintain its influence over competitors, and many potential users avoided using the technology because of fear of losing their competitive advantage.
- There are many loopholes that make users vulnerable to cybercrime attacks, and there are many malwares in the industry that pose a serious risk to users.
- The innovative blockchain network is vulnerable to 51% attacks. According to a 2019 report by a computer science researcher at New York University, 51% attacks could increase because hackers can now rent computing power without having to buy all the equipment.
- Because there is no clear roadmap for implementing blockchain, it is difficult to formulate a strong business strategy centered on technology. Therefore, it is necessary to understand how to integrate this innovative technology into company strategy and personal activities to understand its social impact.
- Buying and selling cryptocurrencies is still difficult. As complex security processes have become obstacles to adopting blockchain, creating a more user-friendly process to safely purchase and store cryptocurrencies remains a serious challenge in the industry.
- Because the blockchain transaction processing speed is slower than the traditional brand VISA, it cannot meet the real-time requirements of processing millions of transactions, so the blockchain faces scalability issues. According to IDC's forecast, by 2022, global spending on blockchain will reach $11.7 billion. Then, to widely adopt the technology,

throughput must be sufficient, and the companies need to consider adopting the technology to achieve scalability.

- The technology cost is very high because the Proof of Work system consumes a lot of computing power, which leads to high energy costs.

- Because blockchain will make government and business operations more accurate, efficient and secure, it is estimated that by 2022 to 2030, the value of at least one innovative blockchain technology–based business will reach between US$10 billion and US$1 trillion.

References

1. Yli-Huumo, J., Ko, D., Choi, S., Park, S., & Smolander, K., Where is current research on blockchain technology? — a systematic review. *PloS one*, 11(10), e0163477, 2016.
2. Behnke, K., & Janssen, M. F. W. H. A., Boundary conditions for traceability in food supply chains using blockchain technology, *International Journal of Information Management*, 52, 101969, 2020.
3. Cermeño, J. S., Blockchain in financial services: Regulatory landscape and future challenges for its commercial application, *BBVA Research Paper*, 16, 20, 2016.
4. Clohessy, T., Acton, T., & Rogers, N.,Blockchain adoption: technological, organisational and environmental considerations, In *Business transformation through blockchain*, Palgrave Macmillan, Cham, 47-76, 2019.
5. Crosby, M., Pattanayak, P., Verma, S., & Kalyanaraman, V., Blockchain technology: Beyond bitcoin, *Applied Innovation*, 2(71), 6-10, 2016.
6. Hughes, L., Dwivedi, Y. K., Misra, S. K., Rana, N. P., Raghavan, V., &Akella, V., Blockchain research, practice and policy: Applications, benefits, limitations, emerging research themes and research agenda, *International Journal of Information Management*, 49, 114-129, 2019.
7. Nakamoto, S., Bitcoin whitepaper, https://bitcoin. org/bitcoin. pdf- (Датаобращения: 17.07. 2019), 2008.
8. Pilkington, M., Blockchain technology: principles and applications, In *Research handbook on digital transformations*, Edward Elgar Publishing, 2016.
9. Marsal-Llacuna, M. L., Future living framework: Is blockchain the next enabling network?, *Technological Forecasting and Social Change*, 128, 226-234, 2018.
10. Abeyratne, S. A., & Monfared, R. P., Blockchain ready manufacturing supply chain using distributed ledger, *International Journal of Research in Engineering and Technology*, 5(9), 1-10, 2016.

11. Lakhani, K. R., & Iansiti, M., The truth about blockchain, *Harvard Business Review*, 95(1), 119-127, 2017.
12. Janssen, M., Weerakkody, V., Ismagilova, E., Sivarajah, U., & Irani, Z., A framework for analysingblockchain technology adoption: Integrating institutional, market and technical factors, *International Journal of Information Management*, 50, 302-309, 2020.
13. Swanson, T., Consensus-as-a-service: a brief report on the emergence of permissioned, distributed ledger systems, Report, available online, 2015.
14. Reyna, A., Martín, C., Chen, J., Soler, E., & Díaz, M., On blockchain and its integration with IoT. Challenges and opportunities, *Future generation computer systems*, 88, 173-190, 2018.
15. Sivarajah, U., Kamal, M. M., Irani, Z., & Weerakkody, V., Critical analysis of Big Data challenges and analytical methods. *Journal of Business Research*, 70, 263-286, 2017.
16. Treiblmaier, H., The impact of the blockchain on the supply chain: a theory-based research framework and a call for action, *Supply Chain Management: An International Journal*, 23(6), 545-559, 2018.
17. Rejeb, A.,Sűle, E., & G Keogh, J., Exploring new technologies in procurement, transport & *Logistics: The International Journal*, 18(45), 76-86, 2018.
18. Casino, F., Dasaklis, T. K., & Patsakis, C., A systematic literature review of blockchain-based applications: current status, classification and open issues, *Telematics and Informatics*, 36, 55-81, 2019.
19. Koteska, B., Karafiloski, E., & Mishev, A., Blockchain implementation quality challenges: a literature, In *SQAMIA 2017: 6th Workshop of Software Quality, Analysis, Monitoring, Improvement, and Applications*, 11-13, 2017.
20. Treiblmaier, H., Combining blockchain technology and the physical internet to achieve triple bottom line sustainability: a comprehensive research agenda for modern logistics and supply chain management, *Logistics*, 3(1), 10, 2019.
21. Rejeb, A., Keogh, J. G., & Treiblmaier, H., How Blockchain Technology Can Benefit Marketing: Six Pending Research Areas, *Frontiers in Blockchain*, 3, 3, 2020.
22. Nowiński, W., & Kozma, M., How can blockchain technology disrupt the existing business models?, *Entrepreneurial Business and Economics Review*, 5(3), 173-188, 2017.
23. Janssen, M., Weerakkody, V., Ismagilova, E., Sivarajah, U., & Irani, Z., A framework for analysingblockchain technology adoption: Integrating institutional, market and technical factors, *International Journal of Information Management*, 50, 302-309, 2020.
24. Chartier-Rueg, T. C., & Zweifel, T. D., Blockchain, Leadership And Management: Business As Usual Or Radical Disruption?, *EUREKA: Social and Humanities*, (4), 76-110, 2017.
25. Andoni, M., Robu, V., Flynn, D., Abram, S., Geach, D., Jenkins, D., ... & Peacock, A.,Blockchain technology in the energy sector: A systematic review of challenges and opportunities, *Renewable and Sustainable Energy Reviews*, 100, 143-174, 2019.

26. Mosakheil, J. H., Security threats classification in blockchains, *Culminating Projects in Information Assurance*, 48, 2018.
27. Chartier-Rueg, T. C., & Zweifel, T. D., Blockchain, Leadership And Management: Business As Usual Or Radical Disruption?, *EUREKA: Social and Humanities*, (4), 76-110, 2017.
28. Zheng, Z., Xie, S., Dai, H. N., Chen, X., & Wang, H., Blockchain challenges and opportunities: A survey, *International Journal of Web and Grid Services*, 14(4), 352-375, 2018.
29. Zhang, Y., & Wen, J., An IoT electric business model based on the protocol of bitcoin, In *2015 18th international conference on intelligence in next generation networks IEEE*, 184-191, 2015.
30. Bigi, G., Bracciali, A., Meacci, G., & Tuosto, E., Validation of decentralised smart contracts through game theory and formal methods. In *Programming Languages with Applications to Biology and Security*, Springer, Cham, 142-161, 2015.
31. Cachin, C., Architecture of the hyperledgerblockchain fabric, In *Workshop on distributed cryptocurrencies and consensus ledgers*, 310(4), 2016.
32. Chris, D., *Introducing Ethereum and Solidity Foundations of Cryptocurrency and Blockchain Programming for Beginners*, Apress, New York, 2017.
33. Freedzai, Nasdaq uses blockchain-based technology to reduce risk and prevent fraud., https://feedzai.com/blog/nasdaq-uses-blockchain-based-technology-to-reduce-risk-and-prevent-fraud/, 2016.
34. Griffiths, M. E., Virtual currency businesses: An analysis of the evolving regulatory landscape, Tex. Tech. Admin. LJ, 16, 303, 2014.
35. Rejeb, A., Keogh, J. G., & Treiblmaier, H., Leveraging the internet of things and blockchain technology in supply chain management, *Future Internet*, 11(7), 161, 2019.
36. Baxter, A., Blockchain-Unchaining the world from fraud?, http://www.thepaypers.com/expertopinion/blockchainunchaining-the-world-from-fraud-/763845, 2016.
37. Camp, C., Bitcoin may help criminals, but blockchain can help thwart fraud., retrieved from: http://www.americanbanker.com/, 2016.
38. Mingxiao, D., Xiaofeng, M., Zhe, Z., Xiangwei, W., &Qijun, C., A review on consensus algorithm of blockchain, In *2017 IEEE International Conference on Systems, Man, and Cybernetics (SMC) IEEE*, 2567-2572, 2017.
39. Marvin, B., "Blockchain: The Invisible Technology That's Changing the World", https://www.pcmag.com/news/blockchain-the-invisible-technology-thats-changing-the-world#:~:text=Think%20of%20blockchain%20as%20a, data%E2%80%94exactly%20as%20it%20occurs. 2017.
40. Walker, M., Distributed Ledger Technology: Hybrid Approach, Front-to-Back Designing and Changing Trade Processing Infrastructure, https://www.risk.net/front-to-back, 2018.
41. Piazza, F., Bitcoin in the dark web: a shadow over banking secrecy and a call for global response, S. Cal. Interdisc. LJ, 26, 521, 2016.

42. Kosba, A., Miller, A., Shi, E., Wen, Z., & Papamanthou, C., Hawk: The blockchain model of cryptography and privacy-preserving smart contracts, In *2016 IEEE symposium on security and privacy (SP) IEEE*, 839-858, 2016.

43. Münsing, E., Mather, J., & Moura, S., Blockchains for decentralized optimization of energy resources in microgrid networks. In *2017 IEEE conference on control technology and applications (CCTA) IEEE*, 2164-2171, 2017.

44. Surujnath, R., Off the chain: A guide to blockchain derivatives markets and the implications on systemic risk. *Fordham J. Corp. & Fin. L.*, 22, 257, 2017.

45. Al-Saqaf, W., &Seidler, N., Blockchain technology for social impact: opportunities and challenges ahead. *Journal of Cyber Policy*, 2(3), 338-354, 2017.

46. Andreasyan, T., ISITC Europe and oasis to define technical standards for blockchain. *Banking Technology*, 13, 2016.

47. Brandman, G., & Thampapillai, S., Blockchain–Considering the regulatory horizon, https://www. law. ox. ac. uk/business-law-blog/blog/2016/07/blockchain–considering-regulatory-horizon, 2016.

48. Buehler, K., Chiarella, D., Heidegger, H., Lemerle, M., Lal, A., & Moon, J., Beyond the hype: Blockchains in capital markets, McKinsey working papers on corporate & investment banking, 2015.

49. Corea, F., AI and Blockchain, In *An Introduction to Data*, Springer, Cham, 69-76, 2019.

50. Deshpande, A., Stewart, K., Lepetit, L., & Gunashekar, S., Distributed Ledger Technologies/Blockchain: Challenges, opportunities and the prospects for standards, Overview report The British Standards Institution (BSI), 40, 40, 2017.

51. Szmukler, D., Applying cryptotechnologies to trade finance: Information paper Euro Banking Association Working Group On Electronic Alternative Payments, https://www.abe-eba.eu/downloads/knowledgeandresearch/EBA_May2016_eAPWG_Applying_cryptotechnologies_to_Trade_Finance.pdf, 2016.

52. Mark, W., Distributed ledgers–Closed POST breakfast event, London: Parliamentary Office,https://www.parliament.uk/documents/post/061216_Distributed-Ledgersv3.pdf, 2016.

53. Shackelford, S. J., & Myers, S., Block-by-block: leveraging the power of blockchain technology to build trust and promote cyber peace. *Yale JL & Tech.*, 19, 334, 2017.

54. SWIFT Institute & Accenture, SWIFT on distributed ledger technologies, SWIFT, http://www.ameda.org.eg/, 2016.

55. Vranken, H., Sustainability of bitcoin and blockchains, *Current opinion in environmental sustainability*, 28, 1-9, 2017.

56. Ametrano, F. M., Barucci, E., Marazzina, D., & Zanero, S., Response to ESMA/2016/773:'The Distributed Ledger Technology Applied to Securities Markets', 2016.

57. Harwood-Jones, M., *Blockchain and T2S: a potential disruptor*, Standard Chartered Bank, 2016.

58. Kiviat, T. I., Beyond bitcoin: Issues in regulating blockchain transactions, Duke LJ, 65, 569, 2015.
59. Radziwill, N., Blockchain revolution: How the technology behind Bitcoin is changing money, business, and the world, *Quality Management Journal*, 25(1), 64-65, 2018.
60. Yeoh, P., Regulatory issues in blockchain technology, *Journal of Financial Regulation and Compliance*, 2017.
61. Kshetri, N., Blockchain's roles in meeting key supply chain management objectives, *International Journal of Information Management*, 39, 80-89, 2018.
62. Mainelli, M., & Mills, S., The missing links in the chains? Mutual distributed ledger (aka blockchain) standards, 2016.
63. Veuger, J., Trust in a viable real estate economy with disruption and blockchain, *Facilities*, 2018.
64. Christidis, K., & Devetsikiotis, M., Blockchains and smart contracts for the internet of things, *IEEE Access*, 4, 2292-2303, 2016.
65. Authority, F. C., Discussion Paper on distributed ledger technology, https://www. fca.org.uk/publication/discussion/dp17-03.pdf, 2017.
66. Knight, W., The technology behind bitcoin is shaking up much more than money,https://www.technologyreview.com/s/604148/thetechnology-behind-bitcoin-is-shaking-up-much-more-than-money/2017.
67. Mainelli, M., & Smith, M., Sharing ledgers for sharing economies: an exploration of mutual distributed ledgers (aka blockchain technology), *Journal of Financial Perspectives*, 3(3), 2015.
68. Mills, D. C., Wang, K., Malone, B., Ravi, A., Marquardt, J., Badev, A. I., ...& Ellithorpe, M., Distributed ledger technology in payments, clearing, and settlement. Retrieved from: https://www.esma.europa.eu/sites/default/files/library/2016-773_dp_dlt.pdf, 2016.
69. Ølnes, S., Ubacht, J., & Janssen, M., Blockchain in government: Benefits and implications of distributed ledger technology for information sharing. *Government Information Quarterly*, 34(3), 355–364, 2017.
70. Shobhit S., Blockchain solutions to grow 75% through 2022: IDC, https://www.investopedia.com/news/blockchain-solutions-grow-75-through-2022-idc/, 2019.
71. Zhang, P., White, J., Schmidt, D. C., & Lenz, G., Applying software patterns to address interoperability in blockchain-based healthcare apps, arXiv preprint arXiv:1706.03700, 2017.
72. Ramachandran, G. S., & Krishnamachari, B., Blockchain for the IoT: Opportunities and challenges, arXiv preprint arXiv:1805.02818, 2018.
73. Hughes, A., Park, A., Kietzmann, J., & Archer-Brown, C., Beyond Bitcoin: What blockchain and distributed ledger technologies mean for firms. *Business Horizons*, 62(3), 273-281, 2019.
74. Lozano, R., Are companies planning their organisational changes for corporate sustainability? An analysis of three case studies on resistance to change

and their strategies to overcome it, *Corporate Social Responsibility and Environmental Management*, 20(5), 275-295, 2013.

75. De Filippi, P., & Hassan, S., Blockchain technology as a regulatory technology: From code is law to law is code, arXiv preprint arXiv:1801.02507, 2018.

76. Yeung, K., Blockchain, transactional security and the promise of automated law enforcement: the withering of freedom under law? *TLI Think*, 2017.

77. Truby, J., Decarbonizing Bitcoin: Law and policy choices for reducing the energy consumption of Blockchain technologies and digital currencies. *Energy Research & Social Science*, 44, 399-410. 2018.

78. Sullivan, C., & Burger, E., E-residency and blockchain. *Computer Law & Security Review*, 33(4), 470-481, 2017.

79. Hyvärinen, H., Risius, M., & Friis, G., A blockchain-based approach towards overcoming financial fraud in public sector services. *Business & Information Systems Engineering*, 59(6), 441-456, 2017.

80. Diallo, N., Shi, W., Xu, L., Gao, Z., Chen, L., Lu, Y., ... & Turner, G.,eGov-DAO: A better government using blockchain based decentralized autonomous organization, In *2018 International Conference on eDemocracy & eGovernment (ICEDEG) IEEE*, 166-171, 2018.

81. Bhupathi, T., Technology's Latest Market Manipulator-High Frequency Trading: The Strategies, Tools, Risks, and Responses, *NCJL & Tech.*, 11, 377, 2009.

82. Casado-Vara, R., de la Prieta, F., Prieto, J., & Corchado, J. M., Blockchain framework for IoT data quality via edge computing, In *Proceedings of the 1st Workshop on Blockchain-enabled Networked Sensor Systems*, 19-24, 2018.

83. Ivan, D., Moving toward a blockchain-based method for the secure storage of patient records, In *ONC/NIST Use of Blockchain for Healthcare and Research Workshop. Gaithersburg, Maryland, United States: ONC/NIST*, 1-11, 2016.

84. O'hara, K., Smart contracts-dumb idea, *IEEE Internet Computing*, 21(2), 97-101, 2017.

85. Savelyev, A., Contract law 2.0:'Smart' contracts as the beginning of the end of classic contract law, *Information & Communications Technology Law*, 26(2), 116-134, 2017.

86. Richard, G. J., Autism spectrum disorders in the schools: assessment, diagnosis, and intervention pose challenges for SLPs, *The ASHA Leader*, 13(13), 26-28, 2008.

87. Carson, B., Romanelli, G., Walsh, P., & Zhumaev, A., Blockchain beyond the hype: What is the strategic business value. McKinsey & Company, 1-13, 2018.

88. Zhang, Y., & Wen, J., The IoT electric business model: Using blockchain technology for the internet of things. *Peer-to-Peer Networking and Applications*, 10(4), 983-994, 2017.

89. Biggs, J., Hinish, S. R., Natale, M. A., & Patronick, M., *Blockchain: Revolutionizing the global supply chain by building trust and transparency*, Rutgers University: Camden, NJ, USA, 2017.

90. Lee, J. H., & Pilkington, M., How the blockchain revolution will reshape the consumer electronics industry [future directions], *IEEE Consumer Electronics Magazine*, 6(3), 19-23, 2017.
91. Mistry, I., Tanwar, S., Tyagi, S., & Kumar, N., Blockchain for 5G-enabled IoT for industrial automation: A systematic review, solutions, and challenges, *Mechanical Systems and Signal Processing*, 135, 106382, 2020.
92. Reyna, A., Martín, C., Chen, J., Soler, E., & Díaz, M., On blockchain and its integration with IoT. Challenges and opportunities. *Future Generation Computer Systems*, 88, 173-190, 2018.

9

A Novel Framework to Detect Effective Prediction Using Machine Learning

Shenbaga Priya[1], Revadi[1], Sebastian Terence[1] and Jude Immaculate[2]*

[1]Department of Computer Science, Karunya Institute of Technology and Sciences, Coimbatore, India
[2]Department of Mathematics, Karunya Institute of Technology and Sciences, Coimbatore, India

Abstract

Prediction in machine learning is a blooming area in the computer field. It is used in almost all areas in order to predict future events. Such prediction will help people to have knowledge about the future, which will enable them to make better decisions. There are several prediction methods that have been proposed by many researchers for various applications. The performance of those systems is pretty good and is helping people to make good decisions. In this paper, we have studied various prediction systems which used machine learning techniques. The performance of these techniques is good but the problem is that the accuracy of the prediction mechanism is greatly affected by various factors such as less datasets, not being implemented in real time, using limited number of parameters, etc. We have proposed a framework which can be used to increase the accuracy of the prediction process by adding several features. Using this proposed system, accuracy of prediction results can be increased. To analyze the efficiency of the proposed framework, we used a web-based interface. In this system we predicted agriculture product price. To predict the price of the product, we used linear regression, random forest.

Keywords: Accuracy, machine learning, prediction, training machine, agriculture

*Corresponding author: juderaj.h@gmail.com

Shibin David, R. S. Anand, V. Jeyakrishnan, and M. Niranjanamurthy (eds.) Security Issues and Privacy Concerns in Industry 4.0 Applications, (179–194) © 2021 Scrivener Publishing LLC

9.1   Introduction

We are living in a world of technology and science, where new innovations are budding up and blooming day by day. In earlier times, people were trained to do a particular job. Now those tasks are made easy with the help of computers. Computers are replacing humans in various fields. In the early stages, computers performed the task based on the instructions given by humans. Now the computers are trained in such a way that they perform the tasks without any human instruction. This has been made possible with the help of machine learning, in which computers are well trained with the help of several algorithms, datasets and methods. Once a computer is trained it can perform the required task more effectively.

Prediction is one of the major advantages of machine learning, and this has been implemented in many areas. Everyone is interested in knowing what the future will bring. It would be really great if future events could be predicted, so that people could make a safe move in the present. Here comes the usage of this prediction technique, which uses several algorithms, methods and datasets to predict the future values. This prediction is really helpful in the area of the stock market. Using this machine learning prediction algorithms, the future value of the stock can be predicted, which would help people to invest in the right category to get high profits. Similarly, prediction is very helpful in the area of healthcare. If it could predict the disease at an early stage, the disease could more easily be treated, and the possibility of the disease being cured would be greatly increased. This prediction method can also be used to predict natural hazards and climatic conditions. There are many more areas where this prediction will be greatly helpful.

The available prediction techniques are really helpful to people involved in that particular event. In this paper, we studied various existing machine learning–based prediction algorithms. From this study, we understand that most of the existing prediction algorithms do not give an exact prediction in most cases. Even though these techniques do not provide exact value, we can improve the accuracy of the traditional system by adding some additional features. Here we have proposed a framework with several features added when compared to the older prediction system. This will help to amplify the reliability of the forecast system. The rest of the paper is organized as outlined below.

9.2   ML-Based Prediction

Machine learning techniques are an emerging area in computer science. The technology today has reached a new level of evolution. In former times, people were trained to do the work. Now it's the computers that are trained to do the tasks with the help of several algorithms and models. It is completely different from the older computer operations, in which instructions were given to the computers to solve a particular problem. Now using, this machine learning method, the computers are trained with the help of several datasets and they use statistical analysis to give the output. The progress of a machine learning–based prediction system is shown in Figure 9.1. This technique is more efficient and helpful when compared to the older ones. There are several methods available in machine learning. We can broadly classify them into three types,

- Supervised learning
- Unsupervised learning
- Reinforcement learning

Prediction of a particular event will definitely be helpful for all of those involved in it, enabling them to make a safe move. There are several steps

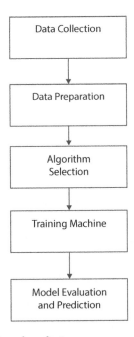

Figure 9.1 Work flow of ML-based prediction.

involved, such as data collection, formatting the data, algorithm selection, training the computer, model evaluation and prediction. Several algorithms are available in machine learning with which we can train the computer and make predictions for a particular event. In supervised learning, the following algorithms are used for prediction.

- Regression
- Random forest
- Decision tree
- Logistic regression
- KNN
- SVM

Machine learning predictions have been used in many areas. They greatly help people to make better decisions. Some of the areas where this machine learning is greatly helpful are listed below:

- Agriculture
- Healthcare
- Economy
- Mammals
- Weather

9.3   Prediction in Agriculture

Agriculture is one of the major occupations which provides employment to a huge amount of the population in a country. Prediction in agriculture helps farmers in many ways. In [1], Kamir et al. projected a mechanism for the prediction of wheat production in a wheat belt located in Australia. The machine learning algorithm used here is support vector regression. This system has resulted in an accuracy of 73% with some constraints. In [2], Zhang et al. came up with an idea for annual crop planting prediction in Lancaster County, Nebraska. The machine learning algorithm used to predict this is multi-layer artificial neural network. This system has resulted in an accuracy of 88%.

In [3], Kakhki et al. used various prediction algorithms such as quadratic and RBF kernals, SVM with linear, Naive Bayes and boosted trees to predict the wound sternness in agribusiness based on some of the machine learning algorithms. They have implemented this technique in the US Midwest and found that there was a 92-98% accuracy. In [4], Khanal *et al.* projected a technique for the spatial prediction of soil properties and corn yield using some of the algorithms such as Neural Network (NN), Support Vector Machine (SVM) and random forest (RF) with radial and Gradient Boosting Model (GBM), linear kernel functions, Cubist (CU). They have implemented this system in the agricultural farm close to London, Ohio, with an accuracy of 97%. In [5] Kim *et al.* projected a technique for the crop pest prediction using several machine learning algorithms such as Multiple Linear Regression, SVM (Support Vector Machine), Neural Network and Bayesian Network–based technique. These techniques of prediction can help farmers in various activities of agriculture.

In [6], Torres *et al.* proposed a technique for analyzing rainfall effects on agricultural income in some of the agricultural fields in Brazil. This is done with the help of the method called the novel hydro economic model. This system clearly presents the relation between water scarcity and agricultural income. In [7], Jiangtao *et al.* projected a technique for the prediction of rice transplanter using the technique called the independence method for modal analysis. With the help of this system the service life was also found out. In [8], Schwalbert *et al.* came up with a solution for the soybean yield forecast in the soybean fields located in Brazil. Machine learning algorithms such as random forest, LSTM neural networks and multivariate OLS linear regression are used for forecasting purposes. With the help of this system, a consistent in-season soybean yield prediction is done.

9.4 Prediction in Healthcare

Machine learning prediction methods are greatly helpful in healthcare in order to predict the diseases that could come in the future and take effective measures to prevent them. In [9], Anand *et al.* came up with a technique for the Prediction of Diabetes which is done using the machine learning algorithm called the CART (Classification and Regression Trees). It was found that this system has come up with 75% accuracy, for a highly categorical dataset. The major defect in this system is that the number of responses collected was less. In [10], Chiang *et al.* came up with an idea for predicting blood pressure using a method called the proposed RF with Feature Selection (RFFS). This system contains only a small prediction error. The only drawback is that this system is too robust for different individuals under some conditions.

In [11], Dinesh *et al.* projected a procedure for the Prediction of Cardiovascular Disease using the machine learning algorithms such as Naive Bayes classifier, Support Vector Machine, random forest, logistic regression and Gradient Boosting. Logistic regression gives the highest accuracy of 91.6%. But better performance can be done with more parameters. In [12], Kaushik *et al.* forecasted age and gender based on Deep BLSTM-LSTM network. This method is giving an accuracy of 93.7% and 97.5%. The major drawback is that this prediction is done only for a particular age group. In [13], Akutekwe *et al.* projected a technique for the Diagnosis of Hepatocellular Carcinoma using the machine learning algorithms such as Dynamic Bayesian Network (DBN) and Support Vector Machine. The accuracy was found to be 100%. But the problem is that the authors used publically available data.

In [14], Mir *et al.* projected a technique to predict Diabetes Disease using several deep learning techniques such as random forest, Naive Bayes, Support Vector Machine, and Simple CART algorithm. Out of all these algorithms, it was found that Support Vector Machine achieved best in forecast of the disease. In [15], Patil *et al.* came up with an idea for the Lifestyle disease prediction using the machine learning algorithm called the support vector machine. This is low-cost technique to detect feasible genetic disorders. This will greatly help in the detection of such diseases at an early stage and can thus lead to effective measures. In [16], Chen *et al.* came up with a method for the forecast of Exudation Failure which is done using the machine learning technique called the Light Gradient Boosting Machine (LightGBM). This system applied some other machine learning techniques such as LR, XGboost, ANN, and SVM.

9.5   Prediction in Economics

The economy plays a vital role in all countries. To analyze the various economic risks, different researchers used many MI-based prediction algorithms. A brief study of prediction in economics is given here. In [17], Barboza *et al.* proposed a technique for bankruptcy prediction in North America. In order to predict this, they used several machine learning techniques such as bagging, SVM, random forest and bagging. After several analyses they have found that random forest gives the highest accuracy of 87%. In [18] Ting-HsuanChen proposed a method for the bank risk prediction using the machine learning techniques such as logistical regression, decision trees, and random forests. This system was implemented in one of the banks located in Taiwan. The biggest disadvantage of this system is that only one bank dataset was used for the prediction.

In [19], Werawithayas *et al.* came up with a technique for Stock Market Price forecast using several machine learning algorithms such as Support Vector Machine model, Multi-Layer Perceptron model, and Partial Least Square Classifier. This system has been implemented in Stock Exchange of Thailand (SET). Partial Least Square is the finest technique for this prediction of stock closing price. In [20], Chandrasekara *et al.* utilized using several machine learning methods such as multi-class under sampling based bagging (MCUB) and Probabilistic neural network (PNN) for the Prediction of a Stock Market Index. This system applied the standard PNN model. In [21] Xiao *et al.* projected a technique for Stock price forecast using various machine learning techniques such as least squares support vector machine synthesis model (ARI-MA-LS-SVM), Support Vector Machine (SVM). This system gives better prediction when compared to the older ones. In [22], Jiang *et al.* came up with an idea for stock index prediction using several machine learning algorithms such as extremely randomized trees (ERT), random forest (RF), light gradient boosting machine (LightGBM), extreme gradient boosting (XGBoost) and recurrent neural networks (RNN), RNN with long short-term memory (LSTM), bidirectional RNN, gated recurrent unit (GRU) layer.

9.6   Prediction in Mammals

We depend on other living beings for our daily needs. The growth and the diseases in these living beings can also be predicted using this machine learning algorithm. In [23], Shahinfar *et al.* projected a technique to predict wool growth and quality in sheep using the machine learning algorithms such as Bagging, Model Tree (MT) and Artificial Neural Networks (NN). This has been implemented in University of New England, Australia. It has been found that MT works best among all the tested algorithms. In [24], Gorczyca *et al.* applied the machine learning technique such as gradient boosted machine, deep neural networks, random forest and generalized linear regression to predict skin, core and temperatures of piglets. Out of all these algorithms deep neural networks gives the highest accuracy.

In [25], Gorczyca *et al.* utilized the machine learning algorithms such as gradient boosted machines, random forests, penalized linear regression and neural networks to dairy cows' behavior. In [26], Chen *et al.* applied machine learning algorithms such as XGBoost, random forest, Support Vector Machine, Quadratic Discriminate Analysis, linear discriminate and Long Short-Term Memory analysis to predict the Bitcoin price. This system predicts with an accuracy of 67.2%.

9.7   Prediction in Weather

The weather plays a major role in many sectors like agriculture, wind power generation, etc. Machine learning techniques can be applied to forecast the various weather conditions. In [27], Richman *et al.* came up with an idea for drought prediction in Cape Town so that it would be more helpful for the people living there. They have used a machine learning technique named SVR (Support vector regression). They have implemented this in Cape Town to predict drought. In [28], Feng *et al.* applied the machine learning algorithms such as wavelet neural network, hybrid mind evolutionary algorithm, original artificial neural network, artificial neural network model, and random forests to predict daily solar radiation prediction. They have implemented this method in China and it helps in managing solar energy solar energy systems.

In [29], Achour *et al.* came up with a technique to predict the accuracy of landslide vulnerability in Algeria. This method is implemented using several machine learning techniques such as random forest, boosted regression tree, and support vector. After several analyses it has been found that the RF model gives the maximum accuracy. In [30], Pham *et al.* provided a solution for the daily rainfall prediction in Vietnam. Several machine learning algorithms such as Artificial Neural Networks (ANN), Particle Swarm Optimization (PSOANFIS), Support Vector Machines (SVM) are used in this technique and it has been found that SVM gave the most accurate value. In [31], Demolli *et al.* projected a technique to predict wind power based on various factors using Support Vector Machines, random forest, Deep learning architectures of long short-term memory networks.

9.8   Discussion

As discussed earlier, machine learning techniques have been applied in many areas for prediction purposes and this has been greatly helpful for the people involved in the respective fields. After several analyses we have found that although these prediction mechanisms have several advantages over the traditional method there are some disadvantages. Some of the prediction methodologies give less accuracy, due to various reasons such as less data sets used in the prediction process, not implemented in real time, utilization of limited parameters, etc. To improve the effectiveness and accuracy of the prediction we have proposed a framework with some more added features. With the help of this proposed framework the accuracy of the prediction can be improved. This will be highly beneficial to the people who are involved in a particular event which is predicted.

9.9   Proposed Framework

As mentioned in Section 8.8, the existing prediction system has lot of disadvantages. To overcome these disadvantages, we have proposed the following framework for prediction. Various blocks of the proposed system are shown in Figure 9.2.

9.9.1   Problem Analysis

This is the first step in the proposed method. In order to provide a solution to a particular problem, the problem must be understood clearly. To understand the problem clearly, the required study should be carried out in the respective field [1].

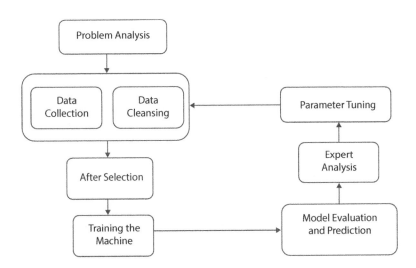

Figure 9.2 Framework architecture.

9.9.2   Preprocessing

The pre-processing includes the following two steps:

- Data collection
- Data cleansing

    Data collection: After understanding the problem, required data need to be collected. To get the accurate result in prediction, a vast dataset is required. The prediction accuracy mainly depends on the amount of data set which is applied in prediction algorithms. So, a vast amount of data needs to be collected before starting the prediction process [1].

    Data cleansing: The collected data cannot be directly used to train the machine. Analyze the collected data and make the required modification so that it can be fed into the machine for further process [2].

9.9.3   Algorithm Selection

Another vital parameter which affects the prediction result is prediction algorithm. The researcher must choose appropriate algorithm before starting the process [7]. The researchers can use multiple prediction algorithms (or) prediction models to get an accurate result.

9.9.4   Training the Machine

Once the data is collected and the required algorithms are chosen, the system should be trained in order to provide the correct results [8].

9.9.5   Model Evaluation and Prediction

To estimate the attainment of the prediction model, the prediction models (or) algorithms can be executed with several data sets. This will help us to find the performance of prediction models [12].

9.9.6   Expert Suggestion

When the system is trained to predict a particular event, it will give us the predicted value as the output and the accuracy of the system will also be known. To increase the accuracy of the prediction, the obtained results should be discussed with experts. The required expert suggestions need to be added to the obtained results.

9.9.7   Parameter Tuning

Based on the obtained results and expert suggestions, the parameters in the dataset need to be updated. The updated data set need to undergo the same process such as pre-processing, algorithm selection, training the machine and model evaluation.

9.10   Implementation

We developed a web-based system to implement the proposed framework. The proposed system consists of the following three modules.

> ➤ Farmers & Sellers
> ➤ Product
> ➤ Price prediction

9.10.1   Farmers and Sellers

Using this website farmers and sellers can create their own account. They can then log in using their credentials, after which they can add the products available with them and the details like

> ➤ Product name
> ➤ Price
> ➤ Size
> ➤ Minimum quantity
> ➤ Availability

Using these details, the customers can get the products from the farmers as shown in Figure 9.3.

9.10.2   Products

The products that are available with the farmers or the sellers can be uploaded in this website. The product detail section consists of details like

> ➤ Name of the product
> ➤ Size of the product
> ➤ Price of the product

Figure 9.3 Product and former details in web portal.

> ➢ Availability of the product
> ➢ Owner's name
> ➢ Contact details

The web-based user interface is shown in Figure 9.4. The farmers and sellers could enter their details through this web portal. The users are able view the products which are given by farmers and sellers. The users are able to forecast the cost of the product with the help of price predictor module.

9.10.3   Price Prediction

To predict the price of the product we applied the following two machine learning prediction algorithms, namely linear prediction and random forest. To implement this prediction algorithm we used python language. The last five years' data such as product details and price details were used for rate prediction. The results of these prediction algorithm details are given in Figure 9.5 and Figure 9.6. This price prediction helps to identify an increase or decrease in the price of the product. It helps formers and users to predict the price of the products and purchase them accordingly.

Figure 9.4 Web interface of proposed system.

```
[21]: X_train, X_test, y_train, y_test = train_test_split(X, Y, test_size=0.2, random_state=2)
      regressor = LinearRegression()
      regressor.fit(X_train, y_train)

[21]: LinearRegression(copy_X=True, fit_intercept=True, n_jobs=None, normalize=False)

[22]: pred=regressor.predict(X_test)

[23]: print(pred)
      [34.08886719 33.14453125 33.37792969 ... 33.45214844 34.61035156
       45.80566406]
```

Figure 9.5 Price prediction using linear regression.

```
[32]: import matplotlib.pyplot as plt

[42]: from sklearn.ensemble import RandomForestRegressor
      regressor = RandomForestRegressor(n_estimators = 100, random_state = 0)
      reg1 = regressor.fit(X,Y)
      print(reg1)

      RandomForestRegressor(bootstrap=True, criterion='mse', max_depth=None,
                            max_features='auto', max_leaf_nodes=None,
                            min_impurity_decrease=0.0, min_impurity_split=None,
                            min_samples_leaf=1, min_samples_split=2,
                            min_weight_fraction_leaf=0.0, n_estimators=100,
                            n_jobs=None, oob_score=False, random_state=0, verbose=0,
                            warm_start=False)

[43]: reg2 = regressor.predict(X)

[44]: print(reg2)
      [32.49250343 47.05168272 47.05168272 ... 33.03962071 33.03962071
       33.03962071]
```

Figure 9.6 Price prediction using random forest.

9.11   Conclusion

Machine learning prediction is a growing area in the field of computer science. Such predictions are used in almost all sectors to predict future events. As we are developing day by day, we need to improve this prediction process in order to make it more effective. The traditional method of prediction is working fine but the problem is that it is unable to provide a high level of accuracy. In order to improve the accuracy, we have come up with the solution. We have proposed a method here with several added features which can be used to increase the accuracy of the prediction process. This will be greatly helpful to people who are looking for the prediction of a particular event.

References

1. Kamir, E., Waldner, F. and Hochman, Z., 2020. Estimating wheat yields in Australia using climate records, satellite image time series and machine learning methods. *ISPRS Journal of Photogrammetry and Remote Sensing, 160,* pp.124-135.
2. Zhang, C., Di, L., Lin, L. and Guo, L., 2019. Machine-learned prediction of annual crop planting in the US Corn Belt based on historical crop planting maps. *Computers and Electronics in Agriculture, 166,* p.104989.
3. Kakhki, F.D., Freeman, S.A. and Mosher, G.A., 2019. Evaluating machine learning performance in predicting injury severity in agribusiness industries. *Safety science, 117,* pp.257-262.
4. Khanal, S., Fulton, J., Klopfenstein, A., Douridas, N. and Shearer, S., 2018. Integration of high resolution remotely sensed data and machine learning techniques for spatial prediction of soil properties and corn yield. *Computers and electronics in agriculture, 153,* pp.213-225.
5. Kim, Y.H., Yoo, S.J., Gu, Y., Lim, J., Han, D. and Baik, S., 2014. Crop pest prediction method using regression and machine learning technology: Survey. *IERI Procedia, 6,* pp.52-56.
6. Torres, M., Howitt, R. and Rodrigues, L., 2019. Analyzing rainfall effects on agricultural income: Why timing matters. *EconomiA, 20*(1), pp.1-14
7. Jiangtao, J., Kaikang, C., Xin, J., Zhaoyang, W., Baoqiong, D., Jingyuan, F. and Xiaojun, L., 2020. High-efficiency modal analysis and deformation prediction of rice transplanter based on effective independent method. *Computers and Electronics in Agriculture, 168,* p.105126.
8. Schwalbert, R.A., Amado, T., Corassa, G., Pott, L.P., Prasad, P.V. and Ciampitti, I.A., 2020. Satellite-based soybean yield forecast: Integrating machine learning and weather data for improving crop yield prediction in southern Brazil. *Agricultural and Forest Meteorology, 284,* p.107886

9. Anand, A. and Shakti, D., 2015, September. Prediction of diabetes based on personal lifestyle indicators. In *2015 1st International Conference on Next Generation Computing Technologies (NGCT)* (pp. 673-676). IEEE.

10. Chiang, P.H. and Dey, S., 2018, September. Personalized effect of health behavior on blood pressure: machine learning based prediction and recommendation. In *2018 IEEE 20th International Conference on e-Health Networking, Applications and Services (Healthcom)* (pp. 1-6). IEEE.

11. Dinesh, K.G., Arumugaraj, K., Santhosh, K.D. and Mareeswari, V., 2018, March. Prediction of cardiovascular disease using machine learning algorithms. In *2018 International Conference on Current Trends towards Converging Technologies (ICCTCT)* (pp. 1-7). IEEE.

12. Kaushik, P., Gupta, A., Roy, P.P. and Dogra, D.P., 2018. Eeg-based age and gender prediction using deep blstm-lstm network model. *IEEE Sensors Journal*, 19(7), pp.2634-2641.

13. Akutekwe, A., Seker, H. and Iliya, S., 2014, October. An optimized hybrid dynamic Bayesian network approach using differential evolution algorithm for the diagnosis of Hepatocellular Carcinoma. In *2014 IEEE 6th International Conference on Adaptive Science & Technology (ICAST)* (pp. 1-6). IEEE.

14. Mir, A. and Dhage, S.N., 2018, August. Diabetes Disease Prediction Using Machine Learning on Big Data of Healthcare. In *2018 Fourth International Conference on Computing Communication Control and Automation (ICCUBEA)* (pp. 1-6). IEEE.

15. Patil, M., Lobo, V.B., Puranik, P., Pawaskar, A., Pai, A. and Mishra, R., 2018, July. A Proposed Model for Lifestyle Disease Prediction Using Support Vector Machine. In *2018 9th International Conference on Computing, Communication and Networking Technologies (ICCCNT)* (pp. 1-6). IEEE.

16. Chen, T., Xu, J., Ying, H., Chen, X., Feng, R., Fang, X., Gao, H. and Wu, J., 2019. Prediction of Extubation Failure for Intensive Care Unit Patients Using Light Gradient Boosting Machine. *IEEE Access*, 7, pp.150960-150968.

17. Barboza, F., Kimura, H. and Altman, E., 2017. Machine learning models and bankruptcy prediction. *Expert Systems with Applications*, 83, pp. 405-417.

18. Chen, T.H., 2020. Do you know your customer? Bank risk assessment based on machine learning. *Applied Soft Computing*, 86, p.105779.

19. Werawithayaset, P. and Tritilanunt, S., 2019, November. Stock Closing Price Prediction Using Machine Learning. In *2019 17th International Conference on ICT and Knowledge Engineering (ICT&KE)* (pp. 1-8). IEEE.

20. Chandrasekara, V., Tilakaratne, C. and Mammadov, M., 2019. An Improved Probabilistic Neural Network Model for Directional Prediction of a Stock Market Index. *Applied Sciences*, 9(24), p.5334.

21. Xiao, C., Xia, W. and Jiang, J., 2020. Stock price forecast based on combined model of ARI-MA-LS-SVM. *Neural Computing and Applications*, pp.1-10.

22. Jiang, M., Liu, J., Zhang, L. and Liu, C., 2020. An improved Stacking framework for stock index prediction by leveraging tree-based ensemble

models and deep learning algorithms. *Physica A: Statistical Mechanics and its Applications, 541,* p.122272.

23. Shahinfar, S. and Kahn, L., 2018. Machine learning approaches for early prediction of adult wool growth and quality in Australian Merino sheep. *Computers and Electronics in Agriculture, 148,* pp.72-81.

24. Gorczyca, M.T., Milan, H.F.M., Maia, A.S.C. and Gebremedhin, K.G., 2018. Machine learning algorithms to predict core, skin, and hair-coat temperatures of piglets. *Computers and Electronics in Agriculture, 151,* pp.286-294.

25. Gorczyca, M.T. and Gebremedhin, K.G., 2020. Ranking of environmental heat stressors for dairy cows using machine learning algorithms. *Computers and Electronics in Agriculture, 168,* p.105124.

26. Chen, Z., Li, C. and Sun, W., 2020. Bitcoin price prediction using machine learning: An approach to sample dimension engineering. *Journal of Computational and Applied Mathematics, 365,* p.112395.

27. Richman, M.B. and Leslie, L.M., 2018. The 2015-2017 Cape Town Drought: Attribution and Prediction Using Machine Learning. *Procedia Computer Science, 140,* pp.248-257.

28. Feng, Y., Gong, D., Zhang, Q., Jiang, S., Zhao, L. and Cui, N., 2019. Evaluation of temperature-based machine learning and empirical models for predicting daily global solar radiation. *Energy Conversion and Management, 198,* p.111780.

29. Achour, Y. and Pourghasemi, H.R., 2019. How do machine learning techniques help in increasing accuracy of landslide susceptibility maps?. *Geoscience Frontiers.*

30. Pham, B.T., Le, L.M., Le, T.T., Bui, K.T.T., Le, V.M., Ly, H.B. and Prakash, I., 2020. Development of advanced artificial intelligence models for daily rainfall prediction. *Atmospheric Research,* p.104845.

31. Demolli, H., Dokuz, A.S., Ecemis, A. and Gokcek, M., 2019. Wind power forecasting based on daily wind speed data using machine learning algorithms. *Energy Conversion and Management, 198,* p.111823.

10

Dog Breed Classification Using CNN

Sandra Varghese* and Remya S

Computer Science and Engineering Department, Saintgits College of Engineering Kottukulam Hills, Pathamuttom, Kottayam, India

Abstract

Dogs are among the foremost common livestock. Due to an outsized number of dogs, there are several issues like social control, decreasing outbreaks like Rabies, vaccination control, and legal ownership. At present, there are over 180 dog breeds. Each dog breed has specific characteristics and health conditions. In order to supply appropriate treatments and training, it is essential to spot individuals and their breeds. This paper presents the classification methods for dogs. It relies on a project that builds a CNN (Convolutional Neural Network) to classify totally different dog breeds. If the image of a dog is found, this algorithm would notice the estimate of the breed. The given system employs innovative strategies in deep learning, also convolutional neural networks and transfer learning. The projected network is prepared to achieve associate accuracy of 93.53% and 90.86%, for two totally different datasets. The result shows that our retrained CNN model performs better in classifying dog breeds.

Keywords: CNN, deep learning, machine learning, artificial neural network, transfer learning

10.1 Introduction

In the US, about 105 million people own one or more dogs, and dog ownership has risen by 29% within the past decade [1]. In Canada, nearly 41% of households have a minimum of one dog [13]. A study conducted by Weiss *et al.* [3], acknowledged that 14% of dogs were lost within the past five

---

Corresponding author: sandra.css1921@saintgits.org

Shibin David, R. S. Anand, V. Jeyakrishnan, and M. Niranjanamurthy (eds.) *Security Issues and Privacy Concerns in Industry 4.0 Applications*, (195–206) © 2021 Scrivener Publishing LLC

years within the US while 7% of them never returned to their owners. The normal means to spot and locate lost dogs are ID collar, microchip, tattooing and GPS tag [15]. The primary three methods include the knowledge of the dog's name and owner's telephone number which can be helpful when shelters find the lost dogs. GPS tags enable owners to locate their lost dogs directly. Nevertheless, the semi-permanent methods like GPS tag and ID collar are susceptible to being lost or damaged. Meanwhile, the permanent means like microchip and tattooing are not prevalent due to their expensive prices [15]. In rural or remote areas of the northern part of Canada, there is less familiarity with tattoos or dog tags, therefore making it difficult to use the identity of the dog to establish ownership. For veterinarians, this presents an obstacle in retrieving the dog's medical records and, accordingly, prevents adequate healthcare. The concept of e-health for animals is among the main driving forces for promoting the creation of electronic medical records for pets [5]. For every record, a photograph of the pet is taken and may be used to verify/identify the identity of every individual pet using image processing techniques. For instance, an individual who has found a dog in a remote area can take its photo employing a multimedia device and send it to a regional veterinary database for identification. Photos of a dog's head or face are often enough to identify that dog, which is analogous to identifying an individual using the person's face. This is often a fine-grained classification which refers to classifying objects sharing similar visual features and belonging to an equivalent basic-level class [16]. Dog owners or veterinarians are more likely to require various pictures of dogs and store these image data for further use like helping to find lost dogs. There also are many apps available within the Google Play Store to seek out lost dogs. As an example, "Pets finder" only requires a report including the situation and an image of the lost or found pet; the report is uploaded to the cloud database where owners can look for their lost pets among all the pet listings within the vicinity. Multimedia image processing and recognition are often applied to not only identify the dog's face but also breed, height and other soft biometric attributes. During this study, we investigate this approach, specifically, how classifying the breed helps improve dog identification by appearance (face). We apply contemporary machine learning like deep neural networks, also the technique called transfer learning [17] which uses information developed for one task (breed identification) to affect another task (dog face identification).

10.2   Related Work

A substantial amount of research has gone into fine-grained classification problems, the bulk of which has focused on increasing the performance or accuracy of the classification by various approaches. Of these works, some have approached the problem similar to [2], where image processing is employed at the beginning of the process [2]. The provided annotations of the Stanford Dogs dataset, which had locations of bounding boxes that outlined the useful information of each image, was used. Specifically, this meant that the information pertaining to the dog could be found inside these boxes. Using this, the images were all cropped to the bounding boxes, and [2] removed any resulting images smaller than 256X256.

Once this image pre-processing was completed, [2] used LeNet and GoogLeNet architectures. However, [2] noted that transfer learning was not used [3]. Researched fine-grained classification of dog breeds using part localization. The method of [3] employed a number of computer vision topics, focusing on the use of dog faces to improve accuracy in classifying the various breeds. [3] found improved performance through the use of their method; however, this method requires a good number of steps and [4] aimed to reduce the complexity of this sort of approach [4]. Used the Grassmann manifold to represent the geometry of dog breeds. Specifically, [4] focused on the geometry of dog faces and found that their method performed on par with other, more complex, approaches.

The main takeaway here is that the goal of all these works was to enhance performance on a fine-grained classification problem. This is an important issue, as discussed in [2], [3], and [4] as it poses a number of problems. Each related work discussed here approaches the problem in a slightly different way; however, the main ideas behind their approaches are all the same. Each work focused on reducing the amount of information analysed, hoping to reduce the amount to just what is important. Focusing on just what's expected provides useful information in classifying dog breeds. However, we have elected to go a different direction with our research. We have decided not to look into a way for optimizing the networks used, instead, we will be investigating what networks find important in classifying the breeds in the Stanford Dogs Dataset.

To examine the performance of recognizing different dog breeds using assorted images, Khosla *et al.* created a dataset of various dog breeds called Stanford Dogs Dataset [7]. Using Stanford Dogs Dataset, Sermanet *et al.* proposed the use of an attention-based model for breed classification

which achieved an accuracy of 76.80% [8]. Another model using depth-wise separable convolutions was proposed in [9] and yielded 83.30% accuracy. Similarly, another dataset, Columbia Dogs Dataset, containing images of different dog breeds, was created by Liu *et al.* [10]. In [10], a breed classification rate of 67.00% can be achieved by using a combination of grey-scale SIFT descriptors and colour histogram features to train an SVM. Furthermore, [11] uses the labelled landmark metadata to improve the accuracy to 96.50% by incorporating Grassmann manifold to help distinguish the different dog breeds using their face geometries. Pet breed classification using both shape and texture was proposed in [12]. A deformable part model was used in [12] to detect the shape and a bag-of-words model to capture the appearance.

For a dataset that includes 37 breeds of cats and dogs, an accuracy of 69.00% was reported. Paper [13] was one of the first to describe dog face identification. It used Fisher Linear Projection and Preservation with One-Shot Similarity for matching and reported 96.87% rank 4 accuracy. The reported dataset is not publicly available, thus making it difficult to perform a proper comparison. Another research [14] was conducted in 2016 aiming at cat face identification by exploiting visual information of cat noses. They designed a representative dictionary with data locality constraint based on a dataset containing 700 cat nose images from 70 cats. This method reached an accuracy of 91.20%. Moreira *et al.* evaluate the viability of using existing human face recognition methods (Eigen Faces, Fisher Faces, LBPH, and a Sparse method) as well as deep learning techniques such as Convolutional Neural Networks (BARK and WOOF) for dog recognition [15]. Using a dataset of two different breeds of dogs, huskies and pugs, Moreira *et al.* show that based on using the WOOF model, an accuracy of 75.14% and 54.38% is obtained for huskies and pugs, respectively.

10.3   Methodology

Even though lot of algorithms are suggests, there are still some problems which make it challenging to realize a satisfying accuracy. We have implemented a CNN model to reinforce the accuracy of dog breed classification [19]. Steps taken in our experiment are,

Step 1: Import Datasets
Step 2: Detect Dogs
Step 3: Create a CNN to Classify Dog Breeds
Step 4: Train a CNN to Classify Dog Breeds (from scratch)
Step 5: Train a CNN to Classify Dog Breeds (via transfer learning)

Step 1: Import Datasets

Our initiative involves loading the datasets that are divided into train, validation and test folders. We would wish to classify dogs into 133 different breeds that are found in our training dataset. We will be using 6,680 dog images to show the models that we will be using. We will be using 835 validation images to fine-tune our parameters, and testing the last word model's accuracy on 836 test images. The test dataset contains images which the model has not seen before.

The datasets contains.

- *Dog Images* - the dog images given are available within the repository within the pictures directory further organized into the train, valid and test subfolders
- *Haarcascades* - ML-based method where a cascade function is trained from tons of positive and negative images, and will detect objects in other images. Therefore the expectation is that a picture with the frontal features clearly defined is required.
- *Test Images* - a folder with certain test images is added to be ready to check the effectiveness of the algorithm
- Pre-computed features for networks currently available in Keras (i.e., VGG19, InceptionV3, and Xception) made available from S3
- Any other downloads to make sure of the graceful running of the notebook are available within the repository. As the next step load the libraries.
- The libraries required are often categorized as follows:
- *Utility libraries* - random (for random seeding), time it (to calculate execution time), os, pathlib, glob (for folder and path operations), tqdm (for execution progress), sklearn (for loading datasets), requests and io (load files from the web)
- *Image processing* - OpenCV (cv2), PIL • Keras and Fastai for creating CNN • Matplotlib for viewing plots/images and Numpy for tensor processing [18].

Step 2: Detect Dogs

Here we use resnet50 pre-trained model in Keras to detect dogs in images. The primary step here is to convert RGB coding of .jpg images into BGR then normalize the three channels supported mean and variance obtained from the large ImageNet database [20]. Luckily, this is often done by the preprocess_input within the applications.resnet50 module in Keras.

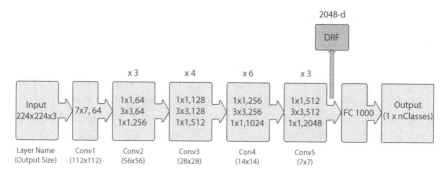

Fig. 10.1 resnet50 model architecture.

Using the resnet50 model we imported from keras.applications library, we will classify the pictures into labels. Within the resnet library any label coded as from 151 to 268 is in effect a "dog". Fig. 10.1 shows the resnet50 model architecture [6]. The function below will give us a real Boolean value if this is the case and False otherwise.

Step 3: Create a CNN to classify dog breeds

We will be using below the bottom Sequential model and designing our CNN networks. We have even used three Convolutional Layers, each followed by a MaxPooling2D to reduce complexity of the stacked model. At the end, we will be using global_average_pooling to convert each feature map within the Max Pooling Layer into a scalar [21]. Fig. 10.2 shows the CNN model architecture.

Step 4: Train a CNN to classify dog breeds (from scratch)

We start training the model we created, and we see that our validation loss constantly lowers, which our accuracy lowers for five epochs, signalling

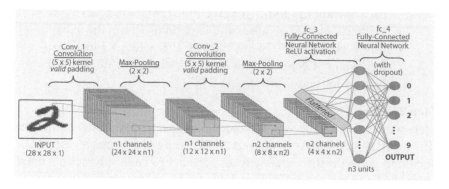

Fig. 10.2 CNN model architecture.

our model is learning. At 20 epochs, it is possible to reach around 4.5% accuracy. Once we run 250 epochs on this dataset, we are ready to reach 40+% accuracy, which does take quite a while even with strong GPU support, which is why we will be using transfer learning as a next step [24].

Step 5: Train a CNN to classify dog breeds (via transfer learning)
Next, we will be using pre-extracted "bottleneck features" which are an output of a pertained library applied on our train, test and validation datasets [22].

We will be using resnet50 library output as an input to our model and train our model using these bottleneck features. We make an easy model by adding a worldwide Average Pooling layer that summarizes each of the previous feature maps into a scalar. The dense layer creates 133 different outputs, one for every needed label. Then, a softmax activation converts each of those into a probability [23].

We then test our algorithm live to ascertain whether it correctly predicts the breed of the dog within the loaded image path [25]. We get a Welsh springer spaniel image loaded into the model, and the neural network correctly classifies the sample dog image that we used [26].

10.4 Results and Discussions

10.4.1 Training

At 20 epochs, it is possible to reach around 4.5% accuracy. Once we run 250 epochs on this dataset, we are ready to reach 40%+ accuracy, which does take quite a while even with strong GPU support, which is why we'll be using transfer learning as a next step.

We are ready to achieve a training accuracy of 93.53% and a validation accuracy of 90.89% using CNN algorithm. Our algorithm is additionally performing excellently on the unseen testing image dataset from Kaggle. (However, thanks to the rationale that labels are not provided for the test assail Kaggle, we are not ready to check the general test accuracy.) The ultimate results seem pretty accurate; we will see that the dog breed prediction for dogs are all correct.

10.4.2 Testing

For 20 epoch, model evaluates a test accuracy of 90.86%. The training accuracy 93.53% is close enough to the test accuracy. Therefore the model can classify images correctly.

Transfer learning works far better than the CNN model. This is mainly because the model from transfer learning is trained by an outsized amount of knowledge, therefore the architecture already understood what features are most representative for an image. This makes the classification process far easier, and we do not have to sacrifice accuracy, albeit we do not have an outsized amount of knowledge. Dog Breed Classification using CNN model was achieved using Keras Library. The model used 20 epoch, i.e., all training dataset skilled aerial and back propagation through the neural network 10 times.

Fig. 10.3 plots the model accuracy and epoch. It is evident that model accuracy increases with the increase in epoch, i.e., here model accuracy is directly proportional to the epoch. Fig. 10.4 depicts the Model loss vs. epoch.

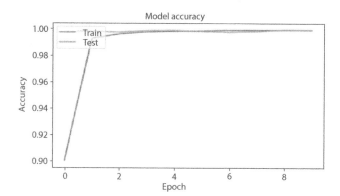

Fig. 10.3 Model accuracy vs. epoch.

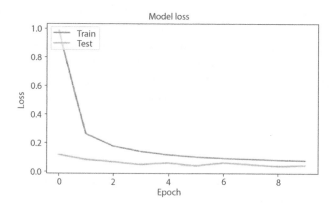

Fig. 10.4 Model loss vs. epoch.

10.5   Conclusions

End-to-end problem solution: this paper offered an answer which may take the image in and then return the breed of the dog. The most interesting aspect of this project is that the magic of transfer learning enables us to produce a better result, albeit we do not have enough data, but still we will train the pre-trained model for our purpose; this is often the most beautiful thing about transfer learning. The convolutional neural networks are often further developed by the following: Generative Adversarial Nets (GAN) [27] to increase the training dataset, using other loss function like centre loss [28], training other convolutional neural network architectures, expanding the dataset with other popular dog breeds, using detectors for locating multiple dogs on a picture and optimizing the server and mobile classification.

The possible improvements on this algorithm might be to urge more data to coach the dog breed classification model. An attempt could be made to tune the model more by using different transfer learning models, and to add more layers to the prevailing architecture. Accuracy is often further enhanced by data augmentation. Data augmentation enables the network to differentiate the features regardless of the orientation and scale. Clearly, building a convolutional neural network using transfer learning yielded much better accuracy than building it from scratch.

There are a couple of breeds that are virtually identical and are sub-breeds. There is also an opportunity of some images being either blurred or having an excessive amount of noise. There is also an opportunity of enhancing the standard by additional image manipulation.

Following the above areas, we could increase the testing accuracy of the model. A simple web application in Flask might be built to leverage the model to predict breeds through user-input images.

References

1. Krizhevsky, Alex, IlyaSutskever, and Geoffrey E. Hinton. "Imagenet classification with deep convolutional neural networks." In *Advances in neural information processing systems*, pp. 1097-1105. 2012.
2. "Latest Canadian pet population figures released," *Tech. Rep.*, 2017.
3. E. Weiss, M. Slater, and L. Lord, "Frequency of lost dogs and cats in the united states and the methods used to locate them," *Animals,* vol. 2, no. 2, pp. 301–315, 2012.
4. S. Kumar and S. K. Singh, "Biometric recognition for pet animal," *Journal of Software Engineering and Applications*, vol. 7, no. 5, pp. 470–482, 2014.

5. B. Yao, G. Bradski, and L. Fei-Fei, "A codebook-free and annotation free approach for fine-grained image categorization," in *IEEE Conference on Computer Vision and Pattern Recognition*, 2012, pp. 3466–3473.
6. L. Torrey and J. Shavlik, "Transfer learning," in *Handbook of Research on Machine Learning Applications and Trends: Algorithms, Methods, and Techniques*, 2010, pp. 242–264.
7. D. Hsu, "Using convolutional neural networks to classify dog breeds," CS231n: Convolutional Neural Networks for Visual Recognition [course webpage]. 2015. [Online]. Available: http://cs231n.stanford.edu/reports/2015/pdfs/fcdh_FinalReport.pdf.
8. J. Liu, A. Kanazawa, D. Jacobs, and P. Belhumeur, "Dog breed classification using part localization," in *Proc. European Conference on Computer Vision [ECCV]*, 2012, pp. 172-185.
9. X. Wang, V. Ly, S. Sorensen, and C. Kambhamettu, "Dog breed classification via landmarks," In *Proc. 2014 IEEE International Conference on Image Processing*, 2015, pp. 5237–5241.
10. Liu, Jiongxin, Angjoo Kanazawa, David Jacobs, and Peter Belhumeur. "Dog breed classification using part localization." In *European conference on computer vision*, pp. 172-185. Springer, Berlin, Heidelberg, 2012.
11. Zeng, Yujun, XinXu, Yuqiang Fang, and Kun Zhao. "Traffic sign recognition using extreme learning classifier with deep convolutional features." In *The 2015 international conference on intelligence science and big data engineering (IScIDE 2015)*, Suzhou, China, vol. 9242, pp. 272-280. 2015.
12. Saravanan, C. "Color image to grayscale image conversion." In *2010 Second International Conference on Computer Engineering and Applications*, vol. 2, pp. 196199. IEEE, 2010.*FLEXChip Signal Processor (MC68175/D)*, Motorola, 1996.
13. Wang, Yu, Qian Chen, and Baeomin Zhang. "Image enhancement based on equal area dualistic sub-image histogram equalization method." *IEEE Transactions on Consumer Electronics* 45, no. 1 (1999): 68-75.
14. Najafabadi, Maryam M., FlavioVillanustre, Taghi M. Khoshgoftaar, NaeemSeliya, Randall Wald, and EdinMuharemagic. "Deep learning applications and challenges in big data analytics." *Journal of Big Data* 2, no. 1 (2015): 1.
15. Gulli, Antonio, and Sujit Pal. *Deep learning with Keras*. Packt Publishing Ltd, 2017.
16. Géron, Aurélien. *Hands-On Machine Learning with Scikit-Learn, Keras, and TensorFlow: Concepts, Tools, and Techniques to Build Intelligent Systems*. O'Reilly Media, 2019.
17. "Pet population and ownership trends in the U.S.: Dogs, cats, and other pets, 2nd edition," Tech. Rep., 2017.
18. A. Khosla, N. Jayadevaprakash, B. Yao, and F.-F. Li, "Novel dataset for fine-grained image categorization: Stanford dogs," in *First Workshop on Fine-Grained Visual Categorization, IEEE Conference on Computer Vision and Pattern Recognition*, vol. 2, 2011, pp. 1–2.

19. P. Sermanet, A. Frome, and E. Real, "Attention for fine-grained categorization," *International Conference on Learning Representation*, pp. 1–11, 2015.
20. A. G. Howard, M. Zhu, B. Chen, D. Kalenichenko, W. Wang,T. Weyand, M. Andreetto, and H. Adam, "Mobilenets: Efficient convolutional neural networks for mobile vision applications," arXiv preprint arXiv:1704.04861, 2017.
21. J. Liu, A. Kanazawa, D. Jacobs, and P. Belhumeur, "Dog breed classification using part localization," in *European Conference on Computer Vision*, 2012, pp. 172–185.
22. X. Wang, V. Ly, S. Sorensen, and C. Kambhamettu, "Dog breed classification via landmarks," in *IEEE International Conference on Image Processing*, 2014, pp. 5237–5241.
23. Y.-C. Chen, S. C. Hidayati, W.-H. Cheng, M.-C. Hu, and K.-L. Hua, Locality constrained sparse representation for cat recognition," in *International Conference on Multimedia Modeling*, 2016, pp. 140–151.
24. T. P. Moreira, M. L. Perez, R. de Oliveira Werneck, and E. Valle, "Where is my puppy? retrieving lost dogs by facial features," *Multimedia Tools and Applications*, vol. 76, no. 14, pp. 15325–15340, 2017.
25. S. Ren, K. He, R. Girshick, and J. Sun, "Faster r-cnn: Towards realtime object detection with region proposal networks," in *Advances in Neural Information Processing Systems*, 2015, pp. 91–99.
26. K. Simonyan and A. Zisserman, "Very deep convolutional networks for large-scale image recognition," *International Conference on Learning Representation*, pp. 1–14, 2015.
27. I. Goodfellow, J. Pouget-Abadie, M. Mirza, B. Xu, D. Warde-Farley, S. Ozair, A. Courville, and Y. Bengio, "Generative adversarial nets," in *Advances in neural information processing systems*, 2014, pp. 2672–2680.
28. Y. Wen, K. Zhang, Z. Li, and Y. Qiao, "A discriminative feature learning approach for deep face recognition," in *European Conference on Computer Vision*. Springer, 2016, pp. 499–515.

11

Methodology for Load Balancing in Multi-Agent System Using SPE Approach

S. Ajitha

Ramaiah Institute of Technology, Bangalore, India

Abstract

In today's scenario a large number of applications are built using Multi-Agent System. The Multi-Agent System (MAS) is a system composed of the coalition and the interaction of several agents distributed in various environments. Thus, there exists the problem of load imbalance between the agents in the system. The load imbalance will result in poor performance of the system. The agents in MAS utilize the system resources such as CPU capacity, memory and communication bandwidth. The agents of the system span the entire machine and so agents do have variable workload patterns depending on the communication among agents. Due to this, some of the agents have more workload while others have less workload. So if the load can be distributed among the agents in such a way that no agent is idle or no agent is overloaded then we can obtain a better performance. In this chapter, we developed an algorithm for load balancing that addresses the load imbalance among agents in MAS using Software Performance Engineering (SPE) approach. The algorithm is implemented using JADE [1] and NetLogo [2]. The results are validated and discussed.

Keywords: Multi-Agent System, Software Performance Engineering, load balancing, JADE, NetLogo

11.1 Introduction

Multi-Agent System is a relatively new paradigm in the field of computer science. This paradigm proposes solutions to highly distributed problems

Email: ajithasankar@gmail.com

Shibin David, R. S. Anand, V. Jeyakrishnan, and M. Niranjanamurthy (eds.) Security Issues and Privacy Concerns in Industry 4.0 Applications, (207–228) © 2021 Scrivener Publishing LLC

in dynamic, open computational domains. Research on multi-agent systems has been mainly concerned with functional properties such as coordination, rationality, and knowledge modeling. Much less attention is paid to research activity on the nonfunctional properties such as performance, scalability and reliability of the MAS. However, as the MAS technologies have gradually matured to be exploited in building practical distributed applications, the non-functional properties of the MAS have become increasingly important, and it is now vital to pay attention to the issues of the non-functional characteristics of agents. The concepts and different applications of MAS are discussed by the authors in [3, 4]. Software Performance Engineering (SPE) is a method for constructing software systems to meet the performance objectives at the early stages of Software Development Life Cycle (SDLC). In SPE, a system does not exist so it is not possible to develop the workload parameters from measurement data. Therefore, models of the system are used to collect the data required to predict the performance. The different data required for the SPE approach are workload scenarios, Performance goals, Software Design concepts, Execution environment and Resource usage estimates. In this chapter we have proposed a methodology to predict the load balancing in MAS by adopting the SPE approach.

11.2   Methodology for Load Balancing

Load balancing is an important factor in predicting the performance of any system. The performance evaluation of the MAS is discussed in [5–7]. Efficient management of load among the agents in MAS requires several mechanisms that decide on the selection policy and location policy. The selection policy deals with which task is redirected whenever there is a need, while the location policy determines to which destination agent the selected task is redirected. If the selection policy is formulated carefully, the desirable effects are that the task selected to redirect will not make the overall situation worse by making the destination more overloaded than the source, and the cost of the redirection will be compensated by the gain in performance. Likewise, the location policy also has to be properly planned; the overall system workload will be more averaged after the redirection of the task. Keeping in view this discussion, we developed an algorithm to determine the load of each agent in the MAS and balance the load among the agents. For the purpose of understanding the scenarios of MAS, we have exploited the features of UML to model the system using UML. A numerical value, called priority, is assigned to every task. If the priority of the task is higher, then that task needs to be executed first, so depending on the load of the agent that task will be redirected to the agent with the lighter workload. The load of the agent is calculated by considering the communication workload and computational workload. Since we are predicting the load of each agent before implementing the software, it can be either in the feasibility study or during the design stage. The communication between the agents in the system for the simulation is represented using appropriate probability distribution. The formula used for the computational load and the communication load is presented below.

$$\textit{Communication load}\ (\lambda) = \sum_{i=1}^{p} (K_i * T_i) \qquad (11.1)$$

where p is the total number of messages, K_i is message size and T_i is the transfer time

$$\textit{Computational Load}\ (\mu) = \sum_{n=1}^{l} \sum_{m=1}^{s} CT \qquad (11.2)$$

where CT is CPU time of operation, l is the size of requests in agent and s is the number of operations requested.

The proposed algorithm for predicting and balancing the load among the agents is presented below.

Algorithm for Load Balancing in MAS using SPE approach

---

1. *Consider the architecture of MAS under study.*
2. *Develop the use case diagram of MAS.*
3. *Develop the sequence diagrams.*
4. *Develop the deployment diagram.*
5. *Compute the Load of each agent*
6.
   6.1 *Compute the communication load of the request by agent using probability distribution or Sequence diagram.*

   $$\textit{Communication load}\ (\lambda) = \sum_{i=1}^{p} (K_i * T_i)$$

   Where p is the total number of messages, K_i is message size and T_i is the transfer time

---

6.2   *Compute computational load of the messages by considering the CPU speed, processing time and number of messages in the queue.*

$$\text{Computational Load } (\mu) = \sum_{n=1}^{l} \sum_{m=1}^{s} \text{CT}$$

Where CT is CPU time of operation, l is the size of requests in agent and s is the number of operations requested

6.3   *Load of Agent = $\lambda + \mu$*

7. *Analyze the queue of requests at Agent and assign priority to the request (a selection of which request to consider for redirection).*

8. *Subject to the priority of the request and the load of the agent the request will be directed to the agent with lower load.*

The architecture of the system is an important parameter when we are assessing the load. There are different architectures available in the literature for Multi-Agent System; for our discussion, we have considered the architecture as RETSINA [8] as presented in Figure 11.1. This architecture consists of three types of agents, namely Interface Agent, Work Agent and Information Agent. An Interface Agent interacts with the user for their specifications and delivering results to the users. A Work Agent formulates the plan and carries out the specified work with the help of other work agents and information agents. The Information agents collect the information needed for the work agents from different information sources.

Figure 11.2 represents the dynamic nature of the agent in MAS. Here we used two different colored agents to represent the nature of the agent. The green color indicates that the agent is lightly loaded and the red color agent says that it is overloaded.

The use case diagram represents an overall scenario of the application. The number of agents in the system and the functionalities of the agents can be identified from the use case diagram. The use case diagram of the case study considered is presented in Figure 11.3. Here we considered

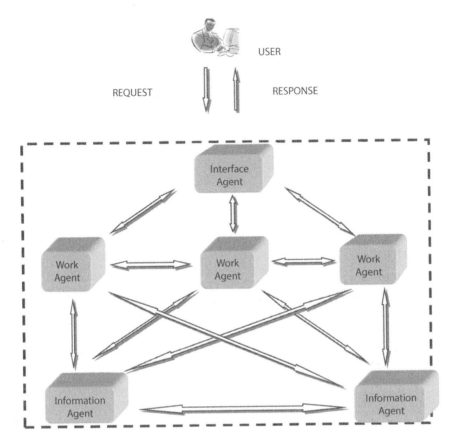

Figure 11.1 Architecture of MAS.

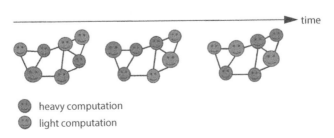

Figure 11.2 Dynamic nature of agents in MAS.

Figure 11.3 Use case diagram for case study.

an MAS with three agents, namely <<Production Agent>>, <<Delivery Agent>> and <<Supplier Agent>>. The functionality of the agents is represented with the respective use cases. Here <<Production Agent>> is considered as interface agent, <<Delivery Agent>> is considered as work agent and <<Supplier Agent>> is considered as information agent.

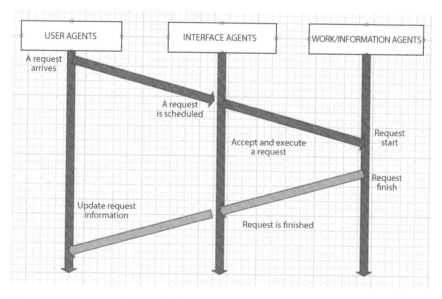

Figure 11.4 Sequence diagram for the case study.

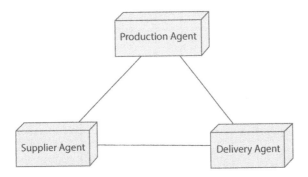

Figure 11.5 Deployment diagram for case study.

From the sequence diagram (Figure 11.4), the interaction between the agents can be realized. At the early stages of the development, this is the diagram which gives a clear interpretation of the communication load between the agents. The deployment diagram (Figure 11.5) specifies the deployment environment where the agents will be deployed after the development of the application. Once we know the number of agents, the functionalities of the agent and the communication between the agents, then finding the communication load (λ) and computational load (μ) is done by using the steps 5.2 and 5.3. The summation of λ and μ gives the overall load of the agent. From the queue of requests, by analyzing the importance and criticality of the request priority values are assigned to the requests. The model is simulated using the software JADE.

11.3   Results and Discussion

11.3.1   Proposed Algorithm in JADE Tool

The simulation is carried out by considering the arrival rates as Exponential, Uniform and Poisson probability distributions. The sample data collected during the simulation is presented in Table 11.1 and Table 11.2. The data in Table 11.1 is collected by considering the redirection of the request on a first-come first-serve basis and the agent selection is done on a random basis. The data in Table 11.2 are collected while executing the proposed algorithm.

The results are obtained for two cases: 1) Proposed load balancing techniques, and 2) first-come first-serve. Figure 11.6 to Figure 11.9 show the results of simulation using the MAS tool JADE. The arrival rate considered for the simulation is uniform distribution.

Table 11.1 Sample data from simulations using first-come first-serve method.

Number of requests	Arrival time (msec)	Response time (msec)	Work load of interface agent (KB)	Work load of work agent (KB)	Work load of info agent (KB)
1	6	17	9	10	4
2	10	27	26	22	2
3	19	26	43	16	7
4	21	37	47	16	1
5	24	39	49	44	5
6	26	44	61	60	8
7	27	45	73	76	10
8	35	57	87	66	1
9	44	56	88	86	1
10	46	57	90	91	7
11	54	59	100	89	2
12	58	59	99	87	4

Table 11.2 Sample data from simulations using the Proposed Algorithm.

Number of requests	Arrival time (msec)	Response time (msec)	Work load of interface agent (KB)	Work load of work agent (KB)	Work load of info agent (KB)
1	3	15	5	2	1
2	7	16	24	7	8
3	8	21	39	18	6
4	17	16	49	2	4
5	26	19	30	7	3
6	35	16	19	3	4
7	38	19	38	7	1
8	47	18	35	13	3
9	54	22	31	1	1
10	58	11	24	1	2
11	60	25	32	2	8
12	62	28	48	1	4

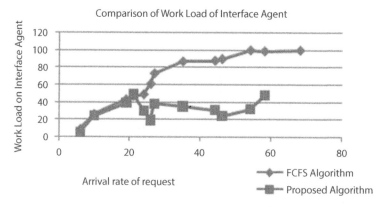

Figure 11.6 Arrival rate of requests versus workload on Interface Agent.

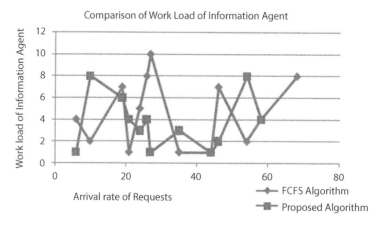

Figure 11.7 Arrival time of requests versus workload on Information Agent.

It is observed that with high arrival of requests, the proposed algorithm is better than FCFS. This means that if the proposed algorithm is applied to MAS the workload of each individual agent can be reduced. This gives better response time and cooperation among agents in MAS.

The Interface agent which interacts with the use cases processes more requests. However, this may not be the case with the information agent. Thus there will be variation of workload in both cases; however, the peak workload obtained with FCFS is reduced in the proposed algorithm. This is a good result we obtained as the information agent in RETSINA architecture needs reduction of workload because it provides the information for all the agents in the architecture. For each agent, the workload is

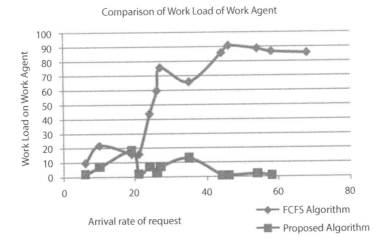

Figure 11.8 Arrival rate of requests versus workload on Work Agent.

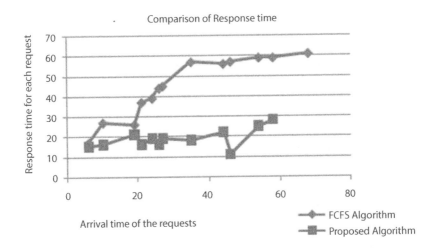

Figure 11.9 Arrival time of requests versus Response time.

compared with the proposed algorithm against FCFS. Moreover, the work-load obtained from the proposed algorithm and FCFS are used to calculate the response time, and the results are presented in the Figure 11.8. It is clear that after applying our algorithm to the agents in the MAS the work-load of agents is balanced and hence a faster response time is observed for the agents in the MAS. Hence load balancing technique has to be employed to the agents in the MAS for obtaining better performance.

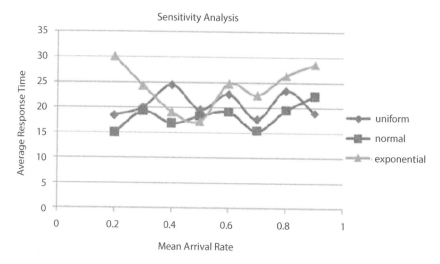

Figure 11.10 Sensitivity analysis for Response Time.

11.3.1.1   Sensitivity Analysis

Sensitivity analysis can help in several ways to assess the uncertainty of the input data. It is a technique for determining which input values, if different, would make a critical difference to the outcome of the performance. We conducted a sensitivity analysis to identify the behavior of the arrival pattern, in terms of giving better performance. In this experiment, we considered three different arrival patterns as uniform distribution, exponential distribution and normal distribution. From the observed results, the normal distribution is giving better performance. The output of the Sensitivity Analysis is presented in Figure 11.10.

11.3.2   Proposed Algorithm in NetLogo

NetLogo is a modeling environment targeted to the simulation of Multi-Agent System. A simulation of BDI communicating agents using NetLogo is addressed in [9]. NetLogo is an excellent tool for rapid prototyping and initial testing of MAS. Basics and usage of NetLogo is available in [10–12].

The Multi-Agent System model we considered is comprised of three different types of agents: Interface-Agent, Work-Agent, and Information-Agent. The RETSINA architecture and the interaction between the agents are presented in Figure 11.1 and Figure 11.4.

Interface-Agent

In this model an Interface-Agent is considered. The Interface-Agent receives the requests from user-agents and forwards to the work-agents to run the tasks. The selection of the work agent for balancing the load depends on the selected scheduling heuristic.

Work-Agent

The Work-Agent is the main agent used to carry out a task. We have used five, six, seven and eight work-agents in this simulation. Each work-agent receives a task assignment request from the interface-agent and updates its available-time, task-time, and idle-time. The number of agents depends on the application. Employing five to eight work-agents in simulation is within a reasonable range to view real-time load balancing activities.

User-Agent

The maximum number of requests used in this simulation is 99,999. Each request arises with a different arrival-time and task-execution time. Different sets of requests are used to represent different run-time environments such as less, moderate and more workload. Also tasks with less and very long execution time, etc. Each request is an independent task. Request are assigned a random execution time, a random arrival time, worst case computation time, and deadline.

11.4 Algorithms Used

We considered three different arrival patterns, Exponential, Normal and Poisson distributions for our simulation in NetLogo. The different algorithms used for the simulation is Round-Robin, Random selection and Mixed selection method which is already existing. In addition to that the algorithm developed by using the principles of SPE, which addresses the load balancing of the system at the early stages of the development of the system, is also used for simulation.

11.5 Results and Discussion

The proposed algorithm is compared with other algorithms such as Round-Robin, Random and mixed selection using NetLogo. We have simulated the model considering Normal, Exponential and Poisson distribution. The various performance metrics such as response time, waiting time and utilization are obtained. The different screen shots and various results are obtained and presented in Figure 11.11 to Figure 11.21.

Figure 11.11 and Figure 11.12 are the user interface screen designed for the simulation. The user interface has the option to select the distribution as Normal, Exponential or Poisson for the simulation. Through user interface, we can add and remove agents from the total number of agents for simulation and the maximum number of requests for simulation. The performance metrics average response time, average waiting time and average utilization values are obtained and displayed in the user interface screen.

The results that are obtained by considering Normal distribution are presented in Figure 11.13, Figure 11.14 and Figure 11.15. The results obtained by considering Poisson distribution is presented in Figure 11.16, Figure 11.17 and Figure 11.18, and the results that are obtained by considering Exponential distribution are presented in Figure 11.19, Figure 11.20 and Figure 11.21. We obtained the performance metrics average response time, average waiting time and average utilization time by considering the number of agents as 5, 6, 7 and 8. We observed from the results that the random algorithm had taken the maximum time for response; the second maximum time for the response is taken by the mixed selection algorithm; the third maximum time for the response is taken by the round robin algorithm and minimum time for the response is taken by the proposed algorithm. Similar results are observed for waiting time also. The server utilization time is obtained by considering the three distributions. When the number of agents is increased the server utilization time is reduced

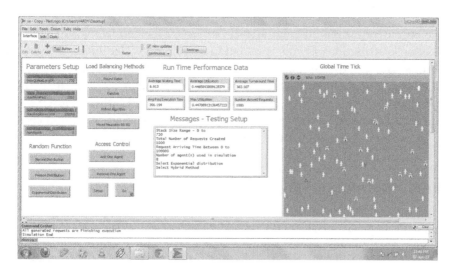

Figure 11.11 Sample screen shots for Proposed Algorithm.

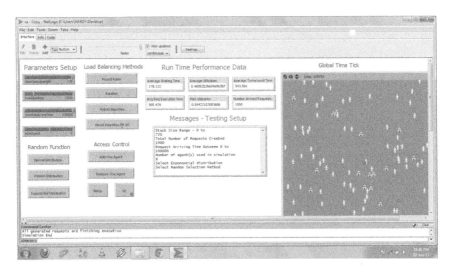

Figure 11.12 Sample screen shots for Random Selection Algorithm.

whatever the arrival rate and algorithm considered. This is because the workload is distributed to a higher number of agents. Also the server utilization results were obtained for the distributions Normal and Exponential. From these observations, we could conclude that the proposed algorithm has given better results.

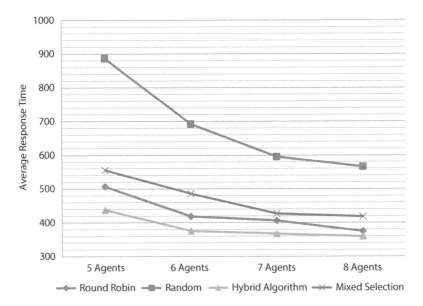

Figure 11.13 Average response time comparison using normal distribution.

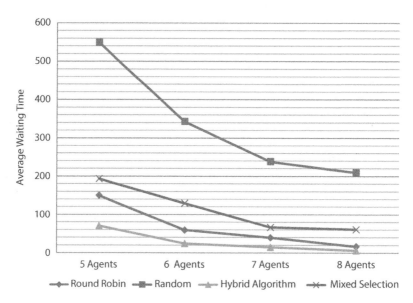

Figure 11.14 Average waiting time comparison using normal distribution.

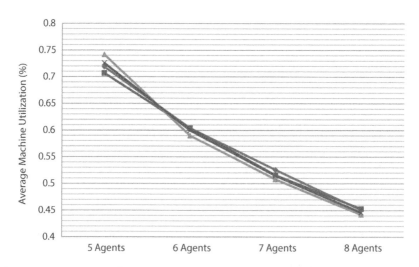

Figure 11.15 Average utilization comparison using normal distribution.

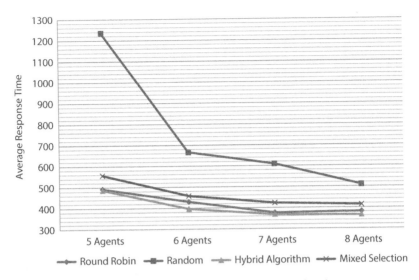

Figure 11.16 Average response time comparison using poisson distribution.

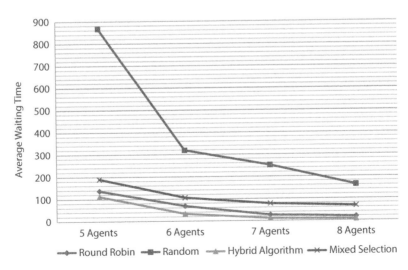

Figure 11.17 Average waiting time comparison using poisson distribution.

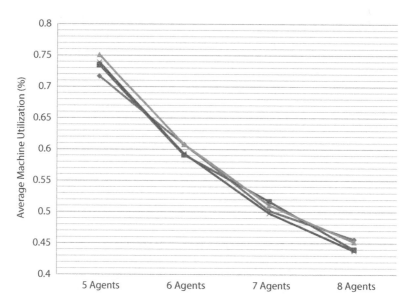

Figure 11.18 Average utilization comparison using poisson distribution.

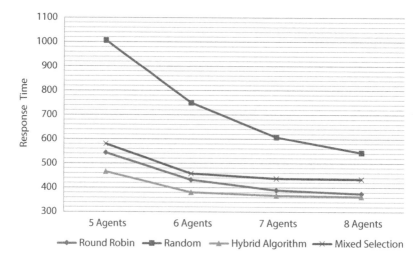

Figure 11.19 Average response time comparison using exponential distribution.

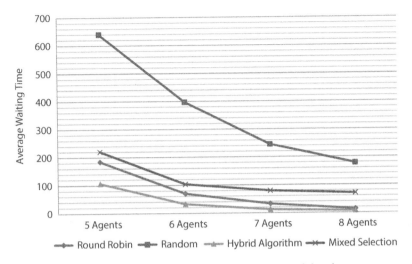

Figure 11.20 Average waiting time comparison using exponential distribution.

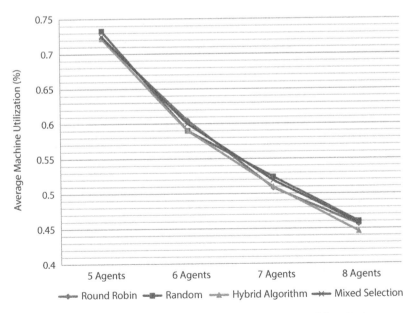

Figure 11.21 Average utilization time comparison using exponential distribution.

11.6 Summary

In this chapter, we discussed two issues: first, a methodology for load balancing in a Multi-Agent System using SPE approach, and second, the comparison of the proposed methodology with other well-known methodologies, using the MAS tool JADE and NetLogo. We have addressed the issue of load balancing by considering the RETSINA architecture of MAS. We have used UML models for representing the system at the early stages of development as per the SPE approach. The proposed algorithm is implemented using the MAS development tool, JADE and the results are obtained by considering the proposed algorithm and by using the first-come first-serve method. From the results, it is observed that the response times of the agents are improved while using proposed algorithm. Sensitivity analysis is carried out for identifying which input pattern is giving better results, and observed that the normal distribution has contributed better results. We obtained different performance metrics such as average response time, average waiting time and average server utilization using NetLogo. From the results obtained we could conclude that the proposed algorithm gives better output.

References

1. Bellifemine F., Bergenti F., Caire G., Poggi A. (2005) Jade — A Java Agent Development Framework. In: Bordini R.H., Dastani M., Dix J., El Fallah Seghrouchni A. (eds.), *Multi-Agent Programming. Multiagent Systems, Artificial Societies, and Simulated Organizations* (International Book Series), vol 15. Springer, Boston, MA. https://doi.org/10.1007/0-387-26350-0_5
2. Website: https://ccl.northwestern.edu/netlogo/
3. A. Dorri, S. S. Kanhere and R. Jurdak, "Multi-Agent Systems: A Survey," in *IEEE Access*, vol. 6, pp. 28573-28593, 2018, doi: 10.1109/ACCESS.2018.2831228.
4. Jing Xie and Chen-Ching Liu, Multi-agent systems and their applications, *Journal of International Council on Electrical Engineering*, 2017, Vol. 7, No. 1, 188–197, https://doi.org/10.1080/22348972.2017.1348890
5. A. Sekala, G.Cwikala and G.Kosti, The role of multi-agent systems in improving performance of manufacturing robotized cells, *IOP Conf. Series: Materials Science and Engineering* 95 (2015) 012097 doi:10.1088/1757-899X/95/1/012097
6. S. Ajitha, T.V. Suresh Kumar, Assessing performance of agents in a MAS: an experimental Study, *International Journal of Advanced Research in Computer Science*, Vol. 9, No. 5, September-October 2018, ISSN No. 0976-5697.

7. S. Ajitha, Modeling the Negotiation of Agents in MAS and Predicting the Performance – an SPE Approach, Informatica, *An International Journal of Computing and Informatics*, Vol. 43, No. 3, 2019.

8. Chang Ouk Kim, Ick-Hyun Kwon, Choonjong Kwak (2010), "Multi-agent based distributed inventory control model", *Expert Systems with Applications* 37 (2010) 5186–5191

9. I.F. Barcelos Tronto, J.D. Simões da Silva, N. Sant'Anna The artificial neural networks model for software effort estimation INPE ePrint:sid.inpe.br/ePrint@80/2006/12.20.23.38 v1 2006-12-21

10. Man-Yi Chen, Ding-Fang Chen, "Early cost estimation of strip-steel coiler using BP neural network", *Proceedings of the first international conference on machine learning and cybernetic, Beijing 4-5 Nov. 2002*

11. Wei Liu, Xiaoling Huang, Guanwang, Tianyou Chai, "The modeling and application of cost prediction based on neural networks", *2004 5th Asian Control Conference.*

12. Evangelin Geetha D, Ch. Ram Mohan Reddy, Suresh Kumar T V and Rajani Kanth K: "JAPET: A Java Based tool for performance evaluation of software systems". *Proceedings of international conference on software knowledge information management and application, 12-15, December 2006 at Chiang Mai, Thailand*, pp. 64-69.

12

The Impact of Cyber Culture on New Media Consumers

Durmuş Koçak

Independent Researcher/Journalist, Ankara, Turkey

Abstract

The aim of this study is to evaluate the effect of cyber culture on the preferences and tendencies of new media consumers based on the information in the literature. In this context, similar studies in the literature were examined and the information obtained from these studies was compiled and transferred.

According to the information obtained in the study, it has been concluded that social networks and new media structures formed on these structures are effective on individuals in many ways. These effects can be given as examples of cultural, social and individual effects. In addition to these, it is noted that individuals' consumption preferences are also affected by new media structures.

Keywords: Cyber culture, consumer choice, consumer tendency, virtual culture, network society

12.1 Introduction

Culture, which expresses the peculiarity of any element that contributes to social life as well as the needs of societies such as eating and drinking, clothing, and shelter, was formed in the first moments when people started living together; it has come through various changes and developments until today. Although more concrete elements are dealt with in the concepts used to define culture, it is also known that culture has an abstract aspect. One of these abstract aspects is that culture is resistant to change. In other words, culture can change, but this change refers to a process that

Email: durmus.kocak@hotmail.com [ORCID ID: 0000-0001-8783-5112]

Shibin David, R. S. Anand, V. Jeyakrishnan, and M. Niranjanamurthy (eds.) Security Issues and Privacy Concerns in Industry 4.0 Applications, (229–248) © 2021 Scrivener Publishing LLC

takes quite a long time. In this context, it is possible to say that there have been changes from the emergence of the first cultural examples until today. However, this change is almost never holistic. As a matter of fact, when the existing cultures are examined, it is possible to see the traces of quite ancient periods in them.

In addition to the change of cultures, it is possible to see an increase in their number. New structures added to the lives of societies as a result of developments cause the emergence of new cultural elements or cultural types. For example, when certain societies start living in an area where people have never lived, a culture specific to that area can emerge. In this context, it is possible to say that the internet, which has spread widely in the 21st century, has also created a new cultural structure. Today, the new cultural phenomenon created by the internet structure used by millions of people and spread in almost all societies is defined as cyber culture (Levy, 2001: 11). This new type of culture is also referred to by different names in the literature, such as "internet culture" (Castells, 2001: 7-8), "virtual culture" and "digital culture" (Jones, 1998: 14). Cyber culture can also be defined as a type of virtual culture that includes structures such as attitudes, behaviors and beliefs that are created through the internet and are developing day by day thanks to information and communication technologies (Rheingold, 1993: 5).

Although it is considered in direct connection with the development of the internet, the emergence of the structure called cyber culture represents a wide change and transformation that cannot be reduced to internet technologies. In this sense, when the literature is examined, it is seen that a basic structure such as globalization is very effective in the emergence of cyber culture.

With the internet, which has a large share in the formation of cyber culture, it has been observed that changes have been made not only in cultural terms but also in many existing traditional structures in the world. One of them is media outlets. The changes that the media type, which is described as the traditional media, has gone through over time has reached its peak with the internet. In this context, the creation of an environment where people can access, comment, and contribute to all kinds of news as they wish has led to the emergence of a structure called interactive media or new media.

The new media formations, which came to the fore with the media mostly called social media, resulted in individuals taking the action of including new media in the cyber culture structure, and these two structures have been in constant interaction with each other. In this context, it is possible to say that cyber culture has many effects on users on new media outlets on the internet.

12.2   The Rise of the Term of Cyber Culture

Cyber culture is conceptually considered as a structure that enters human life with the development of information and communication technologies and causes a cultural change. In this context, it is possible to define the concept of cyber culture as the culture of the computer world in its simplest form. Howard Rheingold, who has studies on this subject, emphasizes that the computer and the internet affect a large number of people and create a culture dependent structure (Rheingold, 1991). Although cyber culture is considered as computer culture, it is also mentioned in studies that cyber culture should be handled with a dual structure in the form of cyberspace (Bell, 2001).

Many studies have been conducted on the subject of cyber culture, which is a current and very common subject. When these studies are considered, it is seen that a common structure is emphasized in almost all studies. This common point is that the developments emerging as a result of the technological studies carried out will reflect on the cultural lives of individuals. In this context, there is a common belief that the technological developments experienced will create opportunities for cultural innovations. However, there are studies that mention that the developments in the past have a shaping effect on cultures, rather than being dealt with only with the current structure (Escobar, 1994: 7-11).

The thoughts that technological developments will affect the cultural structure of societies have been proven with the invention of the computer. As a matter of fact, a culture directly related to computers emerged after this technological development. One of the most obvious examples of this is the transfer of the relationships in people's daily lives to this environment shortly after the invention of the computer. This constitutes the basis of the cultural structure stated as cyber culture (Escobar, 1995: 408-409).

12.2.1   Cyber Culture in the 21st Century

Societies from past to present have lifestyles, unwritten rules, traditions and customs and so on. Although the cultural structure or cultural phenomenon is resistant to change and transformation, it undergoes certain changes over long periods of time by being affected by the changes that societies have undergone. In this context, although we can say that culture does not have a fixed structure for societies, it is possible to say that culture is also open to development.

In the cultural sense, the changes that began in the late 20th century and are continuing to accelerate in the 21st century, are basically related to technological developments. As a matter of fact, the issues that can be qualified as advanced technology that emerged in the mentioned centuries have changed societies, and the changing lifestyles of societies have brought about a change in cultural terms, especially in the 21 st century. It is worth noting that in terms of this century, an aspect of culture blended with technology has emerged and this is gradually increasing.

With the development of technology, cultural phenomena have begun to be included in technological structures or these structures have been included in the culture. As a matter of fact, especially the structures that are described as social networks and used extensively by people constitute the first step of a new cultural structure. The new cultural structures formed on these networks are called "cyber culture" because they are formed in a completely virtual environment.

Cyber culture, which is highly involved in human life as a reflection of people's new life styles, is a cultural formation associated with the internet or thought to be completely specific to the internet. The inclusion of the internet in every field of human life in today's world and the increase in its size in this context increase the impact of cultural formations based on the internet on human life. The effect of this cultural structure, which is so included in human life, in many areas is considered as an inevitable result. In this context, the people and society of cyber culture are subject to effects in many areas, including social, economic, psychological, etc.

12.2.1.1   Socio-Economic Results of Cyber Culture

Considering the economic benefits of cyber culture and the formations included in this cultural structure in the life of the individual and society, the most striking point is the creation of new employment areas, in other words, the creation of new business areas where people will operate. As a matter of fact, a large number of people are employed today in many business areas such as web design, software engineering, web page management, and internet advertising, which are the most known professions with the internet. However, it is possible to talk about a negative situation in this area, which is that the people involved in production activities are replaced by machines with the developing technology. This situation brings with it comments that an environment in which there is an increase in employment with the internet will decrease again with technological developments (Bozkurt, 1999: 97).

Although the mentioned impact issue is valid not only for the internet or new media, but also for the whole of information technologies, it is also accepted that they have an impact nationally and internationally. As a matter of fact, developments defined as information technologies are defined as structures whose effects change economically according to the development level of the countries. In addition, the differences in access to information technologies according to the development level of countries are considered as another reason why the effects of these technologies make a difference (Wallsten, 2003: 1).

It is known that the internet, which creates cyber culture, has social as well as economic effects. The largest of these effects and the most globally influential is the impact on language. When the languages used in communication activities on the internet are examined, it is mentioned that the language with the largest share among these languages is English, and this situation has started to transform English into a global language. However, the issue of impact on language is also the subject of some debate about whether the language is really suitable for this structure and whether it has a universal nature. However, it is worth noting that cultural deformations or assimilations in terms of social impact are also the subject of discussion (Kramarae, 1999: 48). In this context, it is mentioned that language transfer will also lead to the transfer of some cultural issues. However, the reduction of this issue to the internet or cyber culture causes some unfair criticism to spread. It is known that even before the invention of visual media and even media, when people met due to commercial activities, they also affected their societies and culture. In this context, it can be considered a more reasonable approach to mention the characteristics of the structure of the internet and cyber culture, such as diversity in impact and in addition to this, shortening the duration of impact.

12.2.1.2   Psychological Outcomes of Cyber Culture

Psychological effects, which also shape the social effects of the internet, mainly manifest themselves in individual use or non-confrontation. However, the fact that people who spend a lot of time in front of the computer and on the internet exhibit behaviors such as introversion and antisociality, which are accepted as the main problem in this area; it is considered to be one of the most emphasized issues regarding individual effects, although it is the first among the psychological effects of cyber culture (Casalegno, 2003: 19).

Another of the negative effects of cyber culture on individuals is that the individual tries to analyze his own inadequacy perception over the internet, not with his social environment in daily life/real life. In this context, although individuals try to overcome the negativities of this competence perception by communicating with people they have never seen, this issue brings along a different problem. This negativity manifests itself in the way that individuals gain an addiction to this area, in which they partially overcome their disability, and that they cannot feel themselves competent outside of this area. In addition, these people tend to see online structures as safer than real life, which creates an effect that increases the duration and amount of addiction (Caplan, 2003: 628-29).

12.2.1.3 Political Outcomes of Cyber Culture

Another effect of cyber culture in social and individual terms is the political and ideological effect. As a matter of fact, after the spread of cyber culture, it has been determined that there are some political effects in the international community. The main indicator of this is the decrease in blind devotion to leaders in countries where the internet is widespread, while in countries where the internet is not common, it emerges as the public's more tight connection to their leaders (Escobar, 1995: 416). In addition to these, the news that today's social media managers manipulate the elections of countries is also important in terms of showing how serious this issue has become.

12.3 The Birth and Outcome of New Media Applications

When the literature is examined about new media applications that are included in social life after the spread of the internet, it is seen that there are many studies. It is also possible to see that there are some discussions about new media applications within these studies. At the main point of the discussions is the issue of how to distinguish between the media called old or traditional media and the new media. Some researchers make a distinction on the basis of time, while others make a distinction in terms of technique. In this context, while the discussions about new media are continuing, this media formation is referred to as the "second media age" or "the third great revolution" in the historical course of the media (Öztürk, 2011: 196).

Periodic emphasis in naming new media tools is not related to the invention of these media tools. When the literature is examined, it is seen that Mark Poster, who has works on this subject, named the media periods and was the first person to use the expression "second media age" in these periods. As a result of his studies on the concept, with this concept used by Poster in 1995, he argues that capitalism is in a very tight connection with the new media. Poster evaluates the period dominated by traditional media as the first media age, and the media practices that go beyond the traditional as the second media age. According to Poster, the most striking feature of the second media age is that individuals have the opportunity to interact with media practices in this period (Poster, 1995: 3-23).

Essentially, when the history of communication is examined, it is possible to see that the basic acceptance of the separation of communication in the historical process is that every mass media has emerged from the previous tool. For this reason, it can be said that the people who defend the stated opinion actually consider the new media not as a fundamental change in itself, but as an extension of the old media. Ted Greenwald, who reduced the media structures to the first formations in this regard, tied the situation of today's media to quite old times and argued that the first step in the formation of new media was taken with the invention of the printing press (Greenwald, 2002: 18).

Considered in terms of general acceptance, it can be said that the connection from the beginning to the end of the time period proceeds in this way. However, even when examining the functioning of the traditional media structure of the previous period with the functioning of the structure that is described as new media today, it is possible to say that the new media could not have arisen without the invention of the printing press. However, it does not seem possible to connect the past of the two structures. Because while the new media contains a visual, auditory, written and interactive structure within itself, the printing house can be considered as a media structure that stands out only in terms of visuality.

Daniel Bell, who is prominent due to his work on new media, made this structure with the transition to the post-industrial social structure. It evaluates it as a formation that emerged in the second half of the 20th century. Bell emphasizes that during this period, society lost its characteristic of being an industrial society and turned into an information society, and that the period revealed the information age and structure of the information society. However, it also emphasizes that communication technologies and computers occupy a very important place in the information society (Aydoğan, 2010: 6).

Although there are those who deal with the formation of new media together with past media publications or organs and even reduce this structure to the printing press, there are also those that consider new media as a structure that emerged only in a recent period. For Dilmen, one of the researchers on this subject, the new media began to form in the early 1970s. However, he adds that there were no major developments in the 1970s, they accelerated in the 1990s, and he evaluates the new media and the technology called internet technology intertwined. Although Dilmen does not see the internet or computer structure as indispensable for the emergence of new media, he emphasizes that these technological developments have a significant share in the development of new media (Dilmen, 2007: 114).

Manuel Castells, in his book *Information Age*, considers the transition towards new media structure as a revolution in terms of human history. Castells bases this view on the emergence of new media and great advances in technology and, in addition, the reshaping of the material formation in social and social structure with new media. In addition to these views, Castells also states that there is an economic element in the new media, so the new media has an effect that facilitates the diffusion on the capitalist system. In this context, Castells was the first person to use the expression "information capitalism" in the literature.

Schiller is another scholar who has expressed an opinion on the relationship between new media and capitalism. According to Schiller, the reason for the development of new media structures is to reduce the social depression caused by capitalism. In addition, Schiller demonstrated a general approach and stated that all technological developments are directly related to economic structures (Geray, 2003: 81).

When the opinions put forward on the emergence and development of new media technologies are examined, there is an opinion put forward by Marshall McLuhan, which basically covers all opinions in a general sense. This view is "New media changes everything." In this context, it can be said that the media structures created in today's new media environments have a great impact on the society and this occurs in the form of changing the economic and social order. However, it cannot be said that this situation has always had positive results. As a matter of fact, it is emphasized in the studies that the new media has negative as well as positive results regarding the transformations it provides (Hepkon, 2011: 128).

12.3.1   New Media Environments

Social or digital environments, which are called new media environments, represent a structure that spreads over a wide area when evaluated together with the spread of new media. Although they have points in common, these environments, which express quite different structures from each other, can be shown to be created in a computer environment as the most basic determinant and feature of all of them. In addition to this, access to these media, providing access to videos, information, data, and anything shared by other people in these media is also done through a computer.

When examining the place that new media applications have acquired in society, it is possible to say that these environments of new media applications are in a more important position in society compared to traditional media practices and traditional media tools. As a matter of fact, the new media environments that come to the forefront especially with advertising applications come to the fore in economic terms. In the literature, new media environments are listed as follows (Akgün, 2010: 195).

12.3.1.1   Social Sharing Networks

Social networks can be defined as web structures on the internet that mediate the development of relations between people who use these networks. Social networks operating with internet connection or sites that offer social network-like services are among the technological developments that attract the most attention and have the widest usage area in the world today. It can be said that social networks are among the most visited sites today, although there are many different types. Web sites that are downloaded as social networks generally stand out as they are web structures that enable individuals to present their information, news, videos and similar shares to different people and thus interact with them (Finin *et al.*, 2005: 418-19).

Facebook: One of the most well-known sites described as a social network today is Facebook social network site. This structure is defined in the literature as a social network that emerged as a product of globalization and transformation into a network society. Facebook, which enables people to make friends on the internet, in addition to enabling activities such as information sharing and communication, was founded in 2003 by a few students from the Harvard University dormitory (Kırık, 2012: 511).

Facebook, which had a feature of sharing photographs, information and the like among students at Harvard University when it was established, became an inter-university social network in a short time. After being put into general use, it rose to a place that can be considered as the top in terms of social networks in 2006. In this development, Facebook, which reached a more economic and commercial dimension rather than the sharing by students among universities, has gained a general feature of granting the right to be a member of Facebook with an e-mail address with its peak in 2006.

After it was opened to general use, it started to spread at a huge speed. It is mentioned that this social network, whose weight has increased in terms of commercial activities in the world with the mentioned spread, has gained a great income especially from advertisements (Toprak, 2009: 38-39).

Twitter: Twitter, whose establishment dates back to 2006, when Facebook was at its peak, is considered to be a social networking site close to Facebook's social network content. However, it is one of the most popular social networks after Facebook. Although it still has not reached as many members as Facebook, the opportunities it offers to individuals in terms of communication and sharing have brought Twitter to be considered as a social media environment. In fact, Twitter is defined as a microblog site in the literature (O'Reilly, Milstein, 2009: 5).

The most basic feature of Twitter, which offers its users the opportunity to share their feelings and thoughts, pictures or texts, videos or voices, like other social networking sites, is the application of character restriction in the text shares of its users. Due to this restriction, Twitter is generally considered as a short message service available on the internet. Although there is a character restriction, there is no restriction on the number of texts to be shared. In other words, while the text to be written in the message is limited, there is no limit to the number of messages. With this restriction, it is possible to say that Twitter aims to encourage users to act selectively in their posts and to use Twitter more intensively. Twitter stands out in terms of economic and cultural effects as well as being a social network (Altunay, 2010: 32-37).

The shortness of the messages on Twitter results in the rapid response to these messages, which is considered to be the most prominent feature of Twitter for social networks. In this context, it is possible that all the shares presented on Twitter are conveyed to people faster and a faster interaction is received from them (Cömert, 2012: 15).

YouTube: Although social networks such as Facebook and Twitter allow people to post pictures, music videos and similar posts, there are social networks with different content apart from these possibilities. One of the most typical examples of these is the video sharing network called YouTube. YouTube is unquestionably recognized as the most popular video sharing site around the world. The biggest difference of this site from other social networks is that it can only post visual or audio content. However, what makes this structure a social network is that people can write comments under these posts and like and respond to each other's comments with their posts (Kırık, 2012: 74).

What makes YouTube more attractive than other social networks is that people have the opportunity to publish their own products here. However, the fact that it is possible to access YouTube from all platforms such as computers, laptops, tablets and mobile phones, which are defined as new media tools, is also effective in its popularity (Strangelove, 2010: 8).

Instagram: Created later than social networks such as Facebook and Twitter, Instagram was founded in 2010 and was acquired by Facebook in 2012 after its huge user momentum in a very short time. Although Instagram is generally known as a photo and video sharing platform, it is also defined as a social networking site due to the interaction of people through these photos. Unlike other social networks, Instagram, which is described as a more fun social network by people because it is based on photo or video sharing rather than writing, has been easier to access and attracted more attention with the addition of the feature of tagging shared photos since 2013 (Türkmenoğlu, 2014: 96).

As a result of the measurements made on Instagram, it has been concluded that people on this social networking site share around 60 million photos daily and interact with over 1 billion likes. However, it is among the reported information that the monthly active user number of Instagram is approaching 200 million and this number is gradually increasing. The biggest difference of Instagram from other social networks is that it can only be used as a mobile application. In other words, Instagram, whose features cannot be actively used on personal computers, unlike Facebook and Twitter, can only be used effectively with smartphones and tablet computers (Guidry, Jin, 2015: 347). In the researches, it was found that close to 60% of Instagram users visit this site at least once a day, and this result was found to be quite higher than a social media site such as Twitter, which was established before Instagram. In the early days, Instagram has become a more preferred structure with the addition of direct message and video sharing function to its sharing and editing photos features (Huey, Yazdanifard, 2015: 3).

By offering an account privacy feature to its users, Instagram has also ensured that people have the freedom to access their shares by the people they want. In other words, while the posts shared on Instagram can be seen by anyone who visits Instagram, if the user has set their account to be private, only people who are allowed or followed by the account owner will be able to see the posts on this account. Another feature that Instagram offers to its users is the ability to upload photos or videos, but add filters to these posts if they wish. In addition, a feature such as adding hashtag to the relevant part of the shares that the users will make is also provided to the users to find and display their shares with the concepts included in this hashtag. With the tagging feature offered on Instagram, users can tag different users, but with the improvements made, users can add their comments under the posts (Uitermark, 2015: 8). Another feature of Instagram is that it allows its users to share the location of the place where the photo was taken. Based on this location sharing, it is possible to create links to all photos taken in a particular place on Instagram, but a fast way is created for the person to see the photos of the places where the location is given or in the immediate vicinity (Tekulve, Kelly, 2013: 8).

The length of the videos shot on Instagram is limited to 15 seconds; when the user slides the content, the video starts playing automatically and people can watch these videos. However, due to the shortness of this video length by people, the videos can be transferred to the excessive parts and people can watch the video after 15 seconds if they wish (Hellberg, 2015: 21).

12.3.1.2   Network Logs (Blog, Weblog)

Another example of platforms used in the field of new media are blogs. These structures emerged in 1997 by a group of people working in the field of computer programming, based on the idea of publishing the websites they were interested in with short notes on their own web pages. The concept of "blog" created by the combination of the words "web" and "log" is also called "weblog". Blogs, which are considered as an electronic diary in the literature, are managed by the blog owner (Bonnie *et al.*, 2004: 42-43).

12.3.1.3   Computer Games

Although computer games are seen as a game and a non-media structure, these games can be used as a new media tool as a result of the transfer of these games to the internet environment in which they become platforms where many people can play at the same time in the form of online games. Today, new media structures and computer games are added to each other and these games are gradually turning into large advertising platforms. This shows the relationship between the new media and the economy; it means the formation of another field that enables capitalism to use the new media (Prensky, 2001: 21-34).

12.3.1.4   Digital News Sites and Mobile Media

Another medium in which new media structures take place is recorded as mobile devices. Mobile devices are all portable devices with visual and auditory features that benefit from new media environments. Until a short time ago, the mobile structure was limited only to the phone, but with the emergence and wide spread of the internet, tablets, portable computers and so on are included in this structure. Mobile devices are used not only to use new media applications, but also to play the games listed in social space structures. In a study conducted on the use of mobile devices world-wide in 2010, it was concluded that more than 5 billion people in the world are users of mobile communication devices. This result is one of the biggest indicators of the importance of using mobile devices and new media on these devices (Köroğlu, 2011: 375-76).

Not only social networks or games within these network structures, but also television broadcasts with mobile devices are followed through structures called mobile TV. While the mobile TV application enables the spread of new media applications to a much wider area with mobile devices, it also ensures that the effects of this area are larger (Kumar, 2007: 4-6).

12.3.1.5 Multimedia Media

The structure called multimedia refers to a multiple communication structure. In fact, multimedia, which refers to the use of structures such as sound, text, image and painting, which is also the basis of new media applications, can be considered as one of the most effective points of new media in this context (Özçağlayan, 1998: 146).

Multimedia media, as the name suggests, refers to environments where more than one media element is in the same structure. In other words, the mediums that express the transformation of the media organs, which were divided into written, auditory and visual media in the past, under a single roof, are called multimedia media. The only feature of these mediums is not that they bring together different media elements, but that they increase the functionality of the media and its effects on people. As a matter of fact, the effect to be created by one or two of the media organs is not comparable with the structure that will emerge as a result of the combination of all of these and the possibility of interaction with this holistic structure. In this context, multimedia environments are structures that have a more dominant effect on individuals than traditional media (Özçağlayan, 1998: 144-48).

Studies on multimedia show that there are many different definitions expressing these structures. However, what is emphasized in the definitions and expressed as one of the most important features of multimedia is the bringing together of different media environments. As a matter of fact, there is a structure used in all areas of communication when talking about multimedia environments today (Kemaneci, 2018).

12.3.1.6   What Affects the New Media Consumers' Tendencies?

These structures, which are currently in a state of constant change and development, have entered into a faster change and development with the participation of technology in human life and social life. These changes have manifested themselves in individual life and social life, and consequently in consumer structure and behavior. In this context, the traditional consumer turns into the new consumer with the individuals affected by the new media structure, such as the transformation of traditional media into new media. Studies on this subject show that there are many different definitions about the new consumer concept. Although these definitions are different from each other, common points are emphasized—that new consumers are more skeptical, more intelligent and more experienced in marketing activities than traditional consumers. However, while net results can be obtained with the researches on the trends of traditional consumers, the trend issue in new consumers may change constantly. For this reason, there is no clear conclusion about the trends of new consumers. In addition, it is emphasized that the group defined as the new consumer is in a global structure, consumers who attach more importance to information and have a rational approach. In this context, it is possible to say that the knowledge factor underlies the preferences and tendencies of new consumers regarding consumption (Dinç, 2018: 3).

12.3.1.6.1   Formations Determining New Consumer Trends

Continuity in Technology Follow-up: When traditional consumer behaviors are examined, it is emphasized that the individual needs this product primarily in order to make a decision to purchase any product. Therefore, the need is shown as the main factor in consumption for traditional consumers. In consumer behavior based on need, it is not possible to turn to any product without need. It is mentioned that there is a limitation in the preferences of traditional consumers due to the limited information they can use in meeting their needs. In other words, consumption behavior is a restricted behavioral pattern for traditional consumers. In this context, traditional consumers turn to a long research activity aimed at purchasing the product that will best meet their needs at the lowest cost (Dinç, 2018: 6).

The developments in the technological field and the opportunities people have at the point of accessing information have revealed that consumers form a class that is called the new type and has different preferences and actions compared to classical consumers. In this newly formed consumer type, individuals can access all the information about any product or service they need via the internet and shape their preferences and tendencies by comparing this information. Accordingly, after the new types of consumers tend to buy a product or need a product, they experience an information intensity unlike traditional consumers. This brings up many different stages in the consumption process (Dinç, 2018: 7).

Rapid Decision Process and Decision Making: When the experiences of individuals regarding the products they prefer in the traditional consumption process are examined, it is understood that generally they regret the purchased products due to incomplete information. For this reason, individuals in the new consumer type enter a pre-elimination process for these products by reviewing their experiences with the products that different people want to buy with technological tools. It is noted that individuals in the new consumer type, based on the comments made by different people about the same product, have fewer regrets about the products they buy (Dinç, 2018: 7).

Another effect of the new media on the preferences and tendencies of the consumers is that it reveals the advantage of managing the consumption idea of the individuals with the intensity of information about their preferred product or service. Individuals can move to a faster decision stage in the selection process with the information provided or comments made by different people about the same product or service. This brings about the formation of an instant structure in the purchasing tendency when considered in terms of consumers. Instant purchasing behavior also results in the fact that the things preferred by the person go beyond the needs, which shows itself in the way of increasing consumption activities (Dinç, 2018: 7).

Increasing Logic, Loss of Emotion: In activities carried out to affect the preferences of traditional consumers, the thought of drawing their preferences and actions in the desired direction by appealing to the feelings of people in general is dominant. However, with the new media structures, it has been determined that people's emotions are less involved in consumption activities; instead structures such as reason and logic are used more. In this context, by changing the marketing activities, methods based on the emotions used for the traditional structure were developed and marketing strategies that prioritize reason and logic were put into practice. However, this does not mean that new consumers are not under the influence of emotions in any way. In this context, although the emotional structure is partially effective, new consumers generally operate logic and information-based decision mechanisms (Dinç, 2018: 7).

12.4   Result

The cultural structure that people have formed as a result of social relations over time changes with the change of society and can become suitable for the requirements of the time. In this respect, it is not possible to say that the culture remained constant with the structure of the society at the time it emerged. As a matter of fact, many changes that society goes through can have an effect on culture. These changes include social migrations, inter-action with different cultures, wars, diseases, etc. Technological changes experienced over time are also effective on the culture. As a matter of fact, the change in societies with changing and developing technological struc-tures results in the transformation of culture into new structures.

Today, the effect of technological structures on the society has resulted in culture being affected by technological structures, which has resulted in the emergence of a new cultural structure within technological struc-tures. This structure, which is called cyber culture, is a phenomenon that emerges as a result of individuals creating a cultural structure similar to the real environment in cyber environments, and it is accepted as the top point of cultural changes in recent times.

Cyber culture, which emerges as a result of the time and interactions that individuals spend in virtual environments such as social media, can be considered as the product of a global interaction in general. As a matter of fact, people can choose the way of adapting this culture to their lives by interacting with any culture anywhere in the world with technological developments. This results in the cultural structure called cyber culture taking on a global rather than local structure.

This aspect of cyber culture has many effects on new media users. These effects occur in the form of a cultural extinction, especially as a result of the loss of the existing cultural structures of individuals, and the disap-pearance of cultures, which are considered to be the material and spiritual heritage of societies for hundreds of years, can be considered as a situation that causes social concern. However, there is a deformation in the personal structures of individuals due to cyber culture. People's taking on an antiso-cial structure, starting not to behave according to their gender roles, expe-riencing changes in consumption and similar habits can be listed among the negatives caused by cyber culture. This issue manifests itself as direct-ing consumption, especially by manipulating individuals, which results in people engaging in some unintentional consumption activities.

Although the change, which is called the global cultural structure and can be expressed as being free from differences, is seen as a positive situ-ation at first impression, it can be considered as the first step of a social disintegration, due to the lack of people's structures specific to themselves or the society they live in. In this context, due to people breaking away from social ties, feelings of unity and integrity can be damaged, which is against the understanding of being part of a nation. In addition, the decrease in the need for socialization that people feel about social structures in the real world, due to the fact that they are in a virtual socialization in social networks, can cause the social environment to completely shift to the internet, and it can also cause individuals to have an antisocial structure. In addition, since there are effects such as internet addiction, identity confusion, and appearing differently through anonymous identities among antisocial individuals, it would be a healthy approach to deal with these situations under state control.

References

Akgün, Serkan, "Yeni Medya Reklâmlarında Marka Kişiliği", İkinci Medya Çağında İnternet Der. Aydoğan, Filiz, Ayşen Akyüz, 1. Baskı, Alfa Yayınları, İstanbul, 2010.

Altunay, Meltem Cemiloğlu, "Gündelik Yaşam ve Sosyal Paylaşım Ağları: Twitter ya da "Pıt Pıt Net", *Galatasaray İletişim Dergisi*, S. 12, 2010.

Aydoğan, Filiz, "İkinci Medya Çağı'nda Gözetim ile Kamusal Alan Paradoksunda İnternet", İkinci Medya Çağında İnternet, Der. Filiz Aydoğan, Ayşen Akyüz, 1. Baskı, Alfa Yayınları, İstanbul, 2010.

Bell, David, *Introduction to Cybercultures*, Florence KY: Routledge, 2001.

Bozkurt, Veysel, *Enformasyon Toplumu ve Türkiye*, Sistem Yayıncılık, 1999.

Caplan, Scott E.,"Preference for Online Social Interaction A Theory of Problematic Internet Use and Psychosocial Well-Being", *Comunication Research*, Vol. 30, No. 6, 2003.

Casalegno, Federico, "Preference for Online Social Interaction A Theory of Problematic Internet Use and Psychosocial Well-Being", *Communication Research*, Vol. 30, No. 6, 2003.

Castells, Manuel, *The Internet Galaxy: Reflections on the Internet, Business and Society*, Oxford: Oxford University Press, 2001.

Cömert, Hasan, "Kısa Ama Etkili: Twitter"da Edebiyat Mümkün Mü?", *Sabit Fikir Dergisi*, S. 13, Mart 2012.

Dilmen, Necmi Emel, "Yeni Medya Kavramı Çerçevesinde İnternet Günlükleri-Bloglar ve Gazeteciliğe Yansımaları", *Marmara İletişim Dergisi*, S. 12, 2007.

Dinç, Berna, "Dijitalleşmenin Tüketici Alışkanlıklarına Etkisi", *Ekonomistler Platformu*, Ocak 2018.

Escobar, Arthur, "Antropology and the Future, New Technologies and the Reinvantion of Culture", *Futures*, Volume 27, No: 4, Elsevier Science Ltd, 1995, Great Britain.

Escobar, Arthur, "What is Cyber Culture", From Welcome to Cyberia, *Current Anthropology*, Volume 35, S. 3, Haziran 1994.

Finin, Tim, Li Ding, Lina Zhou, Anupam Joshi, "Social Networking on the Semantic Web", *The Learning Organization*, Vol. 12, No. 5, 2005.

Geray, Haluk, İletişim ve Teknoloji Uluslararası Birikim Düzeninde Yeni Medya Politikaları, 1. Baskı, Ütopya Yayınları, Ankara, 2003.

Greenwald, Ted, "Harmonic Convergence", *Living in the Information Age: A New Media Reader*, Bucy, Erik P. (Ed.), 1. Baskı, Ontario: Wadsworth Thomson Learning, 2002.

Guidry J and Jin Y., (2015), "From #mcdonaldsfail to #dominossucks - An analysis of Instagram Images about the 10 Largest Fast Food Companies", *Corporate Communications An International Journal*, 20(3), 344-359.

Hellberg, M., (2015), "Visual Brand Communication on Instagram: A Study on Consumer Engagement", Master Thesis, Hanken School of Economics, Helsinki.

Hepkon, Zeliha, "Yeni İletişim Teknolojileri Tartışmalarının Yeni Olmayan Boyutu: Teknolojik Determinizm", *İletişim ve Teknoloji / Olanaklar, Uygulamalar, Sınırlar Zeliha* Hepkon (Ed.), 1. Baskı, Kırmızı Kedi Yayınları, İstanbul, 2011.

Jones, Steve, *Virtual Culture: Identity and Communication in Cybersociety*, Thousand Oaks, CA: Sage Publications, 1998.

Kemaneci, Ebru, "Multimedya (Çoklu Ortamlar)", https://bote314.files.wordpress.com/2011/ 05/coklu-ortam1.ppt, (Erişim Tarihi: 27.10.2018)

Kırık, Ali Murat, "Gençlerin Sosyal Paylaşım Ağlarındaki Kimlik Sorunu ve Etik Değerlerin İhlali", II. *Medya ve Etik (Medya-Kültür İlişkisinde Etik) Sempozyumu Bildiri Kitabı*, Fırat Üniversitesi, Elazığ, 2012.

Köroğlu, Osman, "Mobil İletişimin Yayıncılık ve Pazarlama İletişimine Etkisi", *Dumlupınar Üniversitesi Sosyal Bilimler Dergisi*, S. 31, 2011.

Kramarae, Cheris, "The Language and Nature of the Internet: The Meaning of Global", *New Media & Society*, Vol. 1, Issue:1, April, 1999.

Kumar, Amitabh, *Mobile TV: DVB-H, DMB, 3G Systems and Rich Media Applications*, 1. Baskı, Oxford: Focal Press, 2007.

Lévy, Pierre, *Cyberculture*, (Trans: Roberto Bonnono), University of Minneapolis Press, 2001.

Nardi, Bonnie A., Diane J. Schiano vd., "Why We Blog", *Communications of the ACM*, Vol. 47, Issue: 12, 2004.

O'Reilly, Tim, Sarah Milstein, *The Twitter Book*, 2. Baskı, Kalkedon Yayınları, İstanbul, 2009, s. 5.

Özçağlayan, Mehmet, Yeni İletişim Teknolojileri ve Değişim, 1. Baskı, Alfa Yayınları, İstanbul, 1998.

Öztürk, R. Gülay, "Yeni Medyanın Reklamcılığa Etkileri: Olanaklar, Riskler ve Sınırlar", İletişim ve *Teknoloji / Olanaklar, Uygulamalar, Sınırlar*, Zeliha Hepkon (Ed.), 1. Baskı, Kırmızı Kedi Yayınları, İstanbul, 2011.

Poster, Mark, *The Second Media Age*, 1. Baskı, Canada: Wiley Publications, 1995.

Prensky, Marc, *Digital Game – Based Learning*, New York: McGraw-Hill, 2001.

Rheingold, Howard, *The Virtual Community: Finding Connection in a Computerised World*, London, Secker and Warburg Pub., 1993.

Rheingold, Howard, *The Virtual Community: Homesteading on the Electronic Frontier*, Menlo Park, CA: Addison-Wesley, 1991.

Scott Wallsten, "Regulation and Internet Use In Devoloping Countries", The World Bank Group, Policy Research Working Papers, 2979, February 24, 2003.

Strangelove, Michael, *Watching YouTube: Extraordinary Videos by Ordinary People*, 1. Baskı, Canada: University of Toronto Press, 2010.

Tekulve, N. and Kelly, K., (2013), "Worth 1,000 Words: Using Instagram to Engage Library Users", Brick and Click Libraries Symposium.

Toprak, Ali, Ayşenur Yıldırım vd., *Toplumsal Paylaşım Ağı Facebook: Görülüyorum Öyleyse Varım!*, 1. Baskı, Kalkedon Yayınları, İstanbul, 2009.

Türkmenoğlu, H., (2014), Teknoloji ile Sanat İlişkisi ve Bir Dijital Sanat Örneği Olarak Instagram, *ULAKBİLGE*, 2(4), 87-100.

Uitermark, J., (2015), Capture and Share the City: Mapping Instagram's Uneven Geography in Amsterdam, RC21 International Conference, 27-29 August 2015, Italy.

About the Editors

Shibin David, PhD

Prof. Shibin David is an assistant professor in the Department of Computer Science and Engineering at Karunya Institute of Technology and Sciences, India. His research interests includes cryptography, network security and mobile computing. He has a good number of publications including being indexed in SCOPUS/SCIE journals. He has been serving as a faculty member for eight years, and involved in research activities for more than five years. He has twice received internal seed-money funding and guided more than ten post-graduate students with research ideas and 43 undergraduate students in his tenure to date. To add feathers to his profile, he has been a Gold Medalist in both his undergraduate and post-graduate years.

R. S. Anand

R. S. Anand worked as an assistant professor at an engineering college, and his obsession with scientific knowledge led him to become a researcher in the mechanical engineering field at Karunya Institute of Technology and Sciences, India. Thermal engineering, heat transfer, two-phase flow, thermal analysis, Artificial Intelligence in thermal appliances, and thermal appliance sensors are his research areas.

V. Jeyakrishnan PhD

Jeyakrishnan works at Saintgits Engineering College, Kottayam. His research area includes cloud computing and grid computing. He has a very good number of publications in reputed journals which are indexed in Scopus and SCI.

M. Niranjanamurthy PhD

M. Niranjanamurthy is Assistant Professor, Department of Computer Applications, M S Ramaiah Institute of Technology, Bangalore, Karnataka. He did his Ph.D. in Computer Science at JJTU, Rajasthan (2016), MPhil in Computer Science at VMU, Salem (2009), and MCA at VTU, Belgaum, Karnataka (2007). His BCA is from Kuvempu University in 2004 with

University 5th Rank. He has eleven years of teaching experience and two years of industry experience as a software engineer. He has published four books with Scholars Press, Germany. He has published 56 papers in various National/International Conferences/International Journals, and filed 15 Patents, two of which have been granted. Currently he is guiding four Ph.D. research scholars in the area of Data Science, ML, and Networking. He works as a reviewer for 22 international journals. He twice received the Best Research Journal reviewer award. He received the Young Researcher award, Computer Science Engineering, 2018. He worked as National/International Ph.D. examiner and has conducted various National Level workshops and Delivered Lecture. He conducted National and International Conferences and is associated with various professional bodies: IEEE Member, Life Membership of International Association of Engineers (IAENG), Membership of Computer Science Teachers Association (CSTA). His areas of interest are Data Science, ML, E-Commerce and M-Commerce related to Industry Internal tool enhancement, Software Testing, Software Engineering, Web Services, Web-Technologies, Cloud Computing, Big data analytics, Networking.

Index

Printed and bound by CPI Group (UK) Ltd, Croydon, CR0 4YY